A SOUTHERNER DISCOVERS NEW ENGLAND

THE MACMILLAN COMPANY
NEW YORK · BOSTON · CHICAGO · DALLAS
ATLANTA · SAN FRANCISCO

MACMILLAN AND CO., LIMITED
LONDON · BOMBAY · CALCUTTA · MADRAS
MELBOURNE

THE MACMILLAN COMPANY
OF CANADA, LIMITED
TORONTO

✵⤙ *NEW YORK* ⤚✵

A SOUTHERNER

DISCOVERS

NEW ENGLAND

By Jonathan Daniels

✵

THE MACMILLAN COMPANY

✵⤙ *1940* ⤚✵

For

L.C.D.

Contents

CONTENTS

A SOUTHERNER DISCOVERS NEW ENGLAND

I

Brash Errand

WE WENT TO NEW ENGLAND LONG AGO, as the first men did, by water. And the landing I remember best was not that one in Nantucket where mother searched the gravestones for the ancestors of Worths and Coffins and Folgers who went South to dislike the slavery they found, nor at Boston where we were directed to be reverent over history and were instead amused by subway trains which were only streetcars running underground, nor at Gloucester where it smelled as if there were more fish on the land than in the sea, but at Bar Harbor where the visitors came for the summer. None were more alien than my younger brother, Frank, and I. I remember we stood, sun-pinked and knotty-kneed and expectant, on the edge of the pool at the swimming club. In we went, and out we came, shivering and certainly Southern with a conviction that people who deliberately and of free choice swam in such gelid waters were not merely Yankees but fools.

We were very young then. Indeed, now the whole country seems to have been young in that time before 1917 and that war. There was a simplicity that made sense, even if not very much sense. He was keeping us out of war. Mills were making millions even if they were also marching to liquidation. Men were working even if they were growing older to idleness and relief. Boys growing up in the last twilight of

1

the blazing memory of the Confederacy could see New England then as the symbolic North, not merely cold-blooded enough to stand cold water, but also home of the abolitionists, home of Harvard, place where the Pilgrims landed and the Puritans remained, and place where General Butler had lived, he who—so they said, and who doubted it?—stole the silver spoons. That was simple enough. It had a counterpart in a simplicity looking South. We are all well escaped from such simplicities. Now, neither Frank nor I nor the president of Harvard nor the men who sit idle in the parks in Fall River know who the Yankees are or what they mean; but all of us know that there remains the New England of their beginning where they carved the ships and the nutmegs from the same trees.

To such a land I went as Southerner. And on a brash errand. But not the first such. Once I wrote a book about the South as a Southerner, and survived. Being the literary native once in a lifetime is enough. It involves a certain responsibility like speaking for the family (when a good part of the family may not be willing to be spoken for). It requires a certain pretension to special knowledge though the true native may know less about his neighbors than he does about other nations. Indeed, the stranger may see things which lie unnoticed (or at least unmentioned), beneath the native's nose. So I went this time to look beneath it. Though I like to think of myself as reporter trying to find answers for myself by looking myself, I am aware that I may be sometimes as much impudent as inquisitive itinerant, knocking unasked at the doors of states and towns and estates in Groton, tar-paper shacks in Vermont and yellow tenements in Lowell, asking questions and even expecting answers, also enjoying the ride and the company regardless of the questions and the answers. Even a native, I knew, might be venturesome to undertake to write a book about a

New England which contained Ralph Waldo Emerson and John L. Sullivan, William Lloyd Garrison and Jim Fisk, Bartolomeo Vanzetti and Cotton Mather, Calvin Coolidge and Phineas T. Barnum. Our South is a simplicity which contains only the multiple variants of black and white, but this New England contains Newport by the sea and Charlestown by the navy yard, not only Adamses but also Aghajanians, more O'Briens than Cabots, almost as many French-Canadians, who slipped over in the dark, as Puritans, who came over in the *Mayflower*. There are not only Saltonstalls but Skoglunds, Steinbergs, Skubinskys, Skoogbergs and Sjodins. There are Langones now as well as Lowells. The land holds wealth and hunger, not only education but violent and blinding bigotry as well.

I set all this down because it is the sensible custom of travelers to emphasize dangers and difficulties; it is also their custom not to be alarmed by them. This journey needed to be made. The whole procession of the American years has been illumined—or at least inflamed—with the works of men who hastened from the North to describe the South. Unfortunately there has been scarcely any perceptible movement from the opposite direction. Either the Southerners were so comfortable at home that they didn't travel, or else they couldn't write. Whatever the cause, New England was denied the corrective influences which she so steadily furnished the South. Obviously this was not New England's fault, but in the fault lay the danger of that malignant hypermetropia, sufferers from which see well at a distance but scarcely at all close at hand.

The New England discoverers of the South—and of cruelty and slavery in it—run down the alphabet of authors from Adams to Whipple, but as far as I have been able to find the only significant early seeing of New England by a Southerner (excepting Captain John Smith of Jamestown in Virginia),

3

occurred just a few years more than a century ago. The man who came and saw and went home and wrote was Mr. Lucian Minor of Virginia, who by a coincidence which pleases me was born in the South just exactly a century before me, lacking two days. "I think," he wrote back to *The Southern Literary Messenger,* "that I have a pretty exact measure of Jonathan's foot." Apparently he did, for Mr. James Russell Lowell fathered the republication of his measurements in 1870 in *The Atlantic* after the war was fought and after Minor was dead. "And this," Lowell wrote in rebuke to his home folks, "was one of the class whom we have heard called barbarians by men who are proud to owe their culture to slaveholding Athens and Rome!"

New England needed such a seeing then. It has too much lacked such a looking since With pretension to none of Lucian Minor's qualifications save his Southernness, I know that the Yankee and the Southerner, the Puritan and the Cavalier, like Mr. Hamilton and Mr. Jefferson and their Republicans and Democrats, remain essential symbols of antagonism in the consideration of American life. As the South has been supposed to hold one set of them, New England has been the last known address of the other. Of course like most symbols in the heads of men these have been vastly oversimplified. Behind the oversimplification are human beings who are by no means symbols only. Men, North as South, are caught in a complexity of problem and difficulty. Even if the legend were true, as a good deal of it is, that the careless Southerner destroyed his land and broke all the rules and so found his way to poverty, there is a possibility that, despite his own traditional thrift, his historical hard-headedness, and the good deal more than myth of the ingenuity of the man among the stones and the snow, the Yankees may be in a serious condition, also. Maybe, after all, the rain does fall on the just and the unjust alike.

4

I did not know, but I wanted to find out. With Lucian Minor I wanted to reverse the general direction of the observers. Definitely I did not want to go North as a carpetbagger from the South swapping a new scolding of New England for an ancient and outspoken superiority toward the South. I had no interest in any spoons General Butler or anybody else may have brought home from Louisiana. As far as I am concerned, the statute of limitations has already run out on every item connected with The War. I wanted to go as sympathetic American to New England, just as I hope I went not merely as Southerner but as American about the South. I was brash enough to believe that such a journey in observation as I proposed might, against the background of what I had found in the South, give a wholeness to a picture of what has happened on this continent to the young, hopeful, brash-also American civilization which began on these shores in the North as in the South not so many generations ago. As I came from Nantucket whalers as well as Roanoke Island fishermen, I was interested in what had happened in the countries behind both of them.

I was anxious to know what New England meant to itself and to America, to try to make some sense for myself and maybe some others out of a region which at a distance seemed compounded of lobster fishing and marble quarrying, dairying and shoemaking, machine tools and tourists and boiled dinners, potatoes and libraries, of Catholicism and the vestigial remains of Puritanism, of much money and meager resources, of the oldest Americans and the foreign-born, maybe of both ingenuity and bewilderment. I hoped to see the other side of new Southern mills in mills shut in the faces of people who have worked in them for generations. I wanted to see if thrift was a word like "gallantry," or a fact like filling a woodshed against certain winter. I wanted to see the courage of people who are facing change and meeting

5

it (if they were), or see the softness of men—"the last run of shad"—who might be living on the fat their fathers had accumulated. I wondered whether men coming up through Groton and Harvard matched those who came in through the hawsehole (even through the cabin window), to the master's berth on the long road to China. I wanted to know what pulp and paper meant to both the people and the forests. As a man from a region where children predominate and schools are the burden, I hoped to understand states in which there are so many more old people that pensions are the plague of the politicians, and where the physical terror must not be rickets in new bodies but cancer in old ones.

I made that journey. But certainly I did not find all the answers. Indeed, my feet remain after the riding firmly planted upon the fact of my foreignness. So far as I know, not a drop of my blood has been involved in biology in New England since the eighteenth century. Those Quakers of my mother came South in trek inland in 1771 because even then there were economic problems in New England which involved the men who depended on the fish. My father's father, a skilled ship carpenter, almost took his blood to Rhode Island from a South in which he said a white man who worked with his hands had no chance for living or dignity among slaves. But he had fallen in love with a girl and he came back to North Carolina to her, came back to help build the *Merrimack* which for that moment before the *Monitor* appeared seemed to threaten the Union: It would have been a joke on grandfather if he had helped preserve the slavery from which he did not quite escape. He died before slavery did because he would not let them amputate the arm which held not only the bullet and the tetanus but also his skill. Stumps do not build ships.

So I went to New England as outlander. I had landed long ago from the sea as a provincial adolescent and gone back to it a chilled one. Later I used to go to Northampton when Belmont Street was younger than it is now. I even took a taxi from Springfield through the snow, being young and not having to make the money the ride cost. It was worth the price. We went more than once to New London for the boat races. We were for Yale. But that was all long ago and far away. This time I dared the dour, the taciturn, the inhospitable, the stingy, the snobbish, the bigoted, the stern Yankee of unfavorable report. I saw his actual land: a country of stone walls and milk cans, of codfish cakes and baked beans (out of cans put up in Camden, New Jersey), of potted geraniums in windows, and of so many elms, some soaring green and high and too many with their roots turned up by the biggest wind since 1815. I saw the town and the Common and the Grange Hall and the Town Hall and the Congregational Church and the house with the mansard roof and the iron dog and the deer in the yard; and I found that the mill that built them was more often than not shut and for sale. Too many boys had gone off to the bigger towns. Not all of them had found work even there.

I went in my car to towns and islands still marked by the memory of the whale. I drove, too, to maple syrup in the Vermont woods and for sale in little jugs by ladies at stands beside the road in little towns. I did not eat enough lobster. I saw the pool at Bangor where they take the first salmon each year for the President. I ate some of those first green peas which Longfellow listed long ago among the excellencies of the best living but which now have lost the premium price, due the early and the rare, to trucks and freezings and California and Florida. Something new and strange has happened since the time when Frederic Tudor sent at a profit ice from his father's pond in Saugus to Calcutta; now the ice comes to New England, with fruit and vegetables in it, on wheels. Pie for breakfast, so far as I could discover, is a myth now if it was ever anything else. I know how at least one farmer feels whose barn was blown down, and that a minimum of three little Polish boys whom I gave a lift home from school to weed onions near Sunderland, have no passion for the onion or the land.

I rode a long way from farms in Connecticut which no longer nourish anything but writers and opera singers to the potato country of Aroostook, that Maine county bigger than Connecticut which waits through hard times with the gambler's memory of a $5–$10 a barrel year. I saw the high tides of Passamaquoddy and the low tides of Salem harbor. Early in the morning of July 5th I watched men raking up the debris of the multitude's delight at Revere Beach. Certainly there is plenty to be seen in this region which runs from a filling station on the Westchester County line to Joe Guerette's beer joint just this side the St. John River bridge in Madawaska, and from the West Quoddy Head Light beyond Lubec in Maine to the slums below the Battery in Burlington, Vermont.

I remember the picture a fat bishop made as he sat, on his way to the confirmation of a churchful of children in North Oxford, in his limousine before a Dutchland Farms place near Worcester and sipped a chocolate ice cream soda. I saw Dr. Charles Seymour, the president of Yale, lank under his striped beach robe, cross the road at Chatham to greet a young female relative with a kiss. I watched the eager meeting of the girls of Eastport, Maine (town from which the native boys have been drawn away by an economic necessity with the pull of the Quoddy tides), and the new boys of the Quoddy camp of the National Youth Administration, who are gathered from New England slums for a brief vocational training for a world which had no place for them and may have no need of their training either. While I watched them

8

it seemed strange to be mosquito-bitten on a night so cold that I shivered.

It is a little country, the maps say, but there are long distances in so brief a land. It is only an afternoon's drive but from one world to another from lady-filled Wiggins Old Tavern in Northampton, where among antiques for sale an American privy is kept as a museum piece (copies of James Whitcomb Riley's nostalgic verse on its passing may be secured at the desk), to John Greenleaf's farm over Vershire in Vermont where the still useful backhouse sits precariously in the front yard high above the field of vetch and timothy almost at the top of the world.

I not only looked and saw. I talked and listened. And the New England which makes this book is not so much mine as it is the land of those who told it to me. They were Yale professors, and solid men of State Street and Post Office Square, and bums and farmers and fishermen, and a fireman who had been a fisherman, even (when he was young) a whaler. There was an Irishman who kept muttering to the irritation of another Irishman, "It's the mick in me." There was the big-handed C.I.O. leader who cursed the Catholic Church for its labor attitude but went devoutly to Mass every morning before he took his place in the hierarchy of John L. Lewis in an office on Tremont Street. Far to the right was the factory manager who said of a high New Deal official who long ago as a labor leader had tried to unionize his shops, "He may be the Honorable Mr. Somebody in Washington but he's the same so-and-so to me."

Maybe they not only told me about New England but also showed me in themselves something approximating the composite New Englander. Certainly I never found a more hospitable land. I slept at the old St. Botolph, ate codfish cakes at the Union Club, and joined the gentlemen of the Tavern in their colored vests in paying Boston's continuing

praises to Messrs. Gilbert and Sullivan. I drank beer as the
guest of a painter and a plumber in Nantucket. By hard luck
I missed both James Michael Curley and the Somerset Club,
but I ate *scaloppini con funghi* on Federal Hill in Providence
and shared the brown beef and the conversation of carnival
employees in a bilingual café close to Canada in French Van
Buren. I never ate a better breakfast than Herb Allan served
in his salmon-fishing camp in Dennysville, Maine. My first
contact with the solemn Vermonter was with Thomas Reed
Powell, professor of constitutional law at Harvard—the same
who said, when the professional patriots of Massachusetts
wanted a law to make every teacher swear to support the
Constitution, that he would be delighted. "Why not? The
Constitution has been supporting me for twenty-five years."

Of course I have run into gelatinous silences, but no more
often in this taciturn North than I came upon such lively
garrulousness as that, for instance, of Charles Carroll, of
Laconia, New Hampshire, former mayor, former member of
the Governor's council and then commissioner of Belknap
County. The New Englander—even the Vermonter—likes to
talk. His laconism is a legend. As Southerner it seemed to me
also that the legend of inhospitality in New England is one
of the first American slanders. It can only be seriously repeated by those who think Southern hospitality means
spreading the board and turning back the counterpane for
every wanderer who rides up or down the road. Old Bob
Toombs set up understandable standards. when he opposed
the building of a hotel in his town of Washington, Georgia.
"We don't need a hotel," he said. "If a visitor's a gentleman,
I'll entertain him; if he isn't, we don't want him in town."
Not quite so severely enforced anywhere, that is a rule of
hospitality everywhere. In New England, as in the South,
people are looking for more people to entertain than there
are entertainable people coming up the road. Naturally they

want to know whether the stranger is armed or unarmed, friend or foe, gentleman traveling or felon fleeing. There are customs which formalize these investigations. Beyond them hospitality is a human and not a geographical phenomenon. New England has its full share of it. But there may be limitations upon welcome. A charming lady showed me that when I first went to Boston.

I was late for the Friday afternoon concert at Symphony Hall. The lights were up and the applause was swelling to greet the returning director when I went in. The orchestra sat against gray walls in subdued light under the pipes of a great gold organ. Before the musicians on the floor and in the two long narrow encircling galleries were many ladies and a very few men. Above the galleries were classic statues in shadowed niches. Below the big orchestra spread from harps to bass viols, from a gray-headed bass violin player to a young man whose business it was to strike the cymbals together. All the music was between the rising and falling of the bows of violins. Serge Koussevitzky moved his body in an accelerating dance of direction until his cutaway tails swung at a wide angle from his spine as his arms and shoulders moved under his bobbing gray head. And the music cried in Boston the story of Pelléas and Melisande, and in the hall the silence seemed to swell as the music did.

At last the lights came up and I went out into the lobbies to see this Boston that listened. There were old ladies smoking cigarettes like the good many young and pretty girls. There were a few boys and young men, but most striking, I thought, in the company were the few well scrubbed and well groomed older men: one man with an ascetic face, bald and Roman-looking; one a clergyman. Most of us that afternoon were middle-aged women chattering in the interval between deep silences. Among music lovers there were remarkably few Jews. Most in a city of many foreign-born

11

looked native, even Yankee, even what they used to call
Back Bay before the well-to-do stopped sleeping in Boston.
I went back to my seat, and I remember that the chattering
mounted and somehow joined the sound of tuning instruments. Behind me I caught a scrap of separate speech:

". . . they are written by men that haven't that lovely vision
that Maeterlinck had, and Debussy."

"And Brahms," said her companion.

Then—it did not seem quite to fit—the first voice said:
". . . and there was something so lovely about the nature of
Thoreau."

I looked about the old hall. Then, brash again, I asked the
charming middle-aged lady next to me how old Symphony
Hall was. She answered as helpfully and as pleasantly as possible that she did not know, that she had come from St.
Louis and had only lived in Boston thirty-five years.

"Does that make you still a newcomer here as it would
in Charleston?"

She smiled. "No. I consider myself a Bostonian," she
said, "but if I really were a Bostonian, I wouldn't be talking
to you."

But Boston did, and Connecticut and Maine, Rhode
Island and New Hampshire and Vermont. I know there is
a world beyond the Symphony, where ladies share a culture
which knows where it came from but not where it is going, even below Harvard, where professors mutter, as the
Puritans' children have muttered, over the character of government they do not make. Away from both there are alleys
narrower than the Merritt Parkway which is New England's
door and lanes beyond the parkway's end which become only
tracks across pastures empty since they sold the cow. Along
them is New England; at the end of them might be some
understanding of it. I crossed from the south into Connecticut to see.

II

New England Vestibule

THE ROAD RUNS INTO CONNECTICUT through the middle of the world. The rock walls run in a procession of aching backs to the American beginning, and tractors pull open the furrows in the fields those backs bent to clear. There is solitude for a singer and her high notes on a hill; there is rest for the broker, quiet for the writer, and, for the painter, stretches of countryside undisturbed and unentered by the mixed multitude which crowds the state's square miles. Machines go on endlessly punching out the brass buttons. Test pilots take the new planes up over Bridgeport, high above the solemn stone over Barnum. Young women make corsets for old women. In peace and with precision the bullets are made that will tear the guts out of a man. A gymnasium which looks like a cathedral backs up in New Haven to a dark yard where boys play ball beside a huge garbage heap where first base ought to be. Czechoslovakians dwell in early American salt-box houses, and American boys go to college in medieval palaces. And yet there is order and content; there might even be security if the rich land like the rich men were not surrounded by a hungry world.

The hungry world, near and far, is not readily seen. A century ago Lucian Minor wrote home to Virginia, "Here is not apparent a hundredth part of the abject squalid pov-

13

erty that our state presents." It is still so. It was simpler to see the young men of Yale than the equal number of young men and women in New Haven who could not find a job. As I entered New England the educated Negro who was still a filling station helper told me: "The Merritt Parkway is merely the Connecticut continuation of the New York parkway."

It is more than that; it is also the gate of New England and with other parkways will one day be a wide canal for cars cut straight through from Broadway to Boston. White lanes of concrete and miles of pretty planting provide the motorist every facilitation to motion; here is avenue of escape from both traffic and reality. One, I suspect, may sometimes be as objectionable as the other. This is progress, and it is also a million dollar parable on progress.

Instead of Connecticut, the rider sees mile after mile of identical right of way prettified with a million dollars' worth of grass and tree. When I rode it, the parkway was twenty-one miles of changeless green procession which looked all the way like those sentimentalized stoneless cemeteries which have made burial a real estate business and added to the economic hazards of quarrying in Vermont. Connecticut escaped the showing and I the seeing of the hamburger and the clam stands, the dine-and-dances, the tourist homes and the automobile graveyards. Maybe this was pure gain. I am not sure. For the man whose only interest in travel is the end of his journey here is perfection. Also served are those who have insisted that New England must be saved from the hot-dog salesman. But I rode as one who wanted not only to go but to see, and as one to whom a hot-dog stand was as much an item in a civilization as a transplanted spruce. This may be heresy. I think it makes as much sense as the doctrine: In order that the traveler may move in this land, he must give up the privilege of seeing it.

14

"He can have this business," the skinny man said. Behind the counter of his clam stand on the road from Westport to New Haven, he put down the bottle of his own beer which he had been drinking. He pushed my clams across the counter. "God knows he's welcome to it."

I had spoken casually about roadside stands of Connecticut.

"There are lots of stands on this road. When you first get off the parkway you realize how many there are."

"Too damn many."

"There's a professor at Yale who says Connecticut has got to get them off the roads if it expects to get the tourists."

My host sneered.

"He can have this business." He looked as if he meant to put the professor forcibly into the clam business. Then his face softened in self-pity. "Christ, all I got's clams! They're good all right, but I've had so many of them that they make me sick. They'll be fine for you, but I've had too many. I got to eat here, and that's about all I get. It's pretty damned easy for college professors to say how pretty things ought to be. But what about us poor bastards? I don't want to sell clams. I hate the sight of the damn things. And I get sick at the stomach watching automobiles riding this road. If they don't like to see me, God knows I don't get any fun out of seeing them. I get so sometimes I don't want any of them to stop. Let 'em keep their damn dimes." He paused. "How 'bout some more? They're good and fresh. A fellow brings 'em to me who digs 'em hisself."

"No, thanks."

"How 'bout a beer?"

"No."

"You been riding a long way," he said, looking at my license. "I got a brother went down South last winter. He ran a Kiddy Ride in a carnival. He liked it. He said the girls

15

were nice, real nice. But I guess he was bragging. Pretty often
he is."

"Maybe not," I said. "I guess I will have a beer."

He opened it.

"He liked it. I hear a lot of people talking about the South.
Some of 'em say the South's going to take our factories away.
Don't you believe it. One thing we got up here is skill. You
can find fellows right around here that can do anything. That
means a lot. I know some of these rich so-and-sos would move
their mills to save a nickel. But we got the skill and they
know it. Hell, I'm not worried!"

I put down my bottle.

"How 'bout some more clams? They're real good today.
I had some myself just before you came."

Though the elms were hardly beginning to be green, old
Connecticut was good to see: the stone walls, the white
houses with the green blinds, the churches and their spires,
and the Common and the Town Hall. The familiar picture
of New England was a real picture on a real road. But the
characters were different. The Italians and the Poles, the
Jews and the Irish move at home on the Yankee scene.

I spoke of this new cast on the old stage to the entirely
native Yale professor who bought my lunch in one of the big
dining halls Mr. Harkness bought for Yale.

"We are all foreigners," he said, "the Yankees most of
all. We are the most unassimilable people in New England.
We act—by golly, we think that Americanization is a process
of becoming like us. How horrible! Obviously we are only
one factor out of the past which must make the New Englander, the American of the future. The wops are another,
the Polacks, the Irish, even your niggers."

"You aren't talking like a professor," I said.

He looked around him at the big dining hall full of students.

"I'm not feeling like one. My Puritan blood pesters me. We Yankees are the ones who hold off most from this so-called melting process. We want everybody to melt but us."

I rode on. There were big trucks on the road with me now, roaring past me down out of New England and Connecticut with tin and silver and brass. There was a boxed airplane engine in a truck parked before a church. At Wallingford like a grim specter a huge "For Sale" sign hung against an old factory's wide brick wall. It was the first such mill I saw in New England, and I remembered a book published when more of us were young called *Get-Rich-Quick Wallingford*. It was possible now to become poor quick, too. Even on this crowded road.

"Don't you believe it," the clam-stand man had said of moving factories. On the rich road where he stood there seemed certainly to be no basis for fear. I remembered, however, that Malcolm Keir of Dartmouth, who had been economic adviser to the New England Governors' freight-rate committee, had used those same words to New England manufacturers, but in warning. There had been losses in textiles and knitting and shoes and leather and paper. Any manufacturer who believed that textile machinery could not follow textile manufacturing or other capital goods industries go after other consumers' goods industries (machine making after the products of machines) was, he suggested, a man riding on a pretty parkway who could not see the world.

"Don't you believe it," Malcolm Keir said.

The men in Meriden apparently did. At least those pouring out of the factories in the late afternoon were as complacent-looking as they seemed well fed. In their American working clothes I could not pick out diverse foreign stocks. As a crowd they looked as American as the factories from which they came. And, wherever they came from, they were. I stood on the sidewalk and let them move by me. One workman was talking about a golf score. A woman said to another, "She can't do that to me." The last man came out smiling and talking to the watchman at the doors. He knew they would open again in the morning.

I came into Hartford under the shadow of the high tower of the Travelers Insurance Company which wears at its top some decoration that looks at a distance like pawnbrokers' balls. In the Bond Hotel I talked with Willard Rogers, who not only runs the hotel but had the official job of talking for publicity for Connecticut.

"He's a B.W.—a Big Wind," said an insurance executive, "an Elk." (As a matter of fact, I don't think he is an Elk; but aristocratic Governor Saltonstall of Massachusetts is.)

I found him in his office, fat and fifty, immaculately and a little sportily dressed, with his little remaining hair brushed over his bald head. His fingernails were shining, I noticed when he moved his hand and the long cigar in it in gesticulation. He is expansive about Connecticut. Polyglot the people may be (thirty nationalities work in his hotels), but they are homogeneous in a sweet reasonableness which extends from the textile workers in hardship in eastern Connecticut through Hartford and the busy Connecticut River valley to New York.

"We don't have any crime. Even when we have strikes— of course the strikers want to win, but we don't have any violence unless outsiders come in and cause it. I was police commissioner of my town of Manchester for twenty years and we never did have but two murders. One of them was a China-man who was killed by an outsider in a tong war. The other case was a man killed in a duel over a girl which two Italians from Hartford came to Manchester to fight."

"Does that apply to all New England?"

"No," he said regretfully. "Over in Providence they had a regular gang of kidnapers and blackmailers. They had a country place with a whole crowd of killers disguised as gardeners. A rich man in Providence came to see my brother and told him that he had gotten a letter saying that if he didn't pay $10,000 they'd kill him and get his daughters, too. My brother told him, 'If it was me I'd get my family out of town and tell these racketeers to go to hell. But since it's you I guess you better pay.' We don't have anything like that in Connecticut. The people are peaceful and reasonable and law-abiding."

I went back to my room, contemplating the productive peace in Babel. From my window I looked out across its capital and my eye fell to a legend printed on the sill:

NOTICE

Persons throwing bottles or other articles from this window will be held responsible.

PLEASE
BE CAREFUL

It was still possible that something might hit the sweetly reasonable below.

The Congregational Church was neither antique nor modern. It belonged to that age of golden-oak interiors, of yellow carved beams, of yellow pews, of yellow pulpit, even yellow walls. North and South, there seems to have been a period when such was the standard coloration of Christianity. Inside the church I might have been in Selma, Alabama, or Clarinda, Iowa. And not only the woodwork. The high-piled menu prepared under the direction of Miss Mary Smith with

19

the assistance of Luces and Bigneys and Fosters and Hulberts conformed to a national church supper standard. When behind me the minister's voice rose in blessing it was not a New England voice but that theological seminary intonation which everywhere seems to me to make a contribution to Christianity similar to that made by golden oak. We ate heartily, plied by the ladies. The three schoolteachers across the table from me were pretty and shy. The retired professional bicycle rider, whose father had been the town's leading surgeon, was a man of information. At the foot of the table sat the frail old man who occupied the highest house on the hill above it; he was the undertaker. They were an old American company, a familiar and not very exciting one. They ate placidly toward the beginning of the scheduled spelling match.

There was a difference here. In this church was the tradition of New England. The line had come down straight to them from the beginning. And not only the succession. They still held the wealth and the library and the schools and the social position. But outside the church the law was in the hands of an Irish chief of police named Joe McCarthy. A man named Howard headed the tree replacement committee but the trees were being planted for the numerous progeny of the Dombroskis and the Zacowiches and the Ratzenoffs. Nick DeRita had just bought the abandoned Stafford Street School.

In the little old American security of the golden-oak room the ladies cleared the dishes, and a knot of men moved out into the vestibule of the church to smoke. My friend took me with them and introduced me to the company of the smokers. I was discovering them, he said. They felt no more than I did like bugs under a glass. But Luce, the son-in-law in the big mill, gave me a cigarette. Another man in the woolen business explained changes in trade practices which

made manufacture more hazardous. Business was not simple
any more, if it ever had been. Labor and merchants and
consumers had all changed. Still the mills were running in
their town. The manufacturer looked modest. The dentist
smiled like a man who knew he was secure. The power company man grinned. Finally we went back in, passing the old
undertaker, who occupied the highest house in town, sitting
in the church auditorium. He sat all by himself in the
yellow room like the last man out of the past.

In north Connecticut on the road to Worcester I could
see the lick New England had been hit when the wind roared
up out of the South. The hurricane had not broken the trees;
it had followed rain, which had softened the earth, to push
them down. Their roots were turned up in the air. An old
buggy still hung in the wreckage of a barn. Not only the
old trees had come down. I stopped at a store in the town
of Union (settled 1727). Two selectmen there were Dorotzak
and Mrakevich.

A wind has been changing New England for a long time.

III

Ring Around the Common

NIGHT

THE ST. BOTOLPH CLUB, Horatio Colony had written me, is a sort of youth hostelry for old men. The description sounded as if it would suit me exactly on my first swift passage through Boston on my way to the New England around it. So straight I came full of music from the Friday afternoon concert of the Boston Symphony Orchestra to get my bags out of the Copley Plaza. Archibald MacLeish, as an agent of Harvard University, had been paying my bill in that excellent establishment in a philanthropic exchange for my part in some (to me) delightful conversation on life and newspapering in the South with the flock of Nieman Fellows in Journalism which MacLeish was shepherding that year. When I stood by my bags waiting for my Plymouth at the Dartmouth Street entrance to the hotel, the short, dark doorman shook his head and spoke to me.

"That fellow"—he nodded toward a slim young man moving rapidly in the direction of Copley Square—"that fellow, he's in a great state of mind."

"How's that?"

"He's my son, and he's been offered three internships in hospitals, and he doesn't know which one to take, and he's got to stand the last of his comprehensive examinations in a few weeks. He just graduated from B.U."

The father beside the door he tended did not seem disturbed.

22

"You look pretty young to have a boy like that."

"He's my youngest. His older brother plays with the Detroit Symphony, but he just joined the New York Philharmonic. Why, I'm a grandfather! They brought the baby here and left it with us for three weeks. They're still complaining that we spoiled him."

He was pleased about that. He was a man, I thought, who stood where the world had beaten a path though not because he had a better mousetrap. He had one, nevertheless. He thanked me for my quarter, and I had the feeling that it would join others to serve the cause of both art and science. Between the symphony and the doorman Boston seemed the earnest and elevating city. But on the sidewalk before the St. Botolph Club an accordion player and a flutist were playing "Alexander's Ragtime Band." An Italian truckman in comic exaggeration was dancing to their music across the sidewalk to his truck. I went up from them—and the Boston they helped make—on the big brownstone steps with the glittering brass hand rails into the delightful mellowed dinginess of the old club. Later in the summer between excursions as close as Concord and as far off as Aroostook it was to be haven as well as hostel.

The pimply-faced Irish boy brought in my bags and stowed them away until I should find Horatio Colony. There were some old men in the hostelry. A rotund white-bearded man was reading *The Transcript,* and another old gentleman in quiet querulousness was giving a politely uninterested man a commentary on the news he had extracted from *The Globe.* It was late afternoon, and there were young men in the dim rooms, too. Two of them with cocktails in their hands watched two others playing at backgammon.

One of the players said softly and sadly, "Well, I've been had." He tapped a bell and ordered himself and his conqueror a drink.

23

Then Horatio came. I had never met him. Once reading galley proofs for a book club I had caught a trivial error in a book of his in time to correct it before publication. I had said in print that I liked the book. He had been unduly grateful. We had corresponded and I was glad to meet him face to face. He was not only a friend but a phenomenon: the modern New Englander at the end of a straight line which went back to Keene, New Hampshire, through manufacturing and education and wealth to that ancestor from Kilkenny who went out from the fort to milk the cows among the besieging Indians when the children needed milk. There was some connection back there between the Colonys and a lady who was hung as a witch. But the mark of neither the witch nor the Indian fighter was on Horatio. Slight and pale and bluntly shy he promptly established me in residence and made the very practical proposal that we go across the street to the Ritz bar for a drink.

A Ritz bar is a Ritz bar, never native nor foreign, but in Boston its pretty women with their scrubbed men emphasized the local color item that outside it in the Athens of America the culture of women does not run to clothes. While I looked at the pretty women in the bar Horatio excused himself and went to another table. He came back with a young man who might have been his brother. He introduced us.

"Mr. Daniels is doing a book about New England."

"We're an odd lot," said the young man calmly.

A jacketed waiter brought two Scotches, and Horatio sent him off for a third. "Well," he asked, "what is there to see in us?"

"I don't know. I've come to find out. I'm riding up the road Monday morning."

The third Scotch came.

"Here's luck," our visitor said.

"I never see a thing in this part of the country," Horatio told us, "being blind to all my own familiar regions—in the South, too, I could only see what I wanted to see."

I doubted his blindness. He saw shrewdly enough, I suspected, behind the young-looking and somehow inscrutable-appearing mask of his face. He smiled just perceptibly as he spoke, chopping his sentences into words and sounds of an accentuation which can only be roughly described as "Harvard."

"Honestly, in my visits South I have always found everything very satisfactory. I like the people down there much better than those up here. Here we have been done to death by reform—our business men as well as our recreationists are beginning to long for your part of the country where the goose of the golden eggs is still capable of laying—and I hope nobody slays her too speedily. In these days it seems as though New England is the only part of the country without a future; and the South will have a great one, I do believe."

"I'm glad you Southerners didn't let Roosevelt purge you," announced the young man who had joined us.

"I'm a New Dealer," I admitted. It was an admission in the Ritz bar in Boston.

He considered me. "I'm sorry, but it doesn't matter."

"Thanks," I said.

He smiled. "The truth is that our present dissatisfaction with your South is the same old jealousy over labor. But like most jealousy we give it a moral sound. The Civil War got most of its fomentation from the clergy, the educators, and the literary people who, always mad for publicity, will champion any cause for the purpose of showing off. Now the people up here crave your advantages while crying out against them. Those able to move down South have done so; those unable to move are the more bitter. The truth of the matter is that Yankee reform (now taken up by immigrant politicians to further their own ambitions) has overreached itself; and business is being murdered in its bed through high wages and high taxes. A person can thrive paying low taxes and high wages, or high taxes and low wages, but not both. The high taxes at least go for dubious and costly social benefits, and now the cry from the Yankees (I'm one, and I'm in the textile business)—that cry is: 'Here we have perfected human society; and these persons who pay the taxes and the wages want to move out—indubitable proof that the manufacturers are wicked, and the places where they want to go are backward.' "

He sighed into his Scotch.

"To me, a costly human society is like a costly house, a yacht, or racing stable, or some other absurd luxury. The essential things can be done very cheaply and simply. Even luxuries can be had at half-price by the knowing; and in the South you have this simplicity; up here all is litter, vacuum, and expense. Education has been perverted into 'more jobs for teachers,' and increased hospitalization to 'more jobs for doctors.' "

"Go on," I said. "I don't think I would agree with a word you say if I were a Yankee, but I'm delighted to hear you. You're one of the things I came to see as well as a Vermont farmer and a Cape Cod cranberry picker."

He laughed. "I suppose I am." But he grew serious. "However, there was much I liked about the old-fashioned Yankee —you find him sometimes even now. He had a keen sense of race and blood. I think his love of property was really a part of that. Now that's been almost completely lost. Why and when he lost his strength, I don't know—probably through lack of understanding of himself and others. In the South you have preserved yourself much better than we— I believe you are less jealous and more strong, and less addicted to pen and paper. You have considered your own flesh and bone and blood rather than your brows."

"It's true we didn't write—" I began.

"Don't now," he advised. "I hope you'll excuse me; I've got to go back to my girl."

I watched him go back to her and the group which included her and did not seem to be missing him. Seeing her, I did not blame him for leaving; but I should have liked to finish my sentence.

"He seems to enjoy his pessimism."

"Maybe," Horatio said. He drained his glass. "Here, let's have another drink."

"What I'd like," I said, "is for you to come to dinner with me at one of the old eating places of Boston."

He looked blank. "I don't know any. I don't think there are any—not any good ones. And the food across the street isn't very good. Let's eat here. You must eat here with me."

"But there must be . . ." I began.

Then Milton Rosenau, Jr., stood by the table. He is a slight, dark, aristocratic-looking Jew, and when we had met him casually in the club before we crossed the street I had felt a geographical closeness to him because his father, the distinguished sanitarian, had gone to the University of North Carolina to do important work for the South after he had passed the retirement age as a professor at Harvard. The younger Rosenau, as a newspaperman on *The Boston Herald* and as president of the Newspaper Guild of Boston, was giving a dinner at the St. Botolph for the same Nieman Fellows to whom I had spoken informally at the Art Club the night before.

"There are thirteen of us at table," he said. I think it was a hospitable lie.

"Oh, I say!" Horatio said. "I think we better not."

But we went. There seemed to be at least twenty at the

table in the big flagon-and-magnum-decorated dining room at the back of the club. It was a good company, and I was glad to be there. Horatio and I had crossed more than the street. The Nieman Fellows seemed like old friends. I was lucky to meet there that gayest Yankee, Thomas Reed Powell, professor of law at Harvard. He represents, I think, a Yankee tradition compounded of gayety as well as good sense which has been almost overwhelmed in popular report by the tradition of the long faces. There were present also three of modern Boston's literary lights: Ben Ames Williams, the novelist who was born in Macon, Mississippi; Edward Weeks, Jr., editor of *The Atlantic,* who was born in Elizabeth, New Jersey; and David McCord, the poet and executive secretary of the Harvard Fund Council, who was born in New York. (That was the night also when I learned that Robert Frost, New England's poet, was born in San Francisco.) I sat between two lawyers, Hector Holmes and Lucius Hill.

We ate well despite Horatio's preference for the food at the Ritz. The talk was good. The Nieman Fellows are not conventional students of journalism learning how to write headlines and news stories but older newspapermen given a chance to study at Harvard with the money of a Milwaukee editor and publisher who made money in the newspaper business while running a paper which won the Pulitzer Prize for distinguished service. The assumption is that such study at Harvard will make better newspapermen in America. Maybe it will. These had also less formally—but not necessarily less profitably—been studying Boston.

"You ought to go down on State Street to see the signs of the estates tied up in the hands of trustees. Bostonians are now living on money their ancestors made and contributing nothing."

"They used to live on the income on their income, and they're sore because they can't now."

"That's just like you fellows. I don't see anything so evil about this inherited wealth. If I hadn't had a little income I'd have had to stuck to money-making, and if I'd stuck to money-making I wouldn't be making half as much money as I am."

"There's something about the influence of inherited wealth on a civilization that you can't laugh off."

"Horse manure!" said a Nieman Fellow from the West.

Someone said of a big New England mill that had failed, "It was looted."

Another spoke of the man who had been at its head when it shut its doors, "He's a pirate."

"But Felix says he's a nice old pirate."

Slowly an argument grew about the United States Supreme Court and its new liberalism. Then something of the meaning in Massachusetts of a man who had come to America as a little Jewish boy of twelve and gone from Boston forty-five years later to the United States Supreme Court came into the conversation. The company was free, but Felix Frankfurter was among friends. A good many of the Nieman Fellows had apparently been studying under him in the Harvard Law School. One of them then was living in his house in Cambridge. Apparently the whole table called him "Felix," and affectionately; but by no means all of them agreed with him entirely.

"Oh, yes, but Felix and some of the others have played the artful dodger in the law for righteousness' sake. Instead of saying of the old cases, 'These decisions were wrong,' they've been writing elaborate foolishness to say that the old cases didn't bar this or that. They've been slipping through the old bad decisions instead of knocking them aside."

The brandy bottle went around. The talk turned to another justice who had their affection, the late Mr. Justice Oliver Wendell Holmes, and to the very human, very masculine vulgarity which they suggested was as much a part of his well loved character as his honesty and his liberalism. They recalled: his description as to how he got his Civil War wound; his comment on modernist painting; his statement when a pompous Puritan was involved with his mother's maid that here was a case of *seductio ad absurdum*.

The brandy bottle went around again. The jokes proceeded from judges to professors and priests and politicians. It was late beyond laughter when at last I went up to the high room to which long before Horatio had sent my bags. Outside my window the spire of the Arlington Street Church, where once William Ellery Channing had preached, stuck up into the night. And Boston was quiet as the stars.

MORNING

I woke in the old room with its high ceiling. The sun came in, warming it. Men who loved good living and good fellowship had been sleeping in that room for fifty years, and except for the telephone beside my bed and the electric light above me the room must have been the same when the gentlemen of St. Botolph moved into this building in 1887. How many and what men, I wondered, had been warmed in Boston winters by fires in the fireplace under the old white marble mantel. Francis Parkman, the historian who had been the club's first president, had been still alive when the club first occupied these quarters. In Boston men had lived well in those days without phones and without electricity. Even the old-fashioned plumbing had been new then. I noticed, baked in the porcelain bowl under the long hanging chain, that the commode in the bathroom had not been patented until 1897. That was four years after Historian Parkman died.

I drank my orange juice and went out into the sun.

Around the corner at the entrance to the parish yard of the Arlington Street Church peddlers were using the gateway as a place to sell flowers: sweet peas and jonquils, a few gardenias white and separate in a box, and little yellow flowers which the churchyard florist said were English primroses. I walked through the Public Garden, which was almost empty then, and stopped to read the scientific labels on the trees which had weeks to wait before they would be richly green. Then I came back by the stretch of Charles Street which separates the Public Garden from the Common, by Boylston Street and stopped for a moment before the statue of Wendell Phillips, bearing the inscription:

> Whether in chains or in laurels,
> Liberty knows nothing but victories.

I wondered about that. Beyond the monument on the Common, Edna St. Vincent Millay had run from a policeman after voicing her indignant protest against the conviction of Nicola Sacco, the shoe worker, and Bartolomeo Vanzetti, the fish peddler. I remembered how indignantly certain I myself had been that they had been railroaded on the murder charge because they were anarchists. I was not quite so sure now, and nobody I found in Boston was sure even where their ashes were. On the Common, too, H. L. Mencken had got the arrest he sought when he peddled the April, 1926, issue of the magazine he edited containing Herbert Asbury's story "Hatrack" which was then too strong for Boston. Across the Public Garden and the Common on Joy Street the Massachusetts Birth Control League had felt the irresistible combination in opposition of the Puritan and the Catholic together.

I went back to the comfortable dark woods and the warm dust of the library in the St. Botolph Club. The shelves were filled with old books, some by members of the club, and a few new ones. There was *The Flowering of New England* by Van Wyck Brooks (born Plainfield, New Jersey), and that *Wickford Point* of John Marquand (born Wilmington, Delaware) which someone said should have been named The Deflowering of New England, and *Sucker's Progress* by that same Herbert Asbury whose "Hatrack" had made Editor Mencken an interesting subject to the Boston police, William Allen White's biography of Coolidge, *A Puritan in Babylon*. While I waited for lunch with the Lawyer and the Literary Man, I read by choice the *Who's Who* biographies of New Englanders. The Cabots seemed the most prolific in brains; James Elliot and Elizabeth Dwight Cabot alone had three sons in the book. Charles Francis Adams, *"g.g.g.s.* of John Adams," seemed to be as solitary in that line as did A. Lawrence among the Lowells. Leverett was the last listed Saltonstall. But James Michael Curley, ex-Governor, had the right to wear the insignia of the Order of the Rising Sun of Japan, the Order of St. Sophia of Serbia, the Order of the Commendátore of the Crown of Italy, and a medal expressive of the gratitude of France.

"Good morning," said the Literary Man.

I put my big book down while he turned with his hands deep in his pockets and looked at the shelves.

"We New Englanders are a bookish people," he said, and then he added as if it were no part of the sentence, "Like hell."

"You read."

"Yes, but we no longer write. Look it up. You'll find that on the lists of Houghton Mifflin and Little Brown and the other Boston publishers there are more people from your South than there are from New England."

He put a cigarette into a holder and pulled a book from the shelf.

"James Truslow Adams. He comes from Brooklyn. Dorothy Canfield Fisher is from Kansas. Thornton Wilder comes from Wisconsin. Of course that's not so new and strange: William Dean Howells came here from Ohio."

He lit the cigarette, and over it looked at me searchingly.

"I'll tell you a secret."

"What?"

"Don't quote me, but I think the whole tradition of New England writing all the way back has been overemphasized. Van Wyck Brooks sentimentalized it in his *Flowering*. Most of the earlier writers were talented amateurs."

"Hawthorne and Thoreau and Emerson and Melville?"

"Well, no," he admitted grinning. He added, "Melville was from New York."

"Longfellow's beard," I said, "drove me off for a long time. I saw it in the school reader, and I guess a million other American children did. It looked like the unpleasant beards Confederate veterans kissed me with. I never liked him or many of his fellows till I read Fredrika Bremer's report of dinner at Longfellow's in Cambridge in 1849. He served champagne made out of Catawba grapes in Cincinnati. It was made by a Mr. Longworth who must have been the great-grandfather of Nick Longworth who became Speaker of the House and married Alice Roosevelt. You remember she said Calvin Coolidge looked as if he had been weaned on a pickle. I've liked all New England literature better since I followed that champagne."

We ate when the Lawyer came. More serious, he was less complacent about the disturbing changes in his world. He could recognize, without liking it, the fact that high taxes and automobiles were taking many of the best Bostonians out of Boston.

"We don't like to think of Commonwealth Avenue as a

street of flats, but maybe it will be. You can buy a house on the water side of Beacon Street for less than anyone ever dreamed. There aren't any buyers."

Not only the big city suffered, but little towns, too. When he was a boy, he said, almost every little town had its mill which fed and built the town. Now not the South but consolidations, the development of bigness, had shut them up.

But both the power and culture of Boston remained, he insisted. Nobody could deny it, he believed. He looked a little as if he pleaded a case. The less ponderous Literary Man smiled.

"I want to show you the Athenaeum," the Lawyer said as if it were not only a sight for a stranger but an item of evidence. It is both.

We walked across the Public Garden to the Mall, across the Common along Beacon Street. Daniel Webster had walked there, and Emerson. The Lawyer stopped and told me about it.

"In the old days," he said, "if a young man and a young lady walked together here, it was a sign they were engaged."

The Literary Man poked the path with his cane.

"Now," he said, "in the summer if you come along here at night, they'll be fornicating." He swung his cane. "I don't know whether that's a sign that they're engaged or not."

We laughed, but the Lawyer did not laugh very heartily. We went on directly then to the Athenaeum, where they have George Washington's books and windows that look out upon the graves of Samuel Adams, Paul Revere, and Mother Goose.

IV

Time and the Wind

THE STORM MARKS SHOWED SLOWLY. There was an elm down. Men worked on a torn barn. Then as we rode farther whole hillsides were bent and broken as weeds might be when a boy swings a stick in the high grass. The wind had seemed as wanton as a boy. Trees stood erect which alone must have withstood the whole blast, and companies of hemlock and pine, close arrayed, had all come down together. Men were working patiently in the path of catastrophe. The first spring stirred muddily around trees that would never bear leaf again.

We had ridden beyond Portland that day to see the woods. The way was by the poet's house on Congress Street. Sixty years before Henry Wadsworth Longfellow wrote his hexameters about the forest primeval, his grandfather began cutting down the pines and the hemlocks with an ax. Old Peleg Wadsworth on the 15,000 acres along the Saco River, which he got for thirteen cents an acre, was neither early nor alone. From the woods that ran back from The Rock the woodsheds of three hundred winters have been filled. The forests were cleared for the corn. The forests were burned for the ash. The forests were shipped by the boatload to the Indies and to England. Two years after Longfellow wrote about the lady Evangeline forever lost in Louisiana the wood of straight New England trees went around the Horn to make shanties

35

for the Forty-niners in California. The forests built the salt-
box houses, McIntire's mansions on Chestnut Street in
Salem, the spiral staircases which Bulfinch built on Beacon
Hill and the clean sweet clippers which slipped down Donald McKay's ways to the first water on the road to China.

Still in 1939 New England remained a forest. You can put
a lot of money into a little vault. A good many people can
be crowded into a tenement. Factories in New England, after
an old fashion, still huddle close together in groups upon a
stream. Even most of the farms seem tight and small. But
the forests go everywhere, and after three centuries of cutting
they occupy 68 per cent of all the land. That sounds like
Yankee thrift. It is Yankee waste instead. The people of New
England at the bottom of depression learned that of an original forty million acres of forest covering, they had cut all
but two million. Not less than fifteen million of these acres
had become farm and pasture, ten million acres of which had
been abandoned later to go back into second growth. The
best of that had also been cut down. There still remained
twenty-seven million acres in woodland, but half of it was
covered with valueless tree and forest weed. Between 1919
and 1929, while the Coolidge boom blessed the land, half
the sawmills of New England had shut up and half the workers had lost their jobs for lack of good-quality timber to cut.
But New England remained a region in which nearly half
the land would never be fit for anything but growing timber.
When the hurricane came that Wednesday afternoon in 1938,
the Yankees had already been before it.

I went to find out what both of them had done. In the
office of the New England Forest Emergency Project in Boston, Vico Isola sat before a big map of what New Englanders
called the blowdown which in vari-tinted townships showed
the swath the storm of September 21, 1938, had cut through
the already wasted woods and where it had hit the hardest.

There was a dark stripe in Connecticut and Rhode Island paralleling the Massachusetts line. A deep triangle cut down into Massachusetts. New Hampshire had been hit hardest. The path of the wind had widened to sweep eastern Vermont and tear at a plug of Maine. The dark towns, I knew, had not only lost church spires and elms; they had also seen an eight years' cut of timber turned up at its roots. The rapaciousness of the past among a supposedly thrifty people did not leave so much timber that the loss in the present could be easily borne. The broken trees would by summer be tinder for fire. The cry for help had risen as the wind died. Now the Yankees and the foresters raced with the summer and the bugs and the fire.

Isola swung his chair around to the map. With a cigarette in his lean hand he followed the wind. I followed his hand. It was as interesting as the map to consider that in this Yankee disaster an Italian, even though a Yale man, should be the forester in charge of information about it. Across the table a fat young man with his hair clipped close to scalp looked across us at the map.

"I'd like to see it," I said. "And not only the hurricane. Down in my country we've been thinking a lot about man's destruction of his forests without the help of any wind. Has that happened in New England, too?"

The slim, gray Isola nodded.

"New England has been importing about 80 per cent of its lumber."

"The hell you say!"

He smiled.

"I do. Why don't you go see it? We'll show you. You can go, can't you, Fleming?"

"Yes, sir," said the fat man with the clipped head. Isola introduced me to his assistant, Hugh Fleming.

So we set out on a dreary April morning in Fleming's

37

Nash, which he complained his mother's chauffeur had almost ruined, and I began to learn about both forests and Fleming. He was in his late thirties and had just come up from Washington, where he had been writing publicity designed to prevent forest fires. His story began long before that, as far back maybe as the cutting of the trees. He told me part of it as we rode. The rest he sent me later in a clipping about his engagement to Mrs. Bettie Randolph Harrison Davis Darling of Wellesley, Massachusetts. "Mr. Fleming," the clip from *The New York Times* said, "is a descendant of General James E. Fleming and Bishop Neely and is a member of the Chew and Johns families of Maryland and the Edward Griswold and Buehl families of Connecticut." He had gone from home in Erie, Pennsylvania, to Groton School and then to the University of Virginia and the School of Journalism at Columbia University. He had been publicity man and newspaper feature salesman, and somewhere along the line, as a sort of tart fruit of both Groton and newspapering, he had acquired a grim sense of humor and a mock insolence from which he derived much delight.

"There are two gals," he said on the road to Portland, "one named Netsa and the other named Nefe. The first one is the New England Timber Salvage Administration and the other is the New England Forest Emergency. I belong to Nefe."

Across the long-strung suburbs of Boston and the cities which are almost a part of its suburbs he told me in the vernacular of one newspaperman talking to another about what his big boss in Washington, F. A. Silcox, chief of the Forest Service until his death late in 1939, had called the Paul Bunyan job of salvaging the billion and a half feet of merchantable "blowdown" timber. That is a lot of lumber. It would build nearly forty such World's Fairs as New York opened that summer. He talked about "tramp iron" found in

some of the trees, old axheads, horseshoes, nails, the staples
with which secret service men had attached alarm wires to
trees when President Wilson had occupied Winston
Churchill's place in New Hampshire, any old metal around
which trees had grown, which would tear out the teeth of a
saw.

We stopped for gasoline beyond a big turreted institution
on a hill.

"It's the Danvers State Hospital for the Insane," said the
filling station man.

No institution anywhere is more appropriately placed, for
in the town of Danvers was old Salem Village where the bad
brats of credulous old Parson Samuel Parris began the Salem
witchcraft trials. The Danvers Hospital is monument to the
time when the whole of Massachusetts was crazy. In maybe
saner times we rode on toward our engagement with the forester in Portland. We went through Newburyport where,
Governor Saltonstall told me later, studies of the changing
New England human stocks were being made and across the
Merrimack River (and I remembered the *Monitor*), which not
only had borne clippers to the sea but had also turned the
wheels of mills in Haverhill and Lawrence and Lowell and
Manchester, and which from such busy flowing had not long
before seemed a stream running through an economic graveyard.

The Merrimack began far off under trees. The foresters
were not merely following the hurricane with a plan to salvage down-timber; they followed also its dramatic emphasis
with plan to fit a forest program into the economics of a New
England which that summer had a million able-bodied men
and women out of a total population of eight million unemployed or on relief who would work if they could get work.
While the foresters bought logs with Uncle Sam's money and
filled ponds with them or sawed them up into lumber piled

up like the cotton surplus, they began also planning toward a forest program which would make sense beyond both the long human waste and the wind's swift blow.

It was chilly on the road. A man from the South could understand the big houses which ran back in long, stay-in succession of woodshed and barn. I was impressed with the wealth which must have built them and with the continuing ability to keep so many of them painted white. All New England could be engaged, I thought, filling their deep and wide woodsheds and painting their long exteriors.

"A lot of them are owned by summer people and retired people, writers and so forth," Fleming thought. "And when they're not, you'd be surprised how many of these people have some good stocks and bonds tucked away somewhere."

We passed a big sign, not meant for us, directing tourists to Hampton Beach. There were not many people on the road, but the empty and shut roadside places indicated that, come summer, many were expected. Summer that day seemed a long way off. Portsmouth looked empty. Some of the grand old houses were shut tight, but the stoop of one which had seen better days made a seat for a whole row of children who needed the sun. We crossed the Piscataqua River. Beyond it the wide white road makes an entrance into Maine cluttered with wayside stands which as effectually hide the land as Connecticut's pretty planting hides Connecticut. They looked gaunt in April like gaudy women in the early morning. Some of the houses along the way were painted with a dirty yellow paint. On a rooftree beyond Ogunquit a row of white birds sat safe and solemn. There were some tarpaper houses, warm enough maybe but hideous certainly. In the Kennebunk Auto Exchange there were old buggies as well as old cars. There were still red flags on the highway fences to guide the snow plows. It was cold. Beside the road there was still some snow. On a hilltop as we approached

Portland the Danish Village, an elaborate tourist camp built after the pattern of its name, looked both grotesque and lonely on that damp day like a gay stage set in an unheated theater.

We passed the Wadsworth-Longfellow House built by the man who cut the primeval forests and lived in by the boy who was to write about them; and, in his office on High Street, we found Paul Bedard. A slight, Latin-looking man in his green forester's uniform, he was in charge of the salvage job in Maine. He is a Northerner by birth and education, but he was on duty at the Jefferson National Forest in Virginia when the phone rang at one o'clock on a Saturday in September. Washington was on the wire. New England was just stirring from Wednesday's storm. He was to be in his car by three o'clock on the road to Maine. He had not been back since. But the Maine job was moving. The state with the biggest forests had been least touched by the wind.

Only four counties and forty towns were directly hit. Even so, the 45,000,000 board feet of timber which the Federal foresters hoped to salvage was enough to build a city in the woods where the trees came down. Maine is a lumberman's land. Maybe gone forever are those lumberjacks who used to come down from the woods with a winter's wages to the Devil's Half Acre in Bangor. Even if the distance a man can spit his tobacco juice into a head wind and hit the mark has diminished, the race still survives that can cut the trees.

Nearly four-fifths of Maine is classed as forest, which is a larger ratio than in any other state in the Union, and a correspondingly high percentage of the people is dependent upon the forests in one way or another for livelihood. So, from the moment men stuck their heads out of their houses to see what the wind had done, there was an awareness of the problem and an understanding of the task. And men to do the job. If also there were some who carried the logic of their opposition to Federal intrusion into the state of Maine (which with Vermont alone had voted against Roosevelt in 1936), to the blowdown business, Republican state officials joined agricultural extension workers in quieting their fears.

"The jam on salvage," said Forester Bedard, "broke when the first checks arrived."

We finished an early lunch at the Eastland Hotel, which also runs the Danish Village on the outside of town and which had Danish atmosphere left over for its hotel dining room. I wondered, when I was in Portland later, if the same architect with this Scandinavian inclination was also responsible for cutting the old-time big bedrooms into three rooms, each just big enough for a skinny traveler.

Outside I shivered in April. "I'm cold."

Bedard laughed. "Maine has three seasons: July, August, and winter. They also say that the Maine weather is pretty good but the sleighing is bad in July and August."

Early American Fleming told the world-wide story: ". . . and in winter it's too cold to fish." A man told it to me once about Siberia. Herbert Elliston, the financial writer who moved from England slowly around the whole world to Boston, asked me if I had heard the Finnish story and told it. It must be a good story or this is a bad world. But it indicates the universal human quality behind the folklore of the world which is not always concerned with the gods.

Bedard took the wheel of Fleming's car and we moved along a noble old residential street and then out into the country and northwest toward North Windham and Raymond. We moved on the same road I was to ride in a greener June to the Luther Gulick Camps where I had a daughter camping, but this time the snow thickened on the roadsides as we moved north; and there was ice in the ponds and on big Sebago Lake. There were no camping children then. They were as gone as the boy Nathaniel Hawthorne who, with a

42

little Negro, had roamed the shore around Raymond long ago. The shore was waiting for the children and the older people, too. The empty-but-waiting quarters for summer visitors stretched in almost continuous line beside the lake under the trees. Thinking of children and trees together, I asked Bedard about the traffic in Christmas trees.

The old idea that the wholesale distribution of Christmas trees meant destroyed forests, like the selling of the seed corn, was no longer held. Cutting trees for Christmas could, if the trees were wisely selected as a part of proper thinning, serve the forests as well as the children far away and put some money into the farmer's pocket for his own Christmas as well. The modern trend was to smaller trees in an apartment-house civilization. Change reached far out into the woods: The forests are no longer merely lumber; increasingly they are pulp. A tree can make a dress as well as a house, a newspaper, a novel. Not far away from where we rode, Bedard said, there was a factory which did a big business in lollypop sticks. (The total production of Maine toothpick factories is about 17,000,000 per day; a cord of sound birch will make 9,000,000 toothpicks. Somebody uses them.)

We passed the narrow-gauge railroad at Bridgton which had been about to end its running forever as unprofitable but took a year more of life from carrying supplies for the Forest Service's salvage job. After its custom the ill wind had blown somebody good. Along the road there were more long houses running back through the capacious woodshed to barn. In the old days, Bedard said, men had stayed inside in the winters, and there had been a good deal of tuberculosis. The winter sports now were pulling the younger people outdoors and improving the general health, he thought. I huddled in my thinking with the old folks about the insalubrious stoves.

Just south of where we rode Peleg Wadsworth's men had

43

cut the trees, and young Longfellow had seen what they left. But beside us the land was black-scarred. A fire in 1934, such as foresters feared from the hurricane's debris in the future, had burned here. It had started from a dynamite cap on the highway and, though it was not a big fire as foresters count big fires, it had almost circled and strangled old Fryeburg, where young Daniel Webster had taught school and wrote as he taught that female company was one thing with which he could "conveniently enough dispense." Webster and New England were both younger then, and both afterwards changed their minds more than once. Time since, I thought, extended all the way from Webster's opposition to tariffs in a seagoing New England and Webster's support of tariffs in a manufacturing New England to a new opposition to the extension of Federal powers and the intervention of the Federal power to save the blown-down timber. There were Yankees among the blown-down trees who had loudly doubted the ability of government to do a businesslike job, and some of the same didn't like it a bit when the government doing a businesslike job rejected the little stick logs they solemnly proffered for sale in salvage. (Straight and six inches through, the government demanded and got.)

From the long houses in Fryeburg which ran back from pleasant street into deep yard we drove on to a dry site near town where the logs the government had bought were piled to wait for the sawmill. The piles looked precarious to me. If a log rolled no human leg would stop it. The logs did not roll. They lay in their piles and, before summer, would be piles of stuck lumber waiting for buyers. (Nobody then seemed to know where the buyers of so much lumber would be.) There were plenty of logs coming for the government's cash. That day two men with axes were clearing away brush to make more room for more logs. Husky young men, they were, but not of any strange roaring lumberjack breed. I

44

suspect that bearded, ribald stock is gone forever outside the books. Their brush fire burned about an old stump, and beside it talking to them was David Bradley. He looked and was in every essential the Yankee, but when Fleming mentioned that he was from Pennsylvania, Bradley grinned to a neighbor.

"I am, too. I'm Potter County."

He had been visiting down there when the hurricane hit, and he was, he said, the first man to enter Maine by Vermont and New Hampshire over the cluttered roads after the storm. What he found on his farms and on the timber rights he owned with his partner, Fred Ella, was worse than he feared. I heard somebody count his losses in millions of board feet. Timber salvage in his case had been Bradley salvage. He and thousands of others had good reason to be friend of the foresters. If the government had not entered the blowdown area with its salvage program, not only would much timber have been lost but the price for that cut would have been disastrous in a land where all men more or less still live upon the woods. Only the government with its "U.S." mark struck into the ends of the logs and the lumber with raised letters on the backs of its axes could have done the job.

Now Mr. Bradley watched the two men clearing the brush and talked to us, grinning and satisfied. In his red Mackinaw over a substantial hard-worn gray suit, he looked playfully guileless as he made a casual and preliminary dicker with Bedard about trucking some logs. He was not pretty. His battered brown hat was pushed back on his big head. His teeth under the gray mustache could have stood some attention. There was warmth in his shrewdness and a dry humor in his eyes. Though, with his hands thrust into his pockets, he was not as erect as a pine, he seemed to grow out of the Maine earth nevertheless. On it he was richer than he looked but, like other men, dependent still on the cut and blown

45

land. He was, I learned, an eligible widower around Fryeburg, and women, who often know the value of timber and
farms as well as any man, petted him, calling him David. I
suspect he liked it and would grin as casually for them as he
would over the sharpness of a lumber trade, recognizing similarity. No wind or woman would blow his head off. The task
of the foresters had been made easier by his help.

He grinned after us as we drove north toward Lovell to
see on a side road the wet storage operations behind booms
on the same Saco River which Peleg Wadsworth had used
long ago. Not all the logs could go to the sawmills. That
spring and summer logs shared the rivers and ponds with the
visitors and boarders and campers. (Wood stains and decay
do not occur when the moisture content of wood is less than
twenty per cent or the wood cells are absolutely full of water.
Like ourselves fungi need both air and water. In lakes and
ponds the logs could wait safe from bugs, rot and stain for
their time at the rasping sawmills and the overloaded market.) In ponds below cottages men walked the precarious
logs untangling and submerging them safe from the warm
air.

Bedard drove down the road and knocked at a door. He
knocked again, but no one came. A young man near the
barn went unconcerned about his work.

"Is Mr. Buzzell here?"

The young man turned slowly. "He ought to be."

Bedard knocked again. We were about to go away when
E. Chandler Buzzell, elderly, fat and sleepy-looking, opened
the door. He gave Bedard familiar welcome, and all of us
went in through the vestibule made tight against cold
weather to a front room which was both sitting room and
Farmer Buzzell's office. The storm windows were still in
place. I had noticed on other houses along the road the in-
sulating walls of earth or of tree branches around the bottoms of the houses. I spoke of the cold.

"I was saying to my boys this morning," Mr. Buzzell said, "I don't remember when there was so much snow so late on the ground. I mind back in May, 1888, it was something like this."

He considered that ancient snow.

"But it's not as cold here when it's 20 below as when it's just zero on the coast."

He sat in a gray suit, gray-headed before an old desk every pigeonhole of which was packed and stuffed with folded papers. There would be the economic history of the Maine farm there, I thought. Those papers might help to explain why the number of Maine farms had been falling since 1880, and why the number of acres under cultivation had fallen, too. Before them Mr. Buzzell sat between an old-fashioned turn-the-crank telephone on the wall and a small modern radio. His thick sweater-vest was buttoned to his throat. He still looked sleepy.

"The storm hit me as hard as it could," he said mildly; "but I didn't have much, just enough to keep me off the town and maybe leave the boys a little."

I knew he was one of the most important men in his region, a country of sweet corn and canneries and trees and tourists. I had heard the story that the car of the Governor of Maine had been sent to take him to the first of the meetings which discussed salvage after the storm. He was a safe distance from being "on the town."

He talked about timber. When he was a boy all these mountains were black with spruce. There had been work for everybody. They used to go up with oxen and bring down the logs. The Diamond Match people had taken pine. In his own years he had made three complete cuttings in his wood lot. But he looked to the future. He wanted to know what the government was going to do about pulp wood. As we went out I noticed that, although the snow had not disappeared from the past winter, his woodshed was packed to

47

capacity for that 20 below zero winter which would certainly be ahead.

The foresters were planning that way, too. While they cleaned up after a wind, their leaders planned a program based not on one blow but upon what the Dean of the Yale School of Forestry had called before the blow "the long continued attrition of past abuse." They planned on the basis of belief that almost three-fourths of New England was suited only to growing trees, but was producing less than a fourth of the high-quality timber it could produce. They began to figure out loud with the amplification the hurricane had given them about the meaning of the woods to watersheds and floods and tourists, about the possibility of re-establishing New England as an important timber producing region which might provide support for 300,000 families in forest farming and the primary manufacture of wood products, about forests which might provide a necessary tax base for an adequate standard of local government. In a waste which went back beyond the hurricane three hundred years, they planned to A.D. 2000 and hoped that men in the 1940's would hear them. Maybe they will.

Dark was coming on when we rode back through Fryeburg and across the state line into New Hampshire, where James Bosworth, another forester (who had done important work in developing mechanical fire-fighting equipment in the West), was to meet Bedard to drive him back to Portland. We found him waiting in the Presidential Inn, which in Conway welcomes summer visitors under the Presidential Range. With him was Gerald Wheeler, a natively witty, dry-talking New Hampshire man on duty in connection with recreation in the White Mountains National Forest. In his civilian clothes his pants gapped below his vest, but his feet were in precise contact with the ground.

In the room named after a President—I think it was

Thomas Jefferson (the Presidential Inn uses Presidents instead of numbers to designate its bedrooms)—we gathered for
a drink. I put the ice into glasses, and Fleming poured the
Scotch. Wheeler, who has the snow top of Mount Washington in his realm, belittled the man-high snow pile outside the
window which seemed to me a sight in April.

"Why, we had a frost in August in New Hampshire," he
said, "that busted the cylinder head out of a tractor."

I felt my leg pulled, and I let him pull. Tall tales can be
good tales, too. Downstairs he told me about a factual and
fabulous New Hampshire while a pretty New Hampshire girl
brought us steak for dinner. Afterwards we walked down the
empty town street which even in the dark seemed waiting
through a weary spring for summertime and summer visitors.
As we came in to go to bed there was a quaint old lady in an
old-fashioned bonnet talking to the clerk at the desk. She
was asking about breakfast.

"When I come into a house," she was saying with a solici-
tous pride—I don't know why, but she looked timid and
afraid—"I suit myself to its convenience."

That might have been a good rule for the people who came
upon a continent, I thought. The Yankees like the Southerners had dealt with the room they used as if nobody else would
ever occupy it after them. A government could provide salvage after a storm but not good sense before it. Maybe not
even after it.

As I went up to my room, named after William Henry
Harrison who was President of the United States for thirty-
one days, I passed a gray-haired traveling salesman who was
showing his samples to some ladies. He was working hard at
his job. He talked devoutly the language of thrift. He looked
old and a little threadbare. He seemed sad, but he did not
keep me long from sleep.

V

Paper and Play

"I THINK THIS WILL BURN OFF LATER IN THE DAY," the forester said.

He threw back his head and searched the sky in appraisal of the morning mist over Conway. I hoped so. The White Mountains in the New Hampshire north country are not the greatest mountains in the world. Their wooded slopes run up to no heights unequaled. My own Southern mountains rise by cove and cabin and hound dog's bark nearer to the sun. But these were mountains made almost articulate by innkeeper and poet, philosophers and passenger agents while other American mountains were merely rising to the sky.

The road which led through the covered bridge into North Conway and toward Mount Washington carried us that gray morning into that country into which men and women had been coming for more than a century for holiday, but in which only a few humans in all that time had stayed in hope of a living out of a wild and beautiful land. I wanted to see its peaks and its people. Despite the prose in its praise the whole White Mountain country remained, I knew, a region with scarcely more humans in it than in the one grimy industrial city of Manchester down the state. But crowds still came to it, many of them the same noisy, unquiet companies which Fredrika Bremer came from Sweden to describe in the 1850's. Then the novelist from Stockholm was a little shocked at the

New Englanders on holiday. They did not seem to understand, she wrote, any other mode of enjoying nature than
talking, laughing, eating, drinking, and all kinds of noisy
pleasure. They posted up the mountain laughing at full gallop, she said, and came down again at full gallop. The horses
are ghosts with the laughter now. Ghosts are those dead gentlemen who let the champagne corks fly in the rambling
hotels, who played cards in the middle of the day; and ghosts,
too, are those ladies who talked all day long about dressmak-
ers and fashions. And so is the disapproving little Swede.
They are better ghosts, I think, than the more famous rural
Willeys who guessed wrong to be engulfed in an avalanche
and to be immortalized by Hawthorne. There are more such
gay outland ghosts making in the same pattern. Winter and
summer now, in their time, they make the same sort of
laughter in the snow and the sun.

But there has been change. It takes poverty to preserve a
resort: The hotels and cottages rise by the sea where the
harbors were too shallow for the ships, and inland where soils
were poor and forested hills ran up too steep and high for
the plow. Today it takes money to develop resorts. North
Conway fortunately produced the man who now produces
the money. It was fifty-seven years that summer since Harvey
Gibson was born in North Conway, to go to school in the old
academy in Fryeburg where Daniel Webster taught, and to
become a rich banker in New York. He comes back and his
money goes back, and both help, in an old summer section
turning more and more to winter skiing, to push the not very
pretty town, which looks on loveliness, toward its share of
the new sport in the snow.

"All kinds of people come," said the native newspaperman
who had gone far off and come back to find content where he
began.

There were not many visiting people in North Conway

when I was there in April. Winter was turning into mud time, and summer was still a long way off. It was a native time then. Jesse Ambrose and his boy Langdon had already made a hundred gallons of maple syrup though the sap was not as sweet as in other years and had to be boiled longer. The first thunderstorm of the year had come early, and the rain with it had taken away a good deal of the snow. But the spring was slow. And snow remained.

"We get college kids who come up with five dollars in their pockets and expect to take a lot of change home. We get rich New York people. There are some sophisticated drunks. Often as not they come with other men's wives."

"What does North Conway think of that?"

He grinned slowly. "There are no Puritans left in New Hampshire," he said.

Nor would there be in any other similar place where the matter involved such a new cash crop as skiing and winter boarders are. Modern farming is impossible in most White Mountain areas, and much of the land has with final wisdom been allowed to go back into forest. Though the White Mountain National Forest harvests its timber under methods which permit profitable operations as well as assure successive crops and appeal to successive tourists, lumbering in the White Mountains is a long way from that time when the New Hampshire lumber king was the richest man in New England. (The timber cut in New Hampshire in 1934 was one-seventh of that in 1907.) Paper sometimes seems going after lumber. The short, skinned, pulp logs are too often no surer of profitable market than the lumber-long ones which go to the mill wearing the bark. The tourist under the trees gradually but not always adequately takes the place of timber for the mills.

We walked in North Conway through the empty corridors of that Eastern Slopes Inn which our newspaperman said

Harvey Gibson had built to make Americans as comfortable
in his home town as he had been in a German Alpine place
where he paid three hundred marks a day. There was no
noisy laughter in it that day nor any feeling that the ghost of
old laughter was there. The inn seemed new and not warmed
by a past. But it would be warm with lights on in it, and
white-shouldered women dressed for the evening in this
bright hostel surrounded by snow. A crowd of schoolteachers,
or women who looked like schoolteachers, were being shown
through the empty rooms that day. They peered over one another's shoulders. They whispered and giggled. Beds were
naked to the mattresses. Rugs were rolled back. Outside,
there was neither summer nor clean snow.

On the road north by Intervale there was snow, and whiter
birch trees among the pines. They gleamed in the woods.
Close to a sign pointing to the ski-tow (which in a sport-lov-
ing but mechanical age eliminates the climb back after the
flight down) was another sign in stern warning against the
defacement of the birches. A man who devotes his life to
both the forests and the visitors spoke with feeling.

"I'll tell you these skiers are so-and-sos. They want everything for nothing. And the bastards carve their names in the
birch trees and peel off the bark for souvenirs."

He spoke with an irritation which almost always accompanies eagerness in resorts. There were of course, as the
editor in North Conway had said, all kinds of people in the
crowds which come in. The White Mountains have made
preparation for them all—and maybe more than all, after a
familiar pattern in cash crops. There were commonplace col-
onies of cabins by the roadside. They needed cleaner snow or
leafy green to make them appealing. They seemed dismal
now, almost abandoned in the margins of the brown woods
lit only by the birches.

There was better accommodation, simple and sound and

not too costly, in Charles Sullivan's place beside the road in
Pinkham Notch (named after that early Joe Pinkham who
came into the region with a trained pig pulling his sled, so
they say). Cheaper still and simpler still were the log bunk-
houses, occupied largely by the young, maintained by the
Appalachian Mountain Club at the height of elevation (two
thousand feet), in the Notch. Young skiers were lounging in
its assembly hall which smelled of young bodies, wet leather,
coffee, and tobacco. Some of them slept in the snow by the
roadside in auto trailers no bigger than kennels for good-
sized dogs.

The snow, though melting slowly, was still thick about the
camp in April. While Wheeler and I talked to the boys,
Fleming had his midmorning coffee. Skiers moved across the
damp snow up toward the dry heights of Tuckerman Ravine
where that year there was skiing until June 25th. There was
a good deal of snow still there on the 19th of July. The con-
sistency of the snow improves, skiers say, as the season ad-
vances.

"Sometimes," Wheeler said, "you'll see the kids skiing in
bathing suits on the Fourth of July."

Certainly the long wait for the boarders from August to
June is closing. The whole year is tourist time. Probably, as
the irritated man suggested, the skiers are in general not so
rich a crop as those who come in summer. Nor are they by
any means so stationary. Even among the older summer folk
now, there is a diminishing proportion of those who once
came in such numbers to sit on the same piazza from June
to September. Even the old move now, and the young fly. By
the very nature of their sport most of the skiers are young.
They are nevertheless part of a general process which is
breaking the long solitude of the snow. The boys at Dartmouth College probably gave the first impetus to the change
as far back as 1910. What followed did not happen with the

speed of a man coming down a mountain on skis. The State
Highway Commission began to keep more and more roads
open in winter. Foresters and CCC boys and chambers of
commerce and cabin owners all stirred themselves. If the
boys and the girls did not bring much money in the breeches
of their skiing clothes, they still brought enough to make
seventy-five towns anxious to share it. In the long New
Hampshire winters most of them need it.

We had come into the White Mountain National Forest
down below Pinkham Notch, and we went out of it briefly
again where the old carriage road ran off to the left to go in
a long curving to the top of Mount Washington. There were
very American ghosts on that road, too, of a fat woman and
a schoolmaster, of six-horse carriages, and a first automobile,
all more concerned with time than beauty in the ascent. The
gatehouse where toll is taken seemed shut for lack of business, and the road was empty. We drove on to the Dolly
Copp Forest Camp which the Forest Service maintains for
summer campers in memory of that pioneer settler woman
who in 1881 on the fiftieth anniversary of her marriage to
Hayes Dodifer Copp declared: "Fifty years is long enough
for any woman to live with a man." She went off to live her
remaining years in Maine and left the forest to others.

They have come to the camp named after her in increasing numbers. Off the main road across Peabody River the
Forest Service provides camp sites for all campers without
charge and without much trouble to the Service. Once on the
summer-crowded camp grounds two fancy ladies briefly conducted their trade. Sometimes campers are careless and in-
considerate of trees and other people. But in general the
mobile masses are neat enough among the tame trees in the
tended wilderness. All the government has asked in return
for their camping was once the answering of a questionnaire.
The replies may indicate much or little about those who

come—and often come again—to camp and fish and swim in
the park. The answers showed that 79.44 per cent of the
campers during the time the government was inquisitive
about it were male; 30 per cent of them said they were professional men; only 5 per cent admitted they were unskilled
workers, and less than 2 per cent said they were unemployed.
The questionnaires were not sworn to but the income status
of the campers as the answers showed was:

Under $1,000	14.39	per cent
$1,000 to $2,000	36.44	
$2,000 to $3,000	21.48	
$3,000 to $5,000	6.67	
Over $5,000	2.89	
No replies	18.13	

A government that wants to please asked for criticisms and
got some. Here are some objections:

To foreigners	0.06	per cent
To lack of privacy	0.55	
Not well enough advertised	0.06	
To thoughtlessness of people	0.32	
To Jews	0.11	
To petting parties	0.10	

Too small to work out even in hundredths of one per cent
were those who thought the government ought to run a beer
parlor and provide individual iceboxes for the campers.

It was a pity, I thought, that some such information was
not available from those who in summer occupy the big,
rambling, white hotels set upon view-commanding emi-
nences. Or maybe the most interesting objections would be
those of the gentlemen who have their money invested in
these hotels. Boarded up on the hillsides that April, placarded
with the warning that the State Police was watching them,

they looked as old-fashioned as would the ladies who first occupied their long porches when they were built long ago—or the whist they played. There seemed to be almost more places where such elderly establishments had burned to the ground than places where they still stood. There seemed to have been a remarkable succession of fires in hotels in a north country where visitors were seeking and getting new and different accommodations. They were new visitors, too, on wheels, who came not for the summer but more often for the night. The White Mountains had been lit not only by fire in the forests but by a remarkable procession of carelessness or incendiarism going back across the years but with an illuminating concentration in the last decades.

We laughed in libel. Somebody recalled that the storage houses for natural ice in Maine had burned with a startling frequency after the development of manufactured ice. Not all change was marked by fire. Wheeler recalled that when he was a boy in Bangor the ships had been docked two deep taking on timber.

"Now," he said, "there's not a real lumber mill on the Penobscot."

There was another barren site where a hotel had been. Another was still standing, waiting for visitors or time or fire. Foresters talked about the new, real menace in the woods about them where the wind had tangled blown timber. The hotels wanted nobody frightened by fear of fire in the woods. But warning and teaching were necessary to reduce hazard. Where did a sensible forester draw the line between warning and frightening?

"I've got that stuck into me and broke off," said Wheeler, "and, hell, I'm no P.R. man."

The Public Relations man himself was not sure.

"You know up here we live a long way from the wigwam," the New Hampshire forester said.

We drove around and back, through these Federal forests so far from the wigwam in Washington and at last out of the National Forest to Gorham where in a hotel before a wide common looking off toward the mountains the elderly manager told us how visitors had come in coaches to the mountains long ago. On his walls he had pictures of the coaches and teams. He remembered the company the horses had pulled through the hills. But tourists were not all. Those were the same years in which, according to a New Hampshire Planning and Development Commission, which talks in terms of New England virtues even when it is discussing New England fault, the forests were "energetically reduced." Now behind the hotel, which looked out toward the big hills where men played, the cut in the forest and change in the world beyond the forest made a tragic threat in a land of pulp and paper to farmers and factory workers and the families which owned big mills which once made money for them all.

One man said, "Netsa's not buying much pulp."

And the other: "I know it, and they are getting a hell of a lot of criticism for it. Pulp was the going concern in New Hampshire before the hurricane, and white pine was already sucking the hind tit."

The forest ranger in the office opposite Marie's Beauty Shop on the second floor of the building in Gorham was pessimistic. This Coos County, most northern in New Hampshire, is bigger than the state of Rhode Island, but in its woods only forty thousand people live, half of them in the town of Berlin, where paper manufacturing had been sick. That meant not only idle men in Berlin but farmers without a market for their pulpwood all around it. By New England standards Berlin, where the Androscoggin River meets a stream called the Dead, is a new town. There were only one hundred and seventy-three people in it when lumbermen from Portland came in in 1852 and began the building of the Brown Paper Company (called the Berlin Company until the Kaiser made the name unpopular). There were only a thousand people there in 1880. Then it boomed in a paper-using world. Other paper companies came. But like some others this boom did not so much burst as escape. There were wage cut and strike and strikebreakers and violence in the International Paper Company's plant in 1921. Then that company moved away. In 1929 the depression hit hard the Brown Paper Company. Competition has grown far away. Around the paper town soft woods are disappearing, and there are technical and transportation problems involved in the greater use of hard woods.

"The moneylenders put a man in charge. The offices are in Portland. Now they're getting a loan from the RFC. The state's been signing the town's notes, and the town's been buying the pulpwood with the state's money, and the town's been letting the mill have it as it could take it. God knows I hope this RFC loan works out. This isn't the Browns' trouble. All the people in the north country are in it." And he added sadly, "I don't know."

We went up the bank of the beautiful Androscoggin River to see the town which in north New Hampshire had suffered in the woods as Manchester, the textile town, had suffered in the more crowded south.

"In Berlin," said a New Hampshire native who rode with us, "there are Italians and Russians and Austrians, some Finns and Polacks, Swedes, a lot of hopping frogs, and a few white people."

I was interested in the prejudice in his distinction and puzzled, too.

"Hopping frogs?" I asked.

He laughed. "French-Canadians."

There were log booms in the wide stream. Long ago it must have been a lovely valley, and there is still beauty in it.

As we came to houses, many of them were unpainted. There were freight cars along the river, and beside them a pile of yellow sulphur, long as two boxcars and higher than the trains. Across the river there were piles of some sort of waste, like slag or pulp strainings. The tenements at the edge of town were not pretty. Higher than any tenement was the young mountain of gray, peeled, pulp logs.

"There must be fifty thousand cords of pulp in that pile."

I thought of the forests and the labor that cut it and piled it there, and what the money for it meant back in the hills on the little steep farms.

There may be places in New England which could have been lovelier than this valley must have been when the river ran unregarded and undeveloped down the gorge between the rocks. I did not see them. Then the forests ran back untouched in first wilderness. It was not only place for beauty; it was also perfect place for production and power. Development had won and, even if development had lost also, beauty's chance seemed gone forever. Man had not put a hand on it but a paw. Now it had been developed and in part discarded. Close to the road lay the ugly ruins of the huge old International Paper plant which had been partially razed as it was deserted. A stranger looking at that half-destroyed mill as a stranger did not need to be a philosopher to wonder at the deliberate ruin. It seemed a queer capitalism and a queer local tax system under which money had to be spent, here as elsewhere in New England, in destruction of property to save taxes on it. In tax reduction the community rewards the property owner who makes an eyesore; the man or company who improves his property pays more taxes. I am sure that must be logical and just. But neither the logic nor the justice seems to make much sense to me.

Up the hill was the abandoned little office building, dirty now, with broken windowpanes, from which executives of the International had bought pulp and made paper and faced strike and diminishing wood supply, and in which, too, they must have carried out the unpleasant orders about shutting up and moving away. We rode the length of the town, past the big Brown plants still equipped and still, though not steadily, running, by the big factory fortress on the stream of the Burgess Sulphite Fibre Company, to the end of the town where the ski jump of the first skiing club in the United States stands as invitation to winter play. There was a Carnegie Library. Westerns and Tarzan pictures were showing at a movie. We rode back from the river in the town which spreads on each side of it. There was a big bulking scabrous tenement on a hill. Another on the steep slope of Elm Street looked like a wooden firetrap, but there were pink satin curtains in one window. I wondered about the woman who had put them there behind the unpainted walls. On the storied porches of all the tenements were bright clotheslines.

Across the river there were names alien to old New Hampshire on the tombstones in the cemetery. All along Goebel Street there were shabby four-story tenements each with its succession of porches. Before them an old Irishman, walking with the bowlegs of rickets, was smoking a pipe. There were signs in French. The names of the tradesmen were Russian and Italian and Polish. Out at the end of Madigan Street part of an unfinished tenement was occupied by a family with many children.

It seemed a sad town, quick-grown with people from all over the earth, but uncertain of its future. It had known strike and depression and the bitter politics along lines of industrial and economic division. In New Hampshire in November, 1938, it had twenty Communist votes. No revolution, but in the state only one ward in Manchester and one in Concord had cast more Communist votes than the third ward in Berlin. Not long before, it elected the only Farmer

Labor city government in the East. From the town in widening circles the forest upon which it depended had been cut. In a real sense it seemed a new frontier town and an industrial town grown old in difficulty, too. Men had been not only worried but angry in it.

"It is entirely possible this might be a ghost city in five years," said one man in the car.

"Yes," said a New Hampshire man, "but I don't think they are going to let it bust. You can't throw thirty thousand people right down on their tails at once."

(In Concord, bald State Forester John W. Foster, a wise quiet man with folds of skin doubling on his eyelids as on an old eagle's eyes, spoke his faith in the ultimate success of the Brown Company and the town of Berlin out of a knowledge of the company and the woods around it. He discounted doom in Berlin. There was a future for paper in Berlin—in New Hampshire—just as there was a deep past behind tourists: The first roadside tourist cabins in the United States, he said, were built in Crawford Notch in 1922 by James F. Donahue and a man named Hamlin of Bartlett, New Hampshire. That did not seem very long ago.)

We moved south and west, back by Gorham and around the border of the National Forest. There was the remnant of a mill village. There were big woodpiles by the poorest houses. Across a field a poor old sway-back white horse was standing by a stone fence in a brown field under a gray sky. The New Hampshire man looked back at a filling station attendant.

"He was a dumb-looking bastard, a typical White Mountain type."

He did not look so much stupid as lost. Near him on the road there were empty houses in which the moss must have crept across the hearths. The big hotel at Twin Mountain did look like a tomb for lost summertimes. We turned east again, on a road that would be crowded that summer, past the Fabyan House, the garage which had once been a tabernacle for the summer preaching of Henry Ward Beecher, and the big Mount Washington Hotel around which the hurricane had blown with a special violence in the woods. A grim man working alone was cutting logs in the grounds of the hotel.

"The Uncle's line is up there half a mile," Wheeler said, pointing where the National Forest and the nation's timber began.

From the Base Station of the Mount Washington Cog Railway which has been carrying scenery lovers up the mountain for sixty years, we turned back to cross a section of the National Forest again and go down the road that runs beneath the Old Man of the Mountain. The Profile House had burned at the beginning of the twenties. The Flume House had burned not long before. But the Pemigewasset still flowed down its beautiful valley. We crossed the river into Lincoln, one of those towns which depend for the materials of its wood and paper industries upon the calculated scientific cutting of the National Forest. We saw where women's shoe heels are made out of trees. In a sad little section of tarpaper houses and poor wooden ones, called the Pig's Ear, snow was melting away to leave bare and ugly the big pile of garbage and tin cans which a restaurant had accumulated through the winter.

Trees had been blown down in a graveyard. But the tomb opening on the roadside to receive the dead when the snow is too deep or the ground is too frozen to permit the digging of graves was solemnly secure. We drove by a paper mill's wood where (so I was told) New Hampshire Yankees met Massachusetts Yankees and won. When they sold the timber resources, the local gossip said, the New Hampshire sellers led the Massachusetts buyers around and around the same twenty acres of trees for days and days. They held all the decent lumber in the whole tract. Down the highway the shut sporting-goods factory was no sign of any Yankee's triumph.

"It was closed by the long noses," the small-town policeman said.

We went on down the road upon which factories and tourist accommodations contested more and more as to which should stamp the quality of the country. And past wide, blue Winnipesaukee we rode into Laconia, which takes its name from the lakes about it but dumps its sewerage into Lake Winnisquam below it. Sewerage disposal plants cost money. Knitting machinery manufacturers do not want to pay more taxes and anyhow the trout are fatter in the lake where the sewerage goes. Tourists are excellent but taxes are terrible.

Below as above Laconia the waters remain beautiful and blue. Colon bacilli are not visible to the naked eye.

VI

Laconism in Laconia

"THEY CAN'T FOOL ME. I'm a licensed embalmer myself, and I used to be in the undertaking business. These undertakers needn't tell me they can't bury the people on relief for forty-five dollars. That's what we'll pay. Seventy-five dollars is too much. The people on relief are arrogant. Here's one family that got fourteen hundred dollars a year. They come up there and tell me what I can do. All right. But as sure as I'm chairman of the County Commissioners of Belknap County, I'm going to balance the budget.

"I'm an Irishman, and I don't pay but twenty-five cents apiece for my neckties; but I'm married to the richest woman in New England. I try—now get this—try to sell some real estate. I sold this hotel to Governor Murphy for seventy-five thousand dollars. I never fooled with the little stuff, and I never took less than 5 per cent. I've been on the town council, mayor of Laconia, member of the Governor's Council. Governor Winant sent me up to Berlin, and I stayed three days looking into things up there for him before the state lent the town a couple of million dollars. I never spent a nickel to get elected to anything in my life. I could have been governor if I'd spent my wife's money; but then she'd been boss.

"They can't fool me. I know. They can do it for forty-five dollars easy. I've got my embalming license. Last year some of the undertakers at their state meeting got a few drinks

65

aboard. They thought it was a joke. I know who it was. They called on me to demonstrate I could still embalm if I wanted to keep my license. I put on my overalls and did it. How about that?

"I've been in the South a good deal. My wife owns a big place down in Florida—in Daytona. She gave the Legion there a big monument. When the police down there found out that I was her husband they apologized to me for getting after me about parking. Bowed and scraped. To hell with them! My wife owns the bank down the street, and when she found out they'd charged me ten cents for cashing a check she made the teller bring the dime out to the house. I'll be damned if I'd have done it. She called me up and said she wanted me to drive to Florida with her. She went to help elect Dave Sholtz governor. He'd be in the Senate now if he hadn't got into a fight with a smart woman over some job in Tallahassee.

"In Daytona at nine o'clock at night you ought to see the niggers run across the bridge. And white men are not much better off in the Negro section. One thing I like about your South: Up here we had a degenerate take a nice Catholic boy to ride, and when the boy resisted he killed him. They didn't find his body for two days, did they, Louie? He was convicted, but now he gets a new trial; and the first trial cost twelve thousand dollars. Now down in your South he'd already have been hung. That's one thing I like about it. Northerners ruin Negroes, then hate them after they've ruined them. I saw one last night pushing his way in the movies, elbowing people out of the way. None of that in Daytona.

"We've got to balance the budget. These people on relief think they can tell the County Commissioners what they can do and what they can't. We haven't got any money to throw around. When did the car plant close up, Louie?

"Well, anyway, we've had plenty of people on relief. There are eleven members of the House in the General Court from Laconia, and three of them are on relief. Of course, the House doesn't amount to anything. There are five hundred members, and two men does it all. Don't pay any attention to the House, the Senate does everything. There's not so much money around here that we can throw it around. Once when I was mayor my wife lent the town fifty thousand dollars and still had half a million in the bank. The banks don't want so much money as they've got. There are only about a hundred men in New Hampshire who lend money. I know one man, a barber here, who got rich lending mileage books to Boston. He'd buy at the mileage book price and charge at the rate for one trip. There're ways to make money. But there's not enough around here for Belknap County to throw any away. We got to balance the budget, and I'm the man to do it.

"If I was this young salesman from Massachusetts, I'd be like I was, an undertaker, and have two funerals a year and sit on my tail and tell the world to go to hell."

VII

Democracy on Tuesday

IN A SMALL ROOM IN THE GRANITE BUILDING with the eagle on its dome she talked very fast and very seriously.

"This young man in our town is an albino. He's mentally all right, but puny and just able to support himself. But he wanted to get married, and his uncle who is a selectman said, 'If you marry, you'll be on the town.' He got married all the same. But they had no children and, over the protest of his uncle who is the selectman, they adopted a child."

"I don't see," said the gray lawyer in the committee chairman's seat, "how they could adopt the child if the selectmen objected. The probate judge—"

But the woman legislator, with hard bright cheeks like New Hampshire crab apples, did not hear him out.

"I don't know how, but they did. The baby *was* adopted, and then another child, too. They had to go to the selectmen for help after they adopted the first child, and then they adopted the other. There was no law the selectmen could find, they said, to keep them from adopting the children. There ought to be a law."

She paused. "This man loves the children. I guess the woman does, too, but not enough to take proper care of them. The year-old baby is covered with sores. We need some kind of adoption law to stop things like that. She's a very slack housekeeper. And he's an albino and not very strong."

68

The chairman thanked her. Then at the rear of the committee room where I sat with attentive citizens, in the State-house of New Hampshire, the woman bent close to me to say unofficially to a friend, "I'd hate to have my neighbors back home hear what I've said, but we need some law to prevent that kind of thing."

Her friend nodded in solemn approval. I followed her out of the room into the crowding Capitol. It was Tuesday, and the members of the General Court of New Hampshire, which boasts of the biggest House of Representatives among American state legislatures, were coming into Concord and the Capitol to legislate and sign the mileage book which assures them every week ten cents a mile for the trip home and back in addition to the two hundred dollars a term which they get in salary.

That year there were 427 members of the House representing the half million people of the state. While I waited for the session to begin, I amused myself with some comparative mathematics. Roughly, there is one member of the House for every thousand people in New Hampshire. If New York State elected its assemblymen on the same basis there would be 12,000 members in its lower house, and if the National Congress used that ratio in representation there would be well over a hundred thousand Congressmen in America. That prospect was so appalling that I worked it backwards: If New Hampshire elected on the New York basis, there would be only half a dozen members in the House, no more than two members if they elected on the same basis as the Congress.

But apparently the size of the House makes everybody happy. No young man need break his heart because of the slimness of the chance of becoming a statesman. Willard Lane, of the town of Stoddard (population 113), where the water on one side of the roof runs into the Merrimack and on the other side into the Connecticut, came to the House as representative of both the Republicans and the Democrats on a grand total of 33 votes. John H. Boothman, Jr., Republican from the mountain town of Randolph (named after John Randolph of Roanoke in Virginia), was elected by 47 votes to represent the entire population of 82. At the other extreme, Joseph O. Gelinas of the Eighth Ward in Manchester got 3,284 votes. All, including the Senators, got the same $200 pay (though the story is told that not long ago when the $200 was paid in a lump sum late in the session a one-armed legislator from Manchester did a lively business helping out his colleagues by buying their pay checks for $150 early in the session). The mileage is something else. The 66 gentlemen who represented the city of Manchester, only seventeen miles from Concord, were only entitled to $3.40 a week; but the Honorable Harvey H. Converse of far northern Pittsburg (population 671) was entitled to around $30 a week—and $30 a week is a lot of money in Pittsburg, New Hampshire, or in the pockets of a Pittsburg man who stays in Concord.

There are only three real working days each week—Tuesday, Wednesday, and Thursday. Even on those days in the past there were often more seats in the big hall than legislators in them. But in 1939 Representative George H. Duncan, Democrat of Jaffrey, introduced a resolution at the first of the session calling for the installation of time clocks in both houses and requiring the representatives of the people of New Hampshire to punch them on penalty of having their compensation reduced to the terms of their attendance. The resolution raised such an uproar among the thrifty Yankees that it was withdrawn; it helped fill the hall during the rest of the session nevertheless.

I had come early across the street from the Eagle Hotel, in the rooms of which the politicians and the patriots, the manu-

facturers and the lumbermen, and the gentlemen of the
Boston & Maine Railroad and the newer power companies
have made across the years something which may be called
history. In the old inn's annals were those days when a boss
like Jethro Bass (whom Winston Churchill made in his novel
Coniston out of Ruel Durkee of Croydon and other tough
and shrewd politicians of tougher if not shrewder times)
dispensed favor and patronage and power. Like a good many
other American hotels, the old Eagle has a lively unwrit-
ten record of plunder and privilege planned in its rooms in
its political past. The rooms were as modern as the politicians who occupied them now. The Boston & Maine was no
longer the political power it once had been. Maybe the new
men of the new power companies were not as political,
maybe not as ruthless, though they might be both. Power in
politics could be more grammatical without being any better.
Even if Jethro Bass was dead and the Throne Room in the
Eagle had been redecorated to suit a salesman as well as a
political boss, there were still men in New Hampshire who
knew what they wanted and how to try at least to get it.

Lawyers in the deep lobby of the Eagle looked prosperous
even when their poor companies needed, as some of them
said, as much help as the members of National Representative Thomas Laite's Townsend clubs—and that month Mr.
Laite of Concord reported to his pension seekers that New
Hampshire was second in the United States in increased
membership. I do not think that the lawyers would have
puzzled Jethro Bass but the organized old folks stirred in
times which might have been bewildering even to him, and,
even to that old realist, maybe a little sad. There were not
any more enriching franchises left to be dispensed. But the
poor had found their way with the rich in supplication to the
State. The farmers from the hills, no longer content with
such little woodchuck bills as they asked under Jethro Bass,

71

had expressed their power in helping to promote Henry Styles Bridges from the secretaryship of the Farm Bureau by way of the State Public Service Commission and the Governor's office to the United States Senate at the age of 38. But in Washington as the people's man, he caused no pain to the plutocrats. When I was in Concord he was in New Hampshire participating in a State Republican rally at Manchester which heard the question: "Which way, America?" The assembled New Hampshire Republicans knew the answer they wanted. Senator Bridges was willing to be the answer himself.

I crossed to the green Statehouse lawn, pockmarked with new grass where old trees had been. A Daniel Webster elm had fallen in the wind and, falling, had almost felled the bronze figure of Daniel himself. A workman showed me where the old tree had hit the statesman's hip. I went on, past Franklin Pierce untouched on his pedestal, into the lobby of the granite and marble Capitol. There in the Hall of Flags I felt, as a Southerner, almost personally intimidated by John A. Dix still crying from his canvas across the years from 1861, "If anyone attempts to haul down the American flag, shoot him on the spot." But the plump gray man in the little waist-high booth greeted me with the official affability of New Hampshire. He was one of the new army of greeters and informers who are put down wherever the tourist is expected, to answer the questions of the tourist—which are expected, also. I leaned on his booth, and we talked about his state and then about his job. He had a book showing the sizes of other Houses of Representatives in comparison with New Hampshire's own. He had written in it, too, some items of ignorance about New Hampshire brought to it as well as the facts which the state wanted taken away.

There had been the breathless woman who arrived in Concord, New Hampshire, amazed at the length of Paul Revere's ride, herself having overshot Concord, Massachusetts, on her ride from Boston after Revere by 53 miles. There had been the whole party of travelers who stopped briefly on their way to Plymouth, New Hampshire, to see where the Pilgrims landed. And it was not only the outlanders who were ignorant: people also came into the Capitol of New Hampshire to see the movies being presented by the Capitol Theatre down Main Street.

"But this," the gentleman in the information box told me blandly, "is nothing. I've got the best job in New Hampshire."

It provided a philosopher a place in which to observe his countrymen, newcomers and the commonwealth. It seemed, as he told his story, that he had been a rich man when the depression of 1929 hit New Hampshire as hard as it hit any other place. But he had in better days (they sounded golden-better) contributed time and money to the advance of politicians on the way to power. They went up as he came down. So he came into the Capitol. He does not mean to leave it. A Senator wanted to take him to Washington, "but I like it up here where it is cool." He remains a man who stays from administration to administration to teach the newcomers how to govern New Hampshire. And to observe how it is governed. He put the observations down in his mind as he put the vagaries and misinformation of the tourists down in his little book. They were as freely shared. All the items seemed like identical entries differentiated only by their place in the succession of his telling: about the new private heating company which warmed the new public buildings (WPA), of state plans for saving decrepid industries and acquiring new ones, of legislative interest in summer boarders and perennial taxes and the collection of mileage in the service of the state, about people and power, politicians and pettifoggers, sharp tricks and slick ones. Listening I had the feeling that while New Hampshire had a place for a philosopher, it presented itself to the public—and quite properly, probably —only in the terms of an amiable chronicler and guide. But amiable certainly. The man and the state had both lost much but both were pleasant still, even a little complacent in pleasantness.

"Now I tell you, I've got some things to attend to now, but why don't you meet me just before eleven o'clock and I'll take you in and show you the House in session? How's that?"

"Fine. Are you sure you have time?"

He smiled indulgently, like a man who could be philanthropic with his valuable time. "I'll be there."

When I came out of the committee hearing where the lady had told us about the albino and the babies, there he was. He knew everybody, and he seemed to be talking to everybody. He saluted the Governor's secretary, recited his unusual accomplishments, and told me how much above the state's secretarial salary the Governor paid him out of his own pocket. We halted down the corridor where he gave—and got —friendly greeting from a benevolent attorney.

The halls were crowding. Members were putting their coats and hats into the wooden cubbyholes provided for them. Governor Francis P. Murphy marched down the picture-hung corridor on the way to his office like a man affable on his way to a fire. He was, he said, busy, busy! But the pressure of public service had not aged him. He looked pink at sixty-two. My guide showed me the huge portrait of Cyrus A. Sulloway, the "Tall Pine of the Merrimack," who looked like a New England Buffalo Bill. Beyond it, in the halls, he pointed out a wig-wearing French-Canadian representative from Manchester who could not speak English, an old white-haired fiddle-playing member, a sleepy-eyed editor member from New Hampshire's little strip of coast, Representative Henry A. Wilson of Hollis "who sends two truckloads of chickens to Boston nearly every day, and eggs, too." There was Senator Curtis Hidden Page, retired Dartmouth professor, in tweeds and spats with a trim beard, a dapper bachelor and a sporty-looking scholar in politics. He was the colorful exception. In general the members, of the House particularly, seemed plain and poor. The women among them seemed old. There were more beards than are usually in evidence today. None of the women, members or clerks, made any such attempts at style as would brighten a Southern legislature. One plump woman, searching in bewilderment for a friend, had her gray hair set in beauty-shop waves, but she had not combed them since she got them.

In the poorer South, I knew, there would be brighter colors, more gayety in the midst of more poverty. But in the South, in general, the deeper poverty would be represented in the legislature only by richer men. The big Negro part of the poverty is not represented by anybody, and a large part of the widespread white poverty never gets to the Capitol. In New Hampshire the people themselves seemed to have come to Concord, and they looked poor as the land from which many of them came. It is a poverty hard to see under the snow or the lush green of sweet short summertimes.

A study of one old agricultural area in the state by the New Hampshire Agricultural Experiment Station showed aspects of a grim rural reality. There were old people living alone on remote and precarious places. And not only the old: One family, living in this region on a place assessed for $300 and selling no farm products, created a special school transportation cost of $144 a year. Around old and young in numbers of New Hampshire towns the forest has been allowed to slip back into the productive fields. Surveyors estimate that 43 per cent of the land in the area studied by the Experiment Station was open in 1860 as compared with 13 per cent in 1934. People are gone. Names have changed. But

75

even in the woods there remain the old cellar holes, the lilacs and rosebushes, the stone walls, the old mill sites, and the little tangled cemeteries. Fortunately sometimes also there are less touching but more tangible summer residents, or a high-tension power line running through the empty town to help pay the taxes. In a good many poor towns, working on the roads that carry the tourists through them is the most important industry left to those who remain on the old land.

Not all the poor are from the country towns which have changed through a long past. There are men to represent the crowded cities which have suffered in a swift present. The men who have come into New Hampshire have not always found more riches than those who were left behind in it. Not only the Carrs and Burleys and Butterfields and Bartletts are the citizens of difficulty on lands which rugged individualism emptied, but the Ouellettes and Bergholtzes and Laframboises and Sullivans and Hurbonoviches are also in the crowded cities which rugged individualism built. The slow continuous departure of neighbors in Dorchester was as destructive, if not as dramatic, as the final closing of the mill doors in the bankruptcy of the vast Amoskeag Mills in Manchester on a Christmas Eve.

That day in the wide hall of the House in Concord, the men and women of town and country, of old New Hampshire and of the polyglot new New Hampshire looked alike. There were, of course, some differences in their dress. A few of the French-Canadians were almost walled off in separation by language; but I had the feeling in the hall that, though only 40 per cent of the people of New Hampshire are of the old stock called Yankee, the Yankee tradition somehow held them all. The purest Yankee stocks in New England come from some of New Hampshire's poorest hills (71 per cent of the farms are still cultivated by the old stock), and the most diverse foreign groups fill its industrial towns. In Concord they met without any difficulty apparent to a stranger in the old ugly legislative hall. The Yankee may be overwhelmed, but his pattern seemed secure. Change in the pattern involved the Yankee and the newcomer together. All their talking made one sound in the room.

The clock moved toward eleven. The big portraits of Washington and Lincoln and Daniel Webster and Franklin Pierce and John P. Hale looked down upon the legislators filling the long semicircular rows of dirty leather, brass nail-bound opera chairs embossed with the seal of the state. The native and the foreigner, the city man and the town man (of course everybody lives in the town in New England, even the last man on the rural road), fused to make a country-looking company. The brass cuspidors gleamed for them on the red carpets. Below the speaker's stand a portable radio in familiarity to them all was blaring, "Coming 'Round the Mountain." One legislator chortled to a group of fellows, "That's all you got to do if you want to know whar he is." All of them laughed. Informal and good-natured, simple and shrewd, they looked together like the gathering commonalty of a democracy. Pictorially they were not pretty, but they looked like the people themselves gathered in a sort of town meeting of the state. The House is the people, I think, but the sleeker, more citified-looking Senate in its more significant, more dignified little green-paneled room is divided by representation from districts where not the number of men but the amount of direct taxes paid is the governing rule.

The radio roared on. The noisy music disturbed nobody. The knots of members went on talking with voices raised above it. Statesmen in New Hampshire like music. There were, my guide said pointing to the piano behind the press table, a House band and a House vocal quartet. But this morning, he had heard, there might not be any song at the session because the second bass was tied up in a long com-

77

mittee hearing—the Judiciary Committee, I think he said. Abruptly the radio's song was sliced off in new silence. Raised voices sounded higher, then hushed. The gavel fell: *bang— bang—bang!*

Almost as abruptly the door beside the rostrum opened, and in came the Governor, grinning, well kept, bald-headed, the Irish Catholic who became a Republican, the packing clerk who became the shoemaking millionaire, one a feat almost as remarkable as the other. He moved briskly across the little stage. Behind the Governor came his council. There was a general good-natured handshaking on the speaker's stand. The clerk shouted, "The Honorable Senate." They came in through the same door and filed to their places in the first rows of seats before the Speaker. A dark youngish chaplain in a gray suit lifted his head above a striped necktie and asked a Unitarian, or Congregational, God to make all the company in the big room "worthy of this beautiful and beloved state where we live together as good neighbors in freedom and safety." Without announcement or accompaniment but with some quaver and uncertainty the House quartet broke into song:

"I need Thee, oh, I need Thee,
Every hour I need Thee . . ."

At the song's end, without more ado the Governor led the way out, grinning, whispering something funny to the last council member as he passed him. The Senate followed, and the gavel fell again for the House alone. There was a monotoning of leaves of absence. There was an announcement about a legislative visit to a normal school. Then a message from the Honorable Senate: The Senate concurred in a bill to regulate fishing through the ice; the Senate refused to concur in an act relating to fishing in Jackson and vicinity.

The routine rolled on. Men were smoking. An old woman adjusted her hair with her hands. A lobbyist took a member to the back of the hall to talk. My guide told me both his name and his desire.

Then this gentleman who had the best job in New Hampshire led me down the hall to show me where an enlightened state required all lobbyists to register in a book. We turned the pages: Cotton, Sulloway, Jones, Whittemore. The list went on. I thought of lobbying and bossing long ago when such a boss as Jethro Bass ruled the fates of men and railroads, taxpayers and jobholders, from the old Eagle Hotel across the street. Times had changed. Patterns had altered. But even New Hampshire was still a state of men, some of whom knew what they wanted. I laughed out loud, and my guide who had the best job in New Hampshire looked surprised at my laughter.

I was remembering what a Concord corporation executive had told me about the descent upon his office and his files of a corps of Federal government investigators. They read and searched and found nothing.

"Isn't it strange," the chief investigator said, "that we don't find any instructions at all to your legislative representatives?"

The New Hampshire man laughed. "Maybe you never heard of Jethro Bass."

But the investigator had.

"Well, then you should remember what he said: 'Don't write—send.'"

In my own particular democracy I had heard the wisdom handed down from a Southern contemporary of old Jethro: "Don't write Sin."

Both rules stand. My guide still could not see what I saw as funny in the lobbyists' book. It seemed to him an evidence of the advancing enlightenment of a wiser people.

That is not merely a New Hampshire view. Maybe new rules and records have put an end to the old-time toughness of the old politicians and the old powers. But in some states under all the new rules the politicians and the powers get together just the same and to the same ends. I started to tell my guide and commentator Jethro Bass' wicked wisdom. In neither old nor new New Hampshire—nor North Carolina—did smart men leave any more tracks than are absolutely necessary. Sometimes, indeed, such tracks as they do make seem only a part of the determined marching of the multitude. It is not always easy to know whether the shrewd move with the simple or the simple move with the shrewd. It is perhaps democracy in either case. But sometimes while half the world is saving democracy I find myself wondering what it is. Certainly there are more ways of running a legislature or a state or a nation than handling it by the scruff of its neck. But to my guide—he is, I learned later from *The Rochester Courier,* "widely and justly known as the Grover Whalen of the State-house"—I said nothing but my thanks. Outside the Capitol, by St. Paul's Church, the State Police headquarters was ugly in the sun, and across the street beyond the Eagle Hotel some smokestacks stuck up to an innocent sky. A robin pecked at the new grass on the Statehouse lawn.

VIII

Money or Men

THE SUN WAS WARMING the long rows of mills and tenements along the Merrimack that morning in Manchester. Old men along the streets sat in it, warming old bones. Children ran in it, shouting. A tall woman with bright arms hung up her wash. From the outside, life seemed to have come back into the procession of brick buildings of the biggest textile mills in the world, whose owners had chosen Christmas Eve in 1935 as the day for application under Section 77B for bankruptcy. That had been a colder day. It must have seemed a day when the world had come to an end. Manchester was the mills, and the gentlemen filing papers about them in the court in Boston then must have seemed no nearer than those men who had begun their building and the building of the town around them more than a century before.

Thomas Jefferson's grandson, T. Jefferson Coolidge, died at eighty-nine in 1920 when there were marvelous millions in the banks to the credit of the huge mills he had built. At least once in his life he had believed what would have shocked his grandfather: "I believed myself to belong to a superior class, and that the principle that the ignorant and the poor should have the same right to make laws and govern as the educated and refined was an absurdity." But his mills had congregated the alien if not the ignorant, and his mills had not made them rich. He died. And, I think, the rich and

81

the refined who remained were as bewildered as the ignorant and the poor.

What lived and lasted in Manchester, as in Mississippi, was the determination of the community to have jobs, even if to get them capital had to come from the community and not from the industrial capitalists. There was another difference that in Mississippi whole communities voted in democracy to tax whole communities for industrial development, while in Manchester the leaders put up the savings of the thrifty without any vote. So in general the little men of the thrifty lower middle class took the chance to give Manchester another chance in which the chief beneficiaries would be the rich above them and the poor below them. I think that is a significant difference, but there was just as significant a similarity in the desperate desire of hungry places for wages on which to feed. Rule might still belong to the rich and the refined, but they were willing to pass the risk down as far as it would go.

The town lived. Nearly two thousand people had slipped away between one census and another. There had been no similar counting from the time the Amoskeag Manufacturing Company shut its last door in the face of its last employee to that May when the sun warmed the old mills. I rode past them. There are more than half a hundred buildings on both sides of the Merrimack for a mile and a half. There was life in them. A new big cotton mill of a big cotton-mill chain had operated in one part of the plant where the biggest cotton mill in the world had failed. Not long before, it had departed, too. There were other industries little and big. There were also signs of warehouses where local retailers enjoyed a spaciousness only possible where there is no great price on space. There were signs hung on the brick walls before the sprawling uncramped quarters of Federal government agencies. Halls were still empty, waiting for the garment maker or the shoemaker and all the congregation of all the little industries, called "diversified," which are almost everywhere now hungrily sought and kindly treated.

Two little red-headed girls waited at the gate while the Boston & Maine passenger train moved north past the mills. Beyond the tracks, close to the long double and triple lines of many-storied red brick buildings, some workmen were digging in the earth to repair a steam pipe or a sewer. After the clatter of the train the mills themselves seemed ominously quiet. Industry is not necessarily noisy, but once there must have been a pulse if not a roar from the seven hundred thousand spindles and more than twenty thousand looms which in good years produced five million yards of cloth a week. That was enough almost to gingham the world while women were willing to be ginghamed.

I parked my car and walked down wide Elm Street. Two midget women turned off Elm into Hanover, and nobody seemed to be regarding them but me; I watched them walk past a Chinese restaurant where an old white man was washing the plate-glass window. Above the stone labels at the second-story levels of Prout's Block and Connor Block there were other windows which would have needed washing if there had been tenants behind them to look out. But on the street there were few more worn workers than on any other city streets. The windows promised them as diverse a merchandise. Printed in French, a placard advertised an amateur opera. A black strand of sooty soft-coal smoke stretched from a puny chimney across the green of Merrimac Common. I took a seat there close to a neat middle-aged man in a shiny blue suit. A fire wagon roared by to make us conversationalists. Beyond fire wagon we talked of Amoskeag.

"Oh, we got another big industry now," he said. "I work for it."

"What's that?"

He laughed. "The WPA." Then he added wearily, "It's crazy. It's crazy. But they got to make us go through the motions. You know they got to make us go through the motions. But sometimes I sit here in the park and think about all those yards of gingham we made they said nobody would buy. Hell, I don't even know whether that fire wagon was going to a fire."

He spoke in bitterness, apathetically.

"They squeezed us and scared us. Some folks are scared yet."

He lit one of my cigarettes and looked back across the smoke at the days when the death rattle seemed in the throat of the town. He told me how high the water had risen in that fatal spring in and around the mills.

He shook his head. "I guess," he said, "you couldn't blame that on the people down in Boston."

"I'm afraid not," I told him.

Of course, the management was responsible for the failure of the mills, he thought. I remember particularly that he mentioned without any affection "old man Dumaine." I was to see Frederic Christopher Dumaine later at his estate in Groton, and I still somehow regard him as less destroyer than rather pathetic figure for the bewilderment which seemed to be implicit in the leadership of New England's economic ruling class. Whatever Mr. Dumaine's business ethics may have been in the financial maze involving both money and men which he made out of Amoskeag, his were the ethics also of his fellows. For in New England he remained, as a director of the First National Bank of Boston, one of the first lords of the land. What he did is formally, if not always privately, approved. I think both he and the other lords who live among poorer men in New England, but who guard the profit on New England money wherever it is, are inevitably caught sometimes in the conflict of profit and people. Amoskeag was

84

merely big enough to be a monumental evidence of their own
uncertainty—and big enough, too, to bring Congressmen to
look at it for the Select Committee on Investigation of Real
Estate Bondholders' Reorganizations (74th Congress, 2nd
session). They listened to the actors in the tragedy.

Perhaps, as Mr. W. Rodman Peabody, member of the law
firm of Peabody, Brown, Rowley & Storey, corporation director and president of the American School of Classical
Studies at Athens, told investigating Congressmen, "Mr. Dumaine was giving his life blood to save the corporation."
Maybe on the other hand, as Charles M. Green, retired engineer and angry small stockholder, declared, "I told Mr.
Dumaine I considered he had absolutely played traitor to
himself as a man, and a traitor, also, to the confidence which
I and other people had put in him, and I believe, also, I
called him a hypocrite." The quality of Mr. Dumaine's
morals is less important, I suspect, than the dilemma in which
he was caught with others even if he escaped with a fairly
whole hide.

That dilemma was not restricted to Manchester or Amoskeag. Undoubtedly Amoskeag suffered from a sort of central-
ized senility in brick and stone, from architectural elephan-
tiasis in a mobile age, from absentee direction, part-time
direction (Mr. Dumaine was running Waltham Watch while
Amoskeag was running down), perhaps from big salaries
(Dumaine drew $100,000 and his son $24,860 a year), and
a definite lag behind the ladies in making what the ladies
wanted and would buy. But the big old mill, which was built
continually bigger until just before it began to die, came out
of the profitable war with millions in cash and Liberty bonds.
It fairly bulged with liquid assets; but the prospect ahead did
not look half as good as the profits in the banks and deposit
boxes. In the twenties the rich and refined who still ran the
banks and the mills had to choose between taking their

money in liquidation or risking their money in a sickening textile industry to keep life in Manchester which depended upon Amoskeag for half its pay roll.

With maybe a surplus of shrewdness, the gentlemen and trustees of Amoskeag under Mr. Dumaine's leadership decided to do both. Perhaps they were right. They had, they said, duties to shareholders as well as jobholders. Certainly, however, in a bewildering complexity of corporate finance shaped in Boston, what the chairman of the Congressional investigating committee unkindly called the "milking process" started. They separated a good part of the money from the mill. Congressional investigators suggested that some of the insiders unloaded on the public and that the loans of big Boston banks, which were close to the mill management, were too precipitately paid. Actually what seems to have happened was that old-fashioned New England financiers tried to save both their money and the mill and were more successful in saving money for themselves than the mill for Manchester.

It is not necessary to vouch for the innocence of financiers to recognize that they were caught in a real box. It may be the box New England will be buried in. Across the years, first from ships and then from expanding mills, the region has accumulated a vast store of capital. In its service New England has also accumulated workers from every part of the world. But in the twenties, even before the depression of 1929, factories in New England, particularly in textiles, were slowing down. Money could not make its profit as easily at home. Although Mr. Dumaine was blaming Southern competition for textile troubles in New Hampshire, he also said as director of the First National Bank of Boston that that institution was lending money to Southern mills. Men, even bankers, joined to save New England industries; but men as bankers, investment counselors, trustees, and individual investors sent money to run industries elsewhere at the very time they organized to lament the results at home of that competition. Men were patriots in New England as elsewhere; but their money went promptly where it made a profit, and not giving much of a damn how. Outside of Manchester, Amoskeag was a dramatic incident in a procession. But in Manchester, villainy was human and suffering was human, also.

"We are fighting for our lives to keep things going," said Mr. Peabody,* the classicist and attorney. John Adams' great-great-grandson, Charles Francis Adams, yachtsman, politician, and trustee of Amoskeag, said, "We might have been damn fools, but we tried hard, and we were not impeded by any stock-market transactions." He added significantly, "We went on longer than we should have gone on in the interest of our stockholders, from loyalty to this city." A great deal depends upon the point of view, and a rich Yankee with a money head and a human heart may be a man caught in his own contradictions. I think very often he is.

The first lords of New England got out, and it makes very little difference to Manchester's story whether they left as unappreciated patriots or as unpunished pirates. The important thing was that they were gone, and that they had shut the mills. Relief rolls rose. Amoskeag's taxes had gone down. Its pay roll had disappeared. Mr. Coolidge's successors had departed. If Manchester was to be saved, it had to save itself. Arthur E. Moreau, who organized the rescue corporation called Amoskeag Industries, Inc., managed the purchase of the mill properties, headed the whole movement, and got the money together, belongs to that big French-Canadian group in Manchester which always had a big place at the looms but none in the management of the mills. The French and Catholic vote was behind him when he was elected mayor. He is, however, no longer a little "hopping frog." A hardware man, he is a Republican, a director of the Public

* Congressional investigation cited above.

Service of New Hampshire and now has an honorary Dartmouth degree.

He did a job. He worked with the little local leaders, bankers, utility vice presidents, one old local millionaire, the local newspaper publishers. These Manchester men, to prevent the dismantling of the mills, got an offer from the master in bankruptcy to sell them the whole physical plant for $5,000,000—$500,000 in ten days and the balance within thirty days. Unless they met the time requirements, he planned to sell the whole thing to anybody anywhere. Manchester then would have to bid against the world. Moreau, the late nonagenarian Frank P. Carpenter (who was the town's first and richest citizen and had been a trustee of Amoskeag), the Public Service of New Hampshire, Frank Knox's *Manchester Union,* a few bankers, and others put up that $500,000 down payment which closed the deal. But unless the master in bankruptcy held them up on the price none of them risked much—or they did not risk it long alone.

The next $4,500,000 was more easily secured. The savings institutions of the city, institutions which are symbols of the thrift of the New England people, took a mortgage on the properties for $4,500,000. At the same time Walter S. Wyman, president of the New England Public Service Company, agreed to buy the mills' power facilities for $2,250,000. The Amoskeag mills had owned its own 16,000-kilowatt hydroelectric plant and other water-power facilities on the Merrimack. Mr. Wyman is a business man not empowered by his stockholders to play philanthropist in Manchester or any other town. Presumably, therefore, he got his money's worth. His payment for power was applied to the mortgage, cutting it to $2,250,000 but reducing the value of the property on which the mortgage was made by the same amount.

The mortgage was increased to $3,000,000, a sum in excess of what the leading citizens had paid for the properties minus the power which was already sold before additional sums were lent by the savings banks. If the bankers made that loan with the cold eyes of bankers guarding depositors' money, the purchasing patriots had bought a bargain even at the money-lenders' appraisal. If the bankers made the loan less cold-eyed as local patriots, they were being patriotic with other little people's money. Whichever, at one time there was a $3,000,-000 mortgage made by the savings banks on properties for which Amoskeag Industries, Inc., had only paid $2,750,000 ($5,000,000 price minus sale of $2,250,000 power properties). Thus, at that time the stockholders of Amoskeag Industries, Inc., held at the bankers' appraisal a property worth $250,-000 more than the trustee in bankruptcy had charged them for it. The savings-bank depositors had provided that difference between what the stockholders paid for the 6,800,000 square feet of manufacturing space and 760 tenements and what they mortgaged them for. Whatever the value, the loss or the profit, the greatest amount risked at the beginning was the savings of the people. Every new industry in the long mills means new jobs; it also means greater value to the property owned by the stockholders in Amoskeag Industries, Inc., and a new consumer for Public Service.

There are new industries. There was, in 1939, still room for more. Sixty per cent of the big emptiness had been filled by sixty-two concerns. There were between 3,900 and 4,000 employed at an annual pay roll of around $3,500,000. But in the summer of 1937 about the same number of workers was reported. In the old Amoskeag days, according to the present Amoskeag owners, there were nearly 17,500 workers. In 1920 the mill's pay roll was $14,000,000. It fell to $4,537,329 in 1935 as the end approached. That dying pay roll was still in excess of the pay roll of all the new industries which had been brought in to fill Amoskeag's hole. Fortunately, two large shoe companies outside the Amoskeag yard had expanded operations. Sadly, some workers had left town hopeless of finding jobs there, and others like my friend in Merrimac Common were on the WPA. Sadly also, Amoskeag Industries, Inc., was not doing so well. By January, 1939, it had reduced its mortgages to $400,000. There was some sale of properties in the reduction of mortgage on the properties. But in 1938 the Pacific Mills plant, which had come in, went out. In the year ending in August, 1938, Amoskeag Industries lost $24,151.29. Losses in the next year rose to $80,-803.74. New indebtedness made to set up operating industrial subsidiaries in the old industrial properties ran the mortgage debt back up to $1,173,000. Also it owed $543,000 to stockholders. "We are still optimistic that the final results will be satisfactory," the management said.

Men were working, making cheesecloth and bandages, tires and pajamas, electrical instruments, metal abrasives, toys, caskets, and soup. Space was being occupied for storage of tonics and dry goods and wool and leather and food. There were even lawyers and real estate men in the old tenements. Maybe some of those who moved in had also moved out of other towns, creating smaller similar problems behind them, like those which their coming helped to solve. Massachusetts had made official complaint about the grabbing. New England as a whole had complained about industries moving South and West. But movement is always welcome at the receiving end in Manchester as in Mississippi. Probably the swift poverty of Manchester cut more cruelly than the long poverty of Mississippi. Men and women in the New Hampshire town knew what jobs were, even if they lacked jobs. Beyond cotton chopping, Mississippi never had had enough jobs. But both situations scar. In Manchester I doubted if any such superior class as that in which Mr. T. Jefferson Coolidge once believed could or would soon erase the mark of the wound.

I spent the day looking for Manchester's story in Manchester's streets. I talked with people up and down the town: a reporter, a policeman, a lawyer, a clerk in the liquor store, and a boy who shined my shoes. I came back to the Carpenter Hotel tired as the fat traveling salesman seemed to be who was waiting for the elevator, too. In my room the view from the window picked me up like a drink. The hotel might have been built to display the wide swing along the river of the Amoskeag Mills. Down below me lay the chimneyed brick tenements with their granite-linteled windows.

They looked somehow beautiful and sad under the nearly naked elms about them. The garbage cans in the yards behind them rather livened than stained the picture. Life remained in the old buildings. But somehow the so-much-lived-in structures which had lasted beyond their first meaning reminded me perversely of the new buildings which John D. Rockefeller had erected to show the past at Williamsburg in Virginia. They had a grace of age which the new buildings did not possess. In a great city someone would remodel them into quaint apartment houses. Ladies in bright rayons would look out of their old windows. In Manchester, however, I had the feeling that more than a Rockefeller would be necessary to their restoration in the terms of their past. Beyond them the old, long, looming factory buildings erected for utility were beautiful, too, with the Merrimack running between them as it ran between my window and the striped red and white brick church steeple with its golden cross far away. In the middle of my picture was a smokeless brick stack lean and beautiful against the sky.

The question of Amoskeag was not its strange loveliness but its possible continuing utility. That remained a question. Old mill properties are old mill properties, and much of Amoskeag is very old. Absentee ownership in a grandiose form was gone but new absentee ownership had been welcome. Diversification has succeeded the blind single-minded preoccupation of Amoskeag with the continued production of a product fewer and fewer people wanted. But little industries which come quickly may move as quickly. Even bigger ones like the Pacific Mills can come and go away, too. Perhaps one of the flaws in old Amoskeag was the huge weight of its anchorage in Manchester. It was an elephant which both the politicians and labor could ride. It even once seemed such a mammoth as could continue to carry absentee management and too-avid profit takers. Wide around its distended corpse a sense of security died, too. Amoskeag Industries, Inc., which labors to fill its rooms, will not quickly fill its place. More than new industries (which help), it needs some magic to bring the sense of safety back.

Manchester, of course, is not the only town where very little men and bigger ones, too, seek that magic. I saw the seeking for it in Manchester in the big Carpenter Hotel where that summer you could get a modern double room and bath for $5.50 a week. That night, with a hard-boiled, pipe-smoking insurance adjuster from Hingham, Massachusetts, I watched in the hotel a company clutching after personality and the stage properties of power.

"The poor dumb clucks!" my companion said. "The pitiful dumb clucks! They pay seventy-five dollars in cold cash for this stuff."

In a banquet room in the Carpenter a professional developer of popularity and prestige was teaching them how to speak, dominate, and charm. The little people, most of them men, each got up in turn and made a speech in the midst of which at a signal from the teacher all the others made a clatter of interruption. The men were most of them turning into middle age, and the few women were thinning or fattening into fixed spinsterhood. Each had his little minute of speech. Each was once the center of the interrupting

92

clatter. Each was hoping hungrily toward power and attractiveness.

My companion punctuated one of the lame speeches.

"Christ!" he said. "That boy better keep his seventy-five dollars. He'll need it."

"How much do you suppose those people make?"

"Not much. But they're afraid they're not worth it. And they're crazy to be worth something. Jesus, everybody wants to be a big shot and most of them aren't sure how long they're going to be able to eat. They're funny, but they depress me."

He knocked out his pipe. The class went on, unaware of us. Hope boomed among them like a ball bouncing. Each was getting his seventy-five dollars' worth of attention from the teacher and the members of the class. Each, at the teacher's direction, declaimed Burke's sentence, "If I were an American as I am an Englishman, I would never bear arms against my country, never, never, never!" The *never's* rose in the scale of emphasis. They roared out across the hotel lobby after us. Even on the street outside, the dramatically determined *never's* of the little people sounded across the parking space between the hotel and the old tenements of the dead Amoskeag Mills.

They did seem foolish. They were, in sparely furnished lives, ready to take delusion to their hearts. They were perhaps that buffoon bourgeoisie lost between the determined and tough at the top and the determined and tough at the bottom. They were not inspiring in Manchester, but I suspect it is their inarticulate hope and timid thrift which carry the world in Manchester as in Mississippi. The thrifty are not the thrilling. They are a little comic as they carry the world. And more than a little sad.

IX

To a Wild Rose

EUGENE BURKE WAS STANDING on the roadside on that Saturday which clotted every corner in Winchendon with Civilian Conservation Corps boys. I almost passed him by. In the corridor of signaling boys I was still thinking about the meaning of the MacDowell Colony in Peterborough, where so many excellent books had been written and where the wind, which is not interested in the arts, had hit such a blow. I saw Eugene hold up his hitch-hiking hand. He wanted to go to Boston to get his baseball shoes before practice began in the camp the next week. There had been little time for baseball so far. They had been busy in the wind-tangled woods—he showed me his hands roughened by the trees. But he had worked no harder than Marian MacDowell, I thought, and she was eighty-one.

I came down toward them both early in the morning from the city sadness of Manchester. Bedford was a big Town Hall and a huge Presbyterian church. Amherst, New Hampshire, was the perfectly preserved old New England town. There was no flaw in it; it might have been preserved in amber instead of that May morning's sunlight. There was place for music in the bandstand in the Milford town square. What impressed me most in all the towns in that countryside were the town libraries. There did not seem people enough in some of the sprawling towns for the books. Books had been there almost as long as the towns. Perhaps the reason for the

94

books was the long shut-in winters when there was little a man or a woman could do but read. I preferred to think that from the beginning there had been a feeling that if the world was far-off over old-time roads, the wise men ought to be brought in their books by the community to give every man a chance to read the world and grow in it from reading. Sometimes it seemed, when I rode, that in alteration of Goldsmith, books had accumulated and men had gone away. In another of its twistings the world had turned around: Now books were not only brought from the cities to the little New Hampshire town, men came to the New Hampshire town to write in its quietness for the world.

For them that spring the old lady played Edward MacDowell's music up and down the land. She was in Florida giving a concert for the benefit of the Colony, and she had been in New York. Music made by her dead husband long ago rose above her old hands on black and white keys. The New Hampshire woods were in that music. Back in Peterborough was the sound of the ax and the saw, the smell of the brush fires. But there had to be peace beyond them, peace for men to make more music, more books, more pictures. The land had to be cleared, the timber removed, the studios repaired. There had to be order. The old lady went up and down the land playing, playing and pleading, also, in order that in the memory of one man others might have the chance to work in guarded quietness in the New Hampshire woods. Edward MacDowell had been dead nearly thirty years when the wind blew. In those years his widow had kept a promise made to him before he died. Between MacDowell's tragic insanity and God's wind she had tended a wood to make it possible for other men and women to have the peace in it he had found and to make it productive as he had done. In those years words and music had come out of her wood as from an enchanted place.

95

(I admired the place but, instinctively, I knew that I should not like it. Congregated poets and painters and pianists make too rich an atmosphere for me. Too much genius —if there is any such thing—in the process of being a genius on paper or in person generates a sort of gas which can be so poisonous you expect it to kill the leaves on the trees.) The ax sounded in it that May morning when I came down the New Hampshire road from Manchester to Peterborough. Mrs. MacDowell was not at the MacDowell Colony when I came.

"I am sorry I was not about when you visited the Colony," she wrote me, "and only wish you might have seen it in its full beauty. I am facing an enormous task, financially and physically, but those two hundred acres have to be cleared before we can open the Colony in 1940—but it must be done!"

I almost missed the Colony as well as its mistress. The old gentleman who sold me the postcards and the homemade horehound candy in Peterborough told me how to go, but I was lost almost as soon as I was out of sight of his store. A woman who displayed the dependable calves of her legs as she bent to brush out the back of her car turned to set me right again. Her directions led me better than she knew, for at the end of them I found young George Wannamaker Pettigrew, late of Florence, South Carolina, late of the forestry school at the North Carolina State College. He had been called from a Federal forest in Louisiana to southern New Hampshire. He and his young wife, who came from my own town of Raleigh, had been living in Nashua, where they had found good board for twelve dollars a week. They were looking for as good a living in Peterborough. He liked the Yankees.

"I don't notice much difference in them," he said, "but they spot me every time."

I am not surprised. I remember how he stood talking to
the one person present at the Colony center to which he led
me. There was a police dog there who came like a wolf roaring at us, but a little dark-skinned woman with smooth dark
hair came out crying him off, "Tilo! Tilo!" The dog with-
drew reluctantly, and Pettigrew addressed her. Under his
green forester's hat, he wore nondescript working clothes
on his slight figure. He stood with his green hat in his hand
talking to the woman. Not merely was his prematurely gray
hair uncovered, also there was a just perceptible bow like a
part of gallantry in his figure. He looked like a man for ro-
mance who had ridden up the road from the South. The
Latin-looking woman opened her mouth in a thick brogue.
She could not let us in to any of the studios, she said. She
could not show us the houses. But there was a studio just a
little way off. She pointed across a hillside where prostrate
juniper grew close to the earth. We could look into its windows.

We walked about the empty place where so much work
had been done. Perhaps the MacDowell Colony began when
Marian Griswold Nevins went to Darmstadt long ago to
study, and to her disappointment found her teacher to be
not a European but another American. The disappointment
did not last, and in 1884 she and Edward MacDowell were
married. It was after his distinguished career back home began in 1888 that they began to go to the wooded farm near
Peterborough where he wrote some of his finest compositions
—"To a Wild Rose," "To a Water Lily." They continued to
go there, in retreat for composition, after MacDowell became
the first professor of music at Columbia University and after
he resigned in 1905 following a faculty division over the place
of music in the curriculum. Then at forty-four he was near
the end of his life. Soon afterwards the mental disorder of
which he died began to plague him. And remembering peace

at Peterborough, he put the idea of the same possibility for others into his wife's hand, and she sealed it with her life. The Colony began with the organization of the MacDowell Association in 1907. In January, 1908, the American composer was dead. The man's idea grew under the woman's tending. Men in the studios worked on scores and sentences until the September afternoon before the storm. Mrs. Mac-Dowell was on the road from Peterborough to Boston in the wind. They saw the wind's waste in the morning. It was still there to be seen in the spring.

When we came back to the center of the Colony there was Emil Tonieri, an Italian who had been active in the two hundred and more acres of the Colony's trees for thirty years. The work was still going on, clearing up the tree tangle which the wind had left. A pleasantly cynical fellow who has seen his share of artists and writers, Tonieri talked about the trees: The Colony would have to sell about 800,000 board feet out of fallen trees which never grew for lumber. Already about $4,000 worth of it had been sold, but behind that price was the cost of cutting and hauling. There was only loss and no salvage whatever in the damaged studios.

Tonieri and his wife, Irish Mary the cook (the food is said to be excellent), have been there a long time. He spoke with a Latin's respect for the effort to make art, a respect which had a little salt sprinkled on it by familiarity with the art makers, of those who across the summers in their time had tenanted the little studios which had been placed in shrewdness to give each seclusion. When the trees stood straight and old, no writer could hear any composer's piano, nor any painter any writer's typewriter. Each worker looked upon a private world around him in which he could chew his pencils and dream about royalties and Pulitzer prizes or brood about his girls and his debts. In an hour the wind had changed it. Men who had left a task in their studios that

September evening could not get back to it over the cluttered paths and roads. It would be nearly two years from that hour before any went back to work in the little separate workshops in the woods. Two years can sometimes make as much change as a wind.

For sixteen dollars a week (and less or nothing, depending on need and talent) some fifty creative artists, chosen on the basis of both performance and promise, had each summer received bed and board and the companionship of other such workers at the center, and the absolute privacy of their individual studios all day long. There were no telephones in the studios, few visitors. Lunch was deposited at the studio doors in baskets. At evening all gathered together. Nobody could go to his studio at night. There were rules against outside social contacts.

"Suppose somebody goes to his studio at night?"

Tonieri spoke like a man quoting the law of the land. "If they don't follow rules we don't speak to them but once or twice. There are too many on the waiting list. These people are artists. They get plenty of time to work in the day."

The result of their work has been the best test of the sense of the system. The MacDowell Colony is, of course, no longer such a solitude as Edward MacDowell himself found long ago. There are still, however, plenty of acres per poet, room enough for the seclusion of writers. It was designed for those who want to work. It is neither such a free congregation of writers and playwrights as grew at Provincetown nor such a school for the hopeful in the arts as is to be found in the summertime for painters on Cape Cod or writers at Bread Loaf. It is a retreat for the already trained who want to work. Probably, as accomplishment has been counted, the Colony seems from the names of Willa Cather, the late Edwin Arlington Robinson who came to the Colony year after year, the Benét brothers (William Rose and Stephen Vincent), the Colums (Padraic and Mary), and Thornton Wilder a gathering of the mature and middle-aged. It will take time for the younger ones to make their impress on the publicity pamphlets, and then they, too, may be older. The Colony is no youth assembly. It seems to have a strong impress of old-fashioned respectability upon it, and of old-fashioned romanticism, too, about genius and the woods. The last, my spies report, can sometimes be a little thick. Bohemia is somewhere else. There are, of course, middle-aged poets who like beer; there was a poetess who wandered, too often like Ophelia, to Peterborough from which Emil and Mary had to bring her back. It is certainly not just a cheaper summer boarding house restricted to the promising (400 apply each year, and 50 are admitted).

Under the trees (too many of which must now be referred to in board feet), Willa Cather wrote most of *Death Comes for the Archbishop,* Thornton Wilder worked on *The Bridge of San Luis Rey,* and Edwin Arlington Robinson wrote the poetry for two Pulitzer prizes. (He has become with Mac-Dowell part of the spirit of the place.) Now the tree that served the shaping of a sonnet may be a bench or a box or a board in the side of a house. Maybe Hervey Allen spoke for other workers as well as himself when he declared that, while *Anthony Adverse* was not written at Peterborough, "it would not have been written if I had never been there." That rule if adopted might also apply to *Naked on Roller Skates* by Maxwell Bodenheim. But taking the good with the bad, certainly few other acres in America in recent years have raised such a crop of respectable literature. The contributions of the musicians working there have not been far behind.

It would be a bold man who would question any aspect of so productive an enterprise as the MacDowell Colony has been; but it did not seem to me necessary to agree with all the philosophy quoted in support of the MacDowell Colony

100

in order to approve its practical results. For instance: "It is not generally recognized by the layman to what extent imaginative incandescence in the artist (sometimes spoken of as 'inspiration') waits upon environment and circumstance. A great artist, said a poet who also thinks, 'is not necessarily a great man, but he is certainly a man with access to a mood in the times of his power.' And the lesser artist, too, is dependent, often tragically dependent, upon access to a mood." I am not sure I know what that means, but I do know that MacDowell Colony has given adequate housing for hard work. That seemed to me enough to justify sadness at the sight of the torn trees and to justify admiration for the old lady moving up and down the land interrupting the peace of her own old age to provide peace for people who she believed might use it to make words or notes or pigments rise and sing.

I had the feeling that the meaning of this place, when the pines and the birches and the spruce had stood where now the land was so much desolated, was that it gave the artist the chance to take strength from touching the earth without losing contact also with his kind. I don't think that is too romantic. I do not like the word "artist." It seems to me always to be a pretentious word which no man or group ought to self-apply. A painter paints. He can only hope that what he paints is art. Even vaudeville actors, such as are left, use the word now. Anybody is an artist who can say the word himself. But all kinds of craftsmen do need association with other craftsmen, and all of them are lucky if they can touch the earth. That long congregation of men and women and trees in the New Hampshire summers meant something at the MacDowell Colony. That May, however, the trees were down, and the earth was torn where their roots had been and where a good many of their stumps still were. The men and women, the writers and the musicians, were not coming in that summer. A year had been pulled up by its roots out of a continuity of craftsmanship. There was something desperate as well as valiant about the efforts of the old lady to heal the waste.

But the woods were still full of the young who were neither valiant nor desperate. They came from the cities (in which there were not enough jobs) to bring their muscle, not to the country to find a mood. There was time in their lives for more trees to grow and not room in their living for any sense of pain over blown trees. They sawed the logs. They burned the brush. They were young in the old woods and eagerly young upon each new free Saturday. I came upon them unexpectedly as I rode down the highway from New Hampshire into Massachusetts.

Beside the road in the first spring men were busily spreading green-brown manure on the fields, and the pungent smell was strangely pleasant in the air. East Jaffrey had an ugly main street, but the Congregational Church and the Ingalls Memorial Library sat as in a park at Rindge. There was not enough village about them to need them, and almost alone there they emphasized that the New England town had long ago been the embodiment of the consolidation of services for town man and country man alike. The towns spread wide over the countryside, but the bulking tenements in Winchendon indicated that men sometimes huddle together also where the winters are cold. In this town devoted to making toys, where once they made more toys than now, the big children from the CCC camp in the hills were waiting on every corner for rides. Eugene Burke, who showed me his rough hands, was one of them. But he was not complaining. Instinctively he knew as well as any writer or musician who ever worked at the MacDowell Colony that he had been given a chance in the woods.

"They run some things funny up at that camp," he said.

"We're supposed to get a rec trip [a recreation trip] once a week, but they don't let us out of camp but once or twice a month. There were some months in the winter we didn't get out but once in a month."

I suggested that they were probably pushing them hard because of the danger of fire in the blown woods in the summer. It was perhaps so, he agreed. He was glad to get out. He was going to Quincy. It was a funny coincidence, I thought, that the one CCC boy I should pick up should come from the neighborhood of the man then at the head of all the CCC. Robert Fechner, director of the corps (the nation and the boys lost greatly when he died late in 1939), had come all the way around from Chattanooga, Tennessee, by Georgia, to Massachusetts, to become head of the machinists' union, and to live near the same Quincy to which Eugene Burke was going for his baseball shoes. Young Burke was one of more than two million young men who had been sent out under Fechner to conserve the land and to have a chance for themselves. They had built dams and defenses against erosion. Half a million of them had left camps to take jobs in private employment before completing the terms of their enrollment. Others had left fed and strong, taught a little, disciplined a little, with maybe a better chance than they had had before they worked in the woods. A pheasant ran across the road before the car near Ashburnham.

"Being in the CCC is hard work," Eugene said, "but it is better than hanging around town. I'd go crazy doing nothing."

I looked at him. He was very young, and somehow, city boy that he was, he reminded me of the swift pheasant which had run before us. He was handsome and dark with his hair not so much brushed as falling into a pompadour. His lean face was sunburned bright red. In his woolen khaki shirt and pants and blue coat, he sat watching the road with his dark eyes. His mother and father were dead, and he lived with his brothers in Quincy. His older brother as relative got half of his pay.

"Can he do what he pleases with it? Could he just throw it away?"

"I'm glad my brother isn't that kind. You see there's a younger brother who's just entering high school, and we want him to get through. I guess my older brother is using some of the money for him and saving some of it for me. My father died when I was nine years old, and my brother kept the house together; and I figure I owe it to him."

That brother must have been a remarkable man. He was (and probably is—I use the past tense out of memory) a machinist on the New Haven Railroad, but he was also the presiding adult over his brothers. He sent them to school. He cooked. He washed. There was no woman in the Quincy home. A fourth brother had married, but he lived in Worcester. The brother in Quincy had sent Eugene through commercial high school. Probably he sent him also into the CCC Eugene was in his first enlistment; but already he had become a group leader, which lifted his pay from thirty to forty-five dollars a month. Half of it went home to Quincy, and Eugene was saving as much as he could of the rest.

"I don't want to get out broke."

He was not sure what he wanted to do when he did get out. He had had a job in Boston with Dun & Bradstreet but that financial firm's ideas about proper pay did not conform to Eugene's. Still he preferred office work to such a job as that of his brother. He did not want to be a machinist. I do not think he was very certain what he wanted to do. He was less certain what the world would have for him. He was more secure in talk about the camp.

"Most of the foremen up there—I don't know how they get their jobs, but they don't know any more about the work than the fellows. They come from the cities, too."

"What cities?"

"Most of us come from Boston, some from New Bedford."

Then he told me a story about a CCC boy who was the camp moneylender. He would lend small sums, but only if he got double his money back.

"He's a funny guy," Eugene said. "He doesn't believe in any God and he goes around preaching his doctrine."

"As a group leader oughtn't you to report his money-lending?"

He looked at me definitely shocked.

"Oh, no! It's all on a small scale. Maybe a guy wants a dollar or fifty cents or wants to go to a movie. I have nothing to do with it, and I figure it's none of my business."

In Fitchburg a velocipede factory was occupying a little space in a big and almost empty ex-textile factory. I remembered that Ed Allen, labor reporter on *The Boston Herald,* had told me that Fitchburg was his home town and that, some years before, Amoskeag had bought a Fitchburg mill. Once fifteen hundred people found work in it. Under the Amoskeag management it had closed its doors in the face of its workers seven years before the big plants had finally shut down in Manchester forty miles away. One of the former owners had begun again making rayon with fifty employees in an emptied mill building which he shared with a trucking company, a wood novelty company and a laundry. The pain per person had been as great in Fitchburg as in Manchester, but the drama of bigness had been lacking. I spoke to Eugene about a big shell of old mill on the street beside us.

"There appears to be no activity in it," he said.

He spoke as apathetically as precisely about an industrial inertness in which he himself was undoubtedly involved, and not very indirectly either. Every shut mill in New England meant boys on the street or luckily in CCC camps. I remember, however, that then I was most impressed by the formality of his English. It was not individual. Everywhere the poorest people often spoke with a trained correctness and a surprising vocabulary. Universal education seemed to have touched them all. The books were available to all in the libraries everywhere. Certainly in the cities education had not entirely eradicated the argot of *dese, dem,* and *dose,* but it seemed to me remarkable how much more widespread were the marks of schooling than the evidences of security. What disturbed me as one out of the too illiterate South was not that in New England the poor were educated, but that so often the educated were poor. Eugene not only showed education in his speech; the schools or the machinist manmother had also taught him good manners as well. He was reluctant about accepting my invitation to lunch. He had eaten, he said. He ate heartily, nevertheless. I was glad for his company and glad, too, as a taxpayer to have a little part in his chance in the woods which that winter and spring he well earned among the twisted trees.

We went on through Fitchburg and rows of the standard storied tenements of New England. Under a bridge the water of a stream was white with floating waste. Eugene and I hurried on over the big road beyond Worcester to friends in Boston and brothers in Quincy. He said good-bye with the grace of a young and handsome poet who hoped to come out of the woods and get a job somewhere in an office which would pay him more than Dun & Bradstreet, whose trade is values, thought he was worth.

I hope he got it.

I hope by now other men are making more music, more books in the studios in the green-again McDowell woods. And that the poet who wants it gets enough beer.

X

Wings on Their Skulls

BEFORE THE HOUSE ON FARMER'S ROAD in Groton a group of men were working at the removal of a big stump which not long before must have been a beautiful tree. One of them stopped digging long enough to warn me about the police-dog bitch which was eyeing me. Then he went back to work. The dog lost interest in me and moved off. I rang the bell and watched a pretty little child who in solemn mimicry of the workmen was digging in the ground with a tiny shovel. I waited, but no one came. I rang the bell again and waited longer. Finally the workman who had spoken to me in the first place sent the child around the back way to tell someone that I waited at the door. An old man deep in the hole about the stump swung an ax vigorously at a thick root. Behind me the door opened, and a servant, still hurrying into his coat, let me in.

The old master of Amoskeag in a worn and faded olive-colored dressing gown was in a little room warmed by an open fire. Frederic Dumaine looked older than he had seemed the one time I had seen him before at a luncheon at the Harvard Club. Then he had come in late and gay, joking about a drink he did not get. He looked then like a man who had lived well and gayly. And, thinking of Amoskeag, I wrote in my journal that, small and round and merry, he had the appearance of a resilient humpty dumpty. He did not seem so resilient now. He looked tired and old; he was suffering from an infection on his legs. He had the same trouble the year· before but had gotten over it. Perhaps this year the saddle straps on his horse had irritated them.

"They tell me," he said, "that in this climate we have what's called old man's itch."

Those legs had carried him a long way. He had begun seventy-three years before in Hadley without any silver spoon in his mouth, in a New England where ancestry in industry has sometimes been as essential to advancement as descendants advanced have been sometimes destructive of efficiency. Mr. Dumaine went from the public schools of Dedham at the age of fourteen to work for the Amoskeag Manufacturing Company. He worked as office boy. He swept floors. Around 1890 he went from the offices of the mills in Boston to learn from the bottom the manufacturing in Manchester. He was twenty-four years old then. At forty he succeeded his patron, T. Jefferson Coolidge, as treasurer of the mills, which is the big job in New England textile companies. The office boy from Dedham had gone a long way. That was thirty years before I talked to him in Groton. Then, he was old, and a whole New England had grown old with him.

That was the conventional success story, and he was it. But he had lived beyond the neat ending. The bright surface of the story was frayed now. It was not a straight line rising to drama. Somehow the story seemed like an old piece of gingham, bright-colored but losing the sharpness of its design. It spread like a piece of old cloth from austere offices in Boston to half-empty brick mills in Manchester. It spread, also, to touch the stories of a multitude of other men. What had happened, I wondered, along that story's margins to all the lively girls and strong boys who had been working over the spindles and the looms when young Fred Dumaine went down from Boston to add knowledge of the details of manufacturing to the more important matters of financing and buying and selling. A good many of those girls were just foreign names on tombstones now. Some of the men were only items in the statistics of old-age assistance in New Hampshire. So far as most of them were concerned, it began not to matter whether Dumaine had been good or greedy.

We left the fire, and in a room of windows overlooking a wide valley, he talked about those years. The valley ran, an orchard of apple trees, down to its bottom and up across more trees to another big house. The trees were late blooming. And the old man wondered, after the wind that had blown them, if they would ever bloom again. It was too early to be sure. He sat looking across them with his spectacles pushed back so that they sat upon his close-cropped gray hair. His head was bullet-shaped. His nose was Roman, almost like a beak. He put an expensive cigar into the pucker of his dry little mouth.

"You talk to people in Manchester—mill people on the streets—and they'll tell you I stole a couple of million dollars." He looked out across the brown orchard. "I wish I had that much money," he said.

His wishing, I knew, would not be everywhere endorsed. Some of those in Manchester who reluctantly agreed at the last to work for $9.60 a week for Amoskeag and still got no work might, I knew, turn his wistful wishing into obscene indignation. But he did not seem rich in his Groton house. If men in Manchester had lost jobs at $9.60 a week, he had lost a job which once paid him $100,000 a year. How much else he had lost or saved, I did not know. He was still employed. Once he testified that his salary as Waltham Watch Company president was $30,000 or $35,000 a year. He had not been sure which. Whichever, however, or whatever it remained, it was probably enough to deny him sympathy in the grimy streets along the Merrimack where there were not even any apple trees that might bloom.

His was a long story, too intricate for me to remember to tell as he told it. It was less a history of a mill than an explanation of its failure. That is what I asked him for, and that is what he undertook to give me. A story of labor seeking better wages and shorter hours, and learning not to work as hard while it worked. A story of women no longer willing to wear the ginghams which they had worn so long, and of which Amoskeag made so much.

"This is gingham." He touched his necktie. It sat like a symbol of an ancient loyalty at his old throat. "It was made at Amoskeag. Women don't wear it any more."

(That week in Boston the windows of Jordan Marsh were a succession of ginghams made into costumes for every summer hour from morning to midnight: Tailored gingham dress with bolero jacket, $25.00. Morning dress, $5.95. Gown for the evening. $10.95. Ginghams—the window dressers quoted *Vogue*—"rise with the sun and never set." I thought, as I stood looking on Washington Street, that *Vogue* and Mr. Dumaine ought to get together.)

The phone rang. His office at the Waltham Watch Company wanted him. He listened and talked. "Well, let him sell at 37. . . . I don't want to make another mistake on this. . . . Yes, I better see that. . . . Put that order in."

He came back from the phone with a parrot on his finger, an old parrot with a profile remarkably like his own.

"He likes to be around me. He's irritable with most people, but he likes to be around me."

With the parrot listening, he went on with his story of stricter and stricter labor laws and of Southerners competing in a South where there were no such laws. It was not a very pretty competition as he told it. Southern mills copied Amoskeag's designs, even Amoskeag's labels, and offered to under-sell them on the copies.

"But I don't blame the Southerners. I don't blame them. There wasn't any law then that could stop them."

Southern labor had improved as New England labor had declined in quality.

"Look at the workers in the Dan River Mills and then look up here. We're down to the Syrians."

"What about the Irish?"

"They're Ambassadors to England," he said.

I laughed.

"The Southern manufacturers live in the towns with the mills. That's right. When I went to Manchester I went straight to the mills and tended to my business. I didn't go much around the town. They talked a lot about absentee ownership by a Boston crowd."

He puffed at his cigar.

"But I don't know. The worst strikes come where the mills have done most for the people."

Then he talked about the effort of a New York crowd which realized in the twenties that the quick assets of the mills made the stock worth more than it was selling for. They wanted to buy it, but he opposed the sale and worked out a plan to give the stockholders some millions of those assets in bonds. That satisfied them but it meant the addi-tion of fixed interest charges to rising labor costs and rising taxes.

Once or twice he said very calmly, "I was a damn fool."

But: "The people of Manchester did not believe the mills were going under till the last moment. They thought we were bluffing. That is, the general run of people."

He got up deliberately and put the parrot on a perch. He poked the ashes off his cigar.

"The people who could tell you about Amoskeag—most of them are dead."

The parrot muttered on his perch and I got up to go.

"A lot of them died in the last two years," he said.

And the parrot made a guttural sound like a cough.

I drove out of the walled grounds ("That wall cost the man who built this place $65,000; that shows how values have fallen"), and down the road to get a glimpse of Groton School. The old apple trees might not bloom again, but there were yellow jonquils in the grass along the road. There were few boys in sight. It was just noon, and I suppose they were still attending classes and learning under old Dr. Endicott Peabody's excellent schoolmasters to be the exclusive young aristocrats they are supposed to be. Franklin Roosevelt had gone from Groton to the White House, and Richard Whitney had gone from Groton to Sing Sing; and there was a tale current among the irreverent that some Groton boys were not sure which had departed most from the Groton pattern. I went in through a gate built by the Auchinclosses and out another built by the Bacons. Between them the school swung in a circle of red brick buildings around a green lawn and a white stone chapel. It was very quiet. I thought of the boys inside the buildings growing over their books to Harvard and the Porcellian Club (maybe, like the President, they would only make the Fly Club), and beyond to the social and economic eminence to which they were entitled by birth and bank account. I wondered what they would do in the world which would continue after Mr. Dumaine.

But there was more hunger than curiosity in me at that hour, so I drove, by roadside stands which were selling everything from eggs to boxes of pansies and from cider to potted plants, the twenty miles to Concord. I ate well in the Colonial Inn and in interesting company. A big middle-aged woman at a table with an elderly, bearded man was reading the

Nation. While she read, he was crumbling bread into his glass of milk with the fixed attention of a philosopher. At the table next to mine were a young couple in love: whispering boy and a girl with plucked eyebrows and a very saucy veil hanging beside her head from a little red hat. A village storekeeper type of man ate in solitude and steadily. A gray professor sat with a wife who bulged in black satin. And one whole end of the dining room rippled with the voices of the luncheon meeting of the Concord Chapter of the D.A.R. Despite the monument in front of the inn which spoke sternly in the philosophers' town of the War of the Rebellion they might have been the D.A.R.'s of Montgomery, Alabama, where the Confederacy began. In the North as in the South, where history is presented the living must be fed. I asked about that, and the manager, in almost automatic action, gave me a map of the town.

"You ought to be here," he said, "in summer when the sight-seeing busses come in."

He did not look particularly pleased at the profitable prospect, and I wondered what Thoreau would have said about the busses and the people in them. Nothing, probably. If he knew modern Concord he would be more concerned about the flood lights for night bathing in Walden Pond. The darkness which pleased him about Concord is not all that has changed. That day the Old Manse where Hawthorne lived had one automobile in the stable and one parked outside. There was a big parking space provided at the entrance to the Concord Battleground, but beside the walk to the bridge where the farmers fired the shot heard 'round the world a man in his back yard was smoking a pipe and digging energetically with a shovel. A goat ate grass in the yard; a shepherd dog slept. There were pigeons. A little trash fire was burning. In the yard there seemed to be both peace and spring. Down the path, near the monument, a woman was buying postcards about the patriots.

Some of those patriots sleep in the Hill Burying Ground, and those who put them there were realistic about the fact that they were dead. There seemed to be almost a rejoicing in decay. I remember the stone of Robert Meriam and the winged skull and the smaller faces like comic-strip angels' faces scratched shallowly into the slate. There were crossbones. Time and death: *Memento mori—fugit hora—all must submit to the king of terrors.* One stone carried the popular verse with which in so many New England graveyards the dead taunt the living:

> "Ho all you that passeth by,
> As you are now, so once was I;
> As I am now so you must be,
> Prepare for death and follow me."

There were many Jonathans, I noticed, in the company. There was John Jack, who must have been one of the earliest Negroes in this cold New England. There was Mrs. Mary Hunt, who "looked well to her own house and meddled not with ye affairs of others." Most of the stones were of slate crudely carved with inscriptions which have stood against time on the hill. One marble stone carried a husband's testimony to a dead wife that her life was as white as the stone. Once she was, too, and probably her husband remembered that as well as the whiteness of her heart. There had been nearly two hundred winters of snow around that stone. But on that afternoon in 1939 it was hot in the graveyard. I remember that when I had pulled up the steep stair of its rows of graves how wet my forehead was under my hat. All the hill was full of sun. As I came down the steep path I saw suddenly a woman's sport shoe, brown and white. It lay among the graves as if it had been kicked off there.

Beyond the founding the flowering of Concord lies in the unremarkable cemetery with the gentle name of Sleepy Hollow. There I found easily enough French's beautiful Melvin Memorial, erected by a private soldier to three soldier brothers who were killed in the war, but I searched nearly an hour for Authors' Ridge, where Emerson and Thoreau, Alcott and Hawthorne all lie together. That afternoon the cemetery was empty except for a little girl of twelve or so who was using its uncrowded hills as a place to teach a younger brother how to ride a bicycle. No better school ground for such a teaching could possibly be found. The last time I passed them, the boy came all the way down a hill before he fell. His sister came running very seriously after him. I found the great at last. Only their names distinguished their graves from the common dead of Concord. The storekeeper lay by the philosopher, the lawyer by the poet, the doctor by the novelist. It was the little town of the dead, and the great were no more than neighbors in the earth.

There may be more democracy in the rich earth than in the changing town. For all the pious preoccupation of the past with mortality, this may not be new. But in that Concord which still breathes and walks and rides in station wagons and works in the mills or in Boston there is a social cleavage based as elsewhere largely on money. Bronson Alcott might not approve, but in Concord today, where the substantial are the suburbanites and not philosophers, a girl must go to the private schools if she wants to go to the best private parties. There is a wall which cannot be seen but can be felt between the well-to-do and the Irish and the other poor across the town. Where the poor live, there also the Catholic Church and one Protestant Church, and there is a divided world behind them. In the green continuity of Concord, there is much that might puzzle the philosophers or disturb the patriots.

Still the good continuity remains. With native friends I found it when we knocked on Ralph Waldo Emerson's door. The very dark but pretty maid who answered and told us that the visiting hours were over reminded me that Louisa May Alcott had tried domestic service before she tried literature as a means of helping feed old, impractical Bronson's brood. But before we reached the gate the maid called us back. Old Miss Helen Legate, who, as the friend of Emerson's daughter, lives in the house, knew my friend and sent word that we were welcome. She showed us through the house herself and gave the boy with us one of the sandwiches she was having with her tea. Long a teacher in the Concord schools, she keeps such a good gayness among the relics that Emerson might merely be out on one of his walks or lecture tours and not gone forever to Sleepy Hollow. During certain hours the house is open to visitors; but tourists can be a plague. There was the insistent woman who came at dinnertime and would not go away. Instead she put her nose to the screen and declined the maid's polite proposal that she come another time. So Miss Legate came to face the woman's persistence.

"I must—I must," the woman said, "I must walk where the great Emerson trod!"

"Well," said Miss Legate calmly, "that's all right. You've already done it. He often came in by the front way."

In the house I remember the picture of Carlyle which looked like a young poet and not like the angry, aging dyspeptic. There was a hobby-horse that some of the Emerson children had ridden. The bookcases were made like boxes which could be quickly carried out in case of such a fire as that which burned the house down once when Emerson was moving toward old age. The present feared fire, too, and a rich part of Emerson's things had been carried across the street to a fireproof museum. Duplicates had been placed in the room so emptied.

The Emerson Heirs are a corporation now. A good many of them are rich despite the steady praying of the philosopher's grandfather that none of his descendants would ever be. But the philosopher's daughter married a Forbes, and from China and railroads and telephones the Forbeses have stored up treasure on this earth. The heirs make decisions by vote and, it is said, the debate over such a proposal as the moving of the furnishings of the study of the philosopher across the street to the museum sometimes exceeds the bounds of the philosophic. However the decision was reached, it should protect Emerson's relics for the future and protect Miss Legate in the present from some of the pressure of the tourists. The fire which he dreaded is kept out. Even time may be warned at the door of the study to stay out, for the calendar hangs as he turned it to the year and month in which he died.

What New England and Concord describe as a "character" began in productive eccentricity the collection which has grown into the museum of the Antiquarian Society. He came between the antique users and the antique collectors. Cummings E. Davis was his name, and what a progressing Concord threw away he gathered and kept. At first it was junk. Then it became a sort of side show in an upper room of the courthouse over which he presided in wig and costume, collecting fees from the curious. As he grew feeble, Concord's past began to grow valuable. Citizens undertook his care in exchange for his collection. The town did not get cheated on that deal.

The procession of Concord's past runs through the precise rooms of the neat museum. I am sure the antiquarians are accurate, but I suspect that all antiquarians pick the past as photographers pick the parts they want of the present. Certainly in these rooms there was little reflection of a past restricted to plain living and high thinking. Beyond the simplicity of the rooms of the settlers, the museum seemed to me to reflect a richly upholstered past. In china and mahogany and looking glass and carpet, living ran back to the settlers through a procession of loveliness and luxury. These things were in that past, but I doubt if they were it. This is no reflection on the antiquarians. But I believe that the past, even in Concord, would be more clearly presented by the junk as well as the jewelry, by the preservation of the poorly nailed as well as the beautifully carved, by the clutter as well as the costly and the chaste. Heirlooms may serve the pride of the heirs better than they preserve the picture of the ancestors. Parts of old Concord must have been as far away as Manchester was in Groton. There were the poor in the past; and I wondered how much truth there was in the dictum that they always loved and honored the rich. It seemed possible that there might be both injustice and envy buried beneath the same dreadful symbols on the old cemetery hill, and in Sleepy Hollow, too.

And maybe as much gentleness remains. We walked before supper on a wide porch which sits in high prospect over the Concord River and two dammed ponds beyond. My friend's children sat between us at dinner, a grave boy, young-wise in that mature age which strangely precedes the immaturity of an older boyhood, and his pretty sister who had just come home from the circus with a head full of memoried wonders. She told us about them at supper. We talked later, with a precious freedom from the sad division which makes the young and the older alien to each other, about the news from Europe and the right of peoples everywhere to rule their own lands even if they did not seem very wise in their rule to other and stronger peoples. The father spoke without bending, and the boy understood without straining. It was good talk over an excellent supper. I remember that we had creamed chicken in a rice ring, new green peas, and a grand upside-down cake with whipped cream. I ate as much as the girl who had just come home from the circus. Mortality and Manchester and Dumaine seemed a long way off.

I drove back toward Boston soon after supper over a road crowded with the movements of a suburban evening. I remembered how dark the road had been as Thoreau described the night way back to Walden from the town. The lights thickened now. Headlights swept the road, and all the houses beside it were lit. Only occasionally was there any night wood's smell on the road. The gasoline fumes filled even the darkness. I came into Cambridge past tenements black around the lights of their windows. For me it was an empty city that I came to at night, and in the Cambridge streets my lonesome thinking went back beyond the children to the old industrialist in Groton and the cemeteries in Concord. I stopped at Harvard Square and asked directions from a placarded picket in a taxi strike. Then I went out Brattle Street into Mount Auburn Street and beyond James Russell Lowell's house to the gate of Mount Auburn Cemetery. I looked inside. It was very dark and I did not go in. But it was not any darker, I thought, than it had been that day when old Emerson had come to Longfellow's funeral and kept wondering aloud whose funeral it was.

XI

Crack in the Rock

PLYMOUTH ROCK SITS, after some pilgrimaging of its own, cemented and safe in a sort of bear pit in a temple. From the east the tide can come in as the Pilgrims themselves came from Provincetown, but on all other sides the stone is guarded against those patriots who might come with hammers in their pockets to knock off a piece to take back to show neighbors in New York or Nebraska. Not even the rail around it and the granite portico above it have always been enough to guard the stone, which bounds our beginning, from Americans far beyond that beginning. One morning Plymouth woke to find the old Rock painted a bright red.

The slim gentleman who was collecting the relatively few quarters that came that day from the visitors at Pilgrim Hall told me about it. He marked his place in Kenneth Roberts' *Trending into Maine* and freed himself for his own storytelling. Massachusetts had responded to the challenge of the merrymaker. Police examined the paint. They traced its source. They looked for places around Plymouth where such paint had been used. Not long before and not far off such a paint job had been finished by a Pennsylvania crew. A landlady had remembered that just as the work was done a foreman had come home late and waking them all with laughter. Next day he had read the papers and laughed more and more. Something was very funny, indeed. But Massachusetts could not take a joke. It reached out to Pittsburgh and pulled him back. A judge without sympathy sent him to nine months in the House of Correction.

"It was really an excellent piece of detective work," the gentleman in the museum said. "He got what he deserved."

He sold me a guidebook for another quarter.

The past is guarded, and properly so and profitably so. But the Main Street of Plymouth, as I rode into it by the cordage mill from Boston, reflects a tawdry present with a great deal more exactitude than the quaint past. True enough, commerce remembers the Pilgrims: There are a Pilgrim Typewriter Co., an Old Colony Laundry, a Puritan Garage, the Plymouth Rock Heating & Plumbing Company, a Mayflower Cleaning Service, and a Priscilla Beach Theatre. I parked my car in Pilgrim Haven Parking Space and set out on my feet to see the town where the Pilgrims began, brave in a bad winter, to build the America which extends from cordage workers and cranberry pickers to the Pittsburgh painter and indignant patriots and the whole scale of the rich and the poor and the reverent and the irreverent. Still in Plymouth after three hundred years there were that spring more than seven times as many pople, whom the town judged so close to hunger that it ought to feed them, as there had been Pilgrims living and dying in the first desperate winter beyond Plymouth Rock.

I walked toward Leyden Street, and a child stopped me.

"Do you know anyone," she asked gravely, "who wants an errand run?"

I considered carefully. "No. I don't. Why?"

She needed a nickel to go to a movie which was soon starting. In fact, I gathered if she were to run an errand it would have to be an exceedingly quick one, if she were to get back in time. I produced a nickel.

"I'll lend it to you. You put it in Sunday school for me."

She closed the deal with a businesslike promptness. I want that in the record even if the nickel never reached the plate. There was a man who got into heaven because once in a long life he gave a starving man an onion. Like a good many philanthropists, I got an extravagant return for my money. I was as warmed by the transaction as if I had given a golden rattle to Peregrine White. It was interesting to consider that, by the time I reached the souvenir stand on wheels of the un-communicative Greek across from The Rock under Cole's Hill, my little Puritan (or Portuguese) was learning about America in a gangster film. It was a great America which the Pilgrims began.

I looked a long time at The Rock, which is split and patched across the middle where they reassembled it after bringing back the piece the patriots had taken up into the middle of the town for propaganda purposes at the begin-ning of the Revolution. Two well dressed women who looked like Daughters of that Revolution came up in a California car and regarded The Rock briefly.

"It's beyond Manomet," one of them said, "and it has a red roof. That's what she wrote me."

"It doesn't sound sensible," the other declared—a trifle testily, I thought.

They went away. The tide was out. It was muddy around The Rock. Somebody had thrown an empty cigarette pack into the pit. There were some peanut shells in the mud. I was thinking about the cleansing effect of tides when the old man came. He looked like Henry Ford; only, if anything, he was stringier and older. He got out of a long car which I think was one of Mr. Ford's Lincolns. Carefully and calmly he re-garded The Rock, the granite canopy above it, the blue bay beyond it, and me.

"Come far, friend?" he asked.

"North Carolina."

"Old American stock," he said. "Did your people come over in The Boat?"

I laughed. "They say so."

He grinned around calm blue eyes. "Mine, too. They must've understood packing in those days. You can count the people, but only God can count the tables and the chairs they're s'posed to have brought."

He walked around to my side of the pit.

"I've just come back to New England for the first time in forty years. That's a long time."

"How do you find it?"

"Shucks, son, it's wonderful! I was born in Massachusetts, and I guess my roots aren't rotted off yet. I'm in the plumbing supply business in Chicago. But I've got a son, and I'm going to let him run things. I'm coming back home to die." He laughed. "Not soon, I hope."

"I understand that's not much fun anywhere," I said.

"No. I guess not." He offered me a cigar, and when I declined lit his own and threw the match into the pit around The Rock. "But you'll like New England."

"I do."

"Yes, you'll like it unless you're too much of a Democrat— and I guess you are, coming from the South. But don't let that worry you; they don't know what a Republican is up here any more than you know what a Democrat is down in your country. And they're not so Yankee either. Take this town." He turned and gestured with his cigar at the town of Plymouth behind the green hill and the statue of Massasoit erected by the Improved Order of Red Men and the restaurants erected by the international order of those who wait in hope of profit out of tourists.

"Take this town of Plymouth. It's a nice little town, and I understand they do a big business in cordage. Well, I'm something of a man for figures, and when I go to these towns up here I get the town reports. I'd rather read 'em than guidebooks. These Yankees aren't so penny-wise. Why, hell, do you know that Plymouth spends more money every year on relief than the whole *Mayflower* trip—boat and supplies and everything, the whole shebang—cost?"

He stuck his head forward in a queer attitude of emphasis.

I was pleasantly intimidated, but I asked, "What does that prove?"

He regarded me solemnly for a moment, then he grinned. "I don't know." He laughed. "I don't know. But I'm going to come back to old Mass. I'm going to like it. I'm going to town meeting every year and be the meanest taxpayer in town."

He flicked his cigar at The Rock in a gesture of almost gay defiance.

"I bet I do," he said. His old head stuck out again emphatically on his thin neck. "I bet I do," he repeated. Then he hit me on the shoulder with a thin, affectionate hand. He went out to his car where a chauffeur helped him in a little too solicitously. As they drove off he waved back at me.

The Rock and I and the Bay were alone for a while then. Across the street the Greek had absolute leisure in his little souvenir store on wheels. A boy went by with a fishpole. I watched a motor boat in the Bay. Off a long way some men seemed to be planting or digging clams. Behind me, very quietly, on the very quiet day two black men came in. They were leaning on the rail about The Rock, talking, when I turned. One of them had whispered something to the other which made him smile. When he answered he spoke the Portuguese patois of the Cape Verde people who began to come to New England with the whalers. But I tried English. They looked as if they ought to understand it as well as men of their color in the Alabama canebrake.

"Are those men digging or planting clams?"

124

They looked at me in surprise, as if they did not understand. But the younger of them said, without looking where I pointed, "Digging."

"Thanks," I said, and both of them smiled.

I offered them cigarettes, and we smoked. They had been working on the preparation of some cranberry bogs near East Carver, but there had not been any work for them today.

"Is it good work?"

They looked at each other and laughed. "It is work." They laughed again.

I asked my question casually. "Are there many Negroes in this section?"

They stopped laughing, but there was no evidence of anger.

"We are not Negroes," the older said. The other added, "No." But the conversation died. We stood awkward for a moment. I looked back at the man digging along the flats of the Bay. One of the men spoke in the Portuguese patois again, and they were gone. I hope I had not hurt them, but they left me sad. They are, of course, as definitely Negro as the old American Negroes in the South. They are called Bravas (after one of the smallest of the Cape Verde Islands where the women, locally celebrated for their dark beauty, long outnumbered the men who emigrated at an early age to America); they call themselves Portuguese. Sometimes, as at Mashpee on Cape Cod, the black blood of the Portuguese Islands has mixed with the blood of the American Indian to make a cranberry picker almost always in a white man's bog.

Alfred Baker Lewis of Boston, a leader among the Negroes there, told me that gradually the pretension I found at Plymouth Rock is disappearing. Among the younger Bravas the language barrier is gone; and they are discovering that in New England, as elsewhere, prejudice is directed at color, not name. He told me a story of the county where the Pilgrims landed and New England civilization began which sounded strangely like stories about the South: "There was an interesting development among the Bravas a few years ago, in 1933, '34, and '35, when they attempted to form a union of cranberry bog workers and pickers; but the strikes which were called by them were defeated with the use of governmental machinery and intimidation. A large portion of these people were on relief, and the local town officials have knocked them off relief when the cranberry season comes along."

From the big cracked steppingstone to freedom, I climbed the hill again to go to the Pilgrim Hall where the gentleman who took the quarters told me the detective story of the painted Rock. In the whole museum there were no other persons except an instructive mother and a weary child. I saw the chairs of Elder Brewster and Governor Carver, Peregrine White's cradle and the Bible of Governor Bradford. But the things that interested me most in the museum were the "Torrent," the first pumping fire engine purchased by the town of Plymouth in 1828 (I'm not sure what it had to do with the Pilgrims), and a copy of Cotton's *Indian Vocabulary* spread open in glass-topped case. Maybe, I thought, the triumph of the white man in New England was not due so much to his superiority, or even the Lord's aid, as to the language of his native adversaries. According to Cotton in Pilgrim Hall's book in the Indian language he learned and reported, "boys will play" is "mukkitchogqŭissog nont puhpŭeg." "To plow" is "wonohchuhamŭnat." If a man stopped to say he was going to plow, he'd never get the corn in.

Plymouth is by no means all history. It is true, of course, that every man, woman and child, servant and sailor among those who settled the town is a historical figure with name preserved for posterity in the books, while not a single modern man of Plymouth was in 1939 included in the company of the American *Who's Who*. The number who filed income-tax returns is about equal to the number who got relief. But there is good life, if not greatness, in the ancient community. The town runs like a loose string along the shore. There are summer places to the south and mill dwellings to the north, and every other house between seems to be a tourist home counting on the American's return to his beginning. One dollar seemed to be the standard price for a bed. There were gay gangs of dark Italian children playing in the mill section of the town. A truckload of green bananas was being unloaded at a store. There was forsythia in bloom, and a wonderful white apple tree. The big Pilgrim's monument on the edge of the town was merely big. There seemed to me to be an air about it which usually attends the abandoned. But on the way back through the town there was a big sign on a lawn, "Welcome, Brother Elk."

I remember I drove out Sumner Street past some old houses, unpretentious and sweet, which had escaped the modern maiming of Main Street. Beyond the town I saw my first cranberry bogs and, in the late afternoon, black men who had been working in them walked along the road. Somehow the bogs reminded me of the rice fields in Louisiana, and the men walking on the road might have been Negroes going home in Lafourche parish. But as the night came on, it was colder, and the black men seemed stranger than ever in the land where even the Puritans nearly froze in the first dark winter of the American beginning.

XII

Or a Stove Boat

NEW BEDFORD KEEPS THE SYMBOLISM of the whale, not the spindle. On the library lawn the eternal whaleman stands in a granite boat with his harpoon forever ready for the ghost of any leviathan which might come up Pleasant Street.

"A dead whale or a stove boat."

There is a simple, if heroic, alternative. New Bedford's sailor, man in every sculptured muscle, stands in the romantic antagonism of man against nature, man against the sea. It is beside the point that at last the boat was not staved; it rotted as whales grew rarer, as the West opened a way for men less than heroes to get out of dirty forecastles, as oil was discovered in Pennsylvania.

But there ought to be, I thought as I looked at the whaleman and the library, a corresponding statue of the textile worker. Soon he might be history, too. It would not be necessary that he be a stoop-shouldered Lancashire Englishman or a slim French-Canadian or a Portuguese. He could be a mythical god like the whaleman, and with the whaleman hide the fact that both of them in their time were men trying to make a living and not finding it always romantic in New Bedford, not even always possible. Not all the men in the whaling ships had a whole whale, as Herman Melville reported, to give their daughters as dowry; and not all the boys who came from Lancashire or Quebec built such a house as Walter

Langshaw, who went to work in the mills at nine, still lived
in up on the hill.

The street lights came on in the town where the spermaceti
candles had burned long ago. I went alone to the Spouter Inn
of the New Bedford Hotel, where the whaleship cabin at sea
is simulated with portholes outside which the lit and painted
marine scenery rises and falls as with rolling ocean. I considered that such a mimicry of sea motion in a taproom might
disturb such a gentleman as the one at the bar who was telling a companion, loud enough for all to hear, about the very
sad funeral he had returned to in this home of his boyhood
and, in quick turn to amusement, about the alligators in the
lobby of the Jefferson Hotel in Richmond, Virginia. If he
was aware of the pretended roll of the room, he did not indicate it.

Over my steak I read *The Standard Times*. In it, behind
Europe and the C.I.O. and twenty-four poison murders in
Philadelphia, I read the obituary of Edward T. Mahoney
who "conducted his own drug store in the North End for
25 years. He was a WPA timekeeper when he was taken ill."
And of Manuel Joaquin Azevedo, sixty-seven: "Mr. Azevedo
was a weaver in a mill in New Bedford. He had lived for the
past six years in East Falmouth, where he operated a strawberry and turnip farm. He was born in St. Michael, Azores."
He hanged himself in his cellar. But in the whaleship cabin
which had never been to sea two ambulant musicians moved
with their music. In the seagoing atmosphere they played
from table to table and from tip to tip. I left the sound of
the swing and the sentiment they made to take a long walk
in the dark down to the fish pier, by the newspaper office
where a slow, puzzled managing editor talked about his town,
up the hill where big houses sat in dark gardens. I came home
early to bed. Down the street below my window the statue
of the past was still waiting for a whale.

The young textile manufacturer called for me on a morning full of bright seaside sun and took me in his car on a pessimistic drive about his town. It was not so much that he was pessimistic, though in important regards he was. It was true undoubtedly that New Bedford had been a fine-goods town in textiles and so had not felt the earliest competition of the South. It had never been quite a one-industry town. But since 1925 twelve mills employing fifteen thousand people had shut their doors, and not all those surviving the shutting were sure of the continuance of their jobs or of the mills in which they worked.

In the daylight the old houses sat high and lovely on the hill, patrician as they had seemed to Melville long ago; but the patricians in them, my manufacturer said, were disturbed. As old patricians died there were few who wanted the big houses any more. There were problems of servants and of taxes and upkeep and incomes. The same thing seemed true of too many of the monumental mills of brick and granite down on the flat land nearer the shore. The mill companies had not moved away. In the whole town only one mill had moved South. The rest had died where they stood; the lawyers call it "liquidation." And liquidation had left not only empty mills.

That spring there had been more than seven thousand people depending upon the general relief of the town for food. The Irish Mayor, who had been a loom fixer, and his council were fighting over the proportions of the town's participation in WPA. A rich young Irishman was leading the fight against big outlays by the town. The mills that were failing had been sometimes getting their taxes rebated as a result of the pressure of their employees on the politicians. The Reconstruction Finance Corporation was lending money to keep collapsing plants in competition with still successful ones. The RFC had got for keeps some of the plants it took in hock.

The employers and the unions fought over the rules surrounding the remaining jobs.

The old-time manufacturers of Yankee stock did not like the new-time manufacturers, often of Jewish stock, who were taking little places in the big empty mills. Taxpayers fought the Mayor. Even in the desperate quest for new industries to take the place of old ones, the town was split with two industry-seeking civic organizations which were scarcely on speaking terms with each other. From the black Bravas scratching in their gardens on the edge of Buzzards Bay to the troubled Yankees in the Wamsutta Club, New Bedford seemed that May rent like Babel. The wound may have come from without, but the town seemed split within. Still I remember that an ancient Yankee, head of an old manufacturing family, grinned in the Wamsutta Club and took consolation in the confusion of tongues.

"I told my friends down South," the pert old man said, "that they could look forward to greater labor troubles than New England, for labor in the North is divided into English, Irish, French-Canadian, Portuguese, Italian, and so forth. They don't understand each other, which keeps them divided. But in the South they're all the same people."

(It was interesting, I thought, that at that moment in my own North Carolina and in prison, from which I thought he should be released, was Fred Beal, the ex-Communist, who as Communist had helped organize the big 1928 strike of the Textile Mill Committees in the New Bedford Mills. I had first heard of the Wamsutta and the Whitman Mills in his story. He had organized Portuguese, Greeks, Englishmen, and French-Canadians in New Bedford and the wholly homogeneous Southern workers in Gastonia. Later the Communists loved him no more than the conservatives. New Bedford was a long way from the Caledonia Prison Farm. I wondered

what had happened to Beal's comrade in arms and in the
New Bedford jail, Bessie Katsikaras, she who sang:

"Strawberry shortcake,
Huckleberry pie,
Who gave the bosses a punch in the eye?
We did, we did!
Who are we?
We are members of the T.M.C."

Bessie and New Bedford and Beal were nearly a dozen years
older in 1939.)

We ate our lunch, fish chowder and filet of sole. Maybe
sole is, as Joseph Chase Allen wrote in consideration of New
Bedford fishing, merely the once detested pug, or flatfish,
glorified. Glorified or not, it was good that day. Difficulties
in industry did not dull our appetites any more than they
had dulled the hungers of those of the people who ate at the
expense of the town. At last my host smiled beyond talk'
black as our coffee.

"But here," he said, "not all the interesting things about
New Bedford are disturbing. Let me show you something."
So we looked at a case of old baseballs bearing dates and
scores. In 1867, the Wamsuttas had beaten the Mutuals 70
to 26. That must have been a game! At any rate the competition then had not been so close that everybody could not
produce.

He drove me down the hill to the Board of Commerce,
but the manager of the industrial development division was
still at lunch; so I crossed the street to the offices of the Industrial Development Legion. They are bitter rivals. The
Board of Commerce is the older organization, and it still
represents (though some citizens support both) an older, more
conservative business element in the town. The Industrial
Development Legion is closer to local politics and maybe also

a little closer to the rank and file of the town from whose pockets was collected a good deal of the money to set it going.

A very blonde secretary let me in and gave me some interesting scrapbooks of industrial progress to read while I waited for T. A. Haish, the managing director. *The Morning Mercury* reported a quarrel (to be found almost everywhere) between the little fishermen and the trawlers; it reported that that spring the public welfare department was caring for 850 more cases than at the same time the year before, that there had been 115 burials at city expense in 1938.

Haish came in. He is a tall, lean Jew with a mop of graying hair which almost covers the bald spot on the back of his skull. He wore a small mustache. Across the desk (an immaculate urban desk), he looked alive and shrewd; and he seemed at the same time a go-getter and a cynical realist. New Bedford had brought him from Middlesex County, New Jersey (that's the county of New Brunswick and Perth Amboy), where he had been industrial commissioner. He had received his education at the University of Illinois.

"When Mayor Carney got the idea of such an industrial legion," he said, "there were a lot of local people who wanted this job. They didn't get it."

He paused impressively. And I understood that modesty halted him.

"One reason I was glad to come was that the campaign for funds resulted in contributions from forty-three hundred people. Every teacher, every fireman, every policeman—there may have been a few exceptions—all of them gave."

"Was it an 'or else' campaign?"

He looked surprised.

"Oh, no! Of course it was the Mayor's idea. They urged them to give. But nothing like 'Give or lose your job.' Nothing like that."

"Can you get industries?"

"You can get industry, but you've got to buy it."

"Subsidize it?"

"Um—well," he said. He spread his hands wide above the desk to emphasize the obvious—to express the willingness as one man of the world to another to leave deduction to me.

"That's not so different from what Mississippi's doing."

"No. You have to go out and get it."

"No taxes? Free rent?"

"Oh, no, we just pay moving costs. We put up $42,500 to move Aerovox from New York City, but it cost them $200,-000."

(C.I.O. workers were distributing pamphlets indicating that the Aerovox Corporation, which makes electrical condensers and resisters, had run away from C.I.O. in Brooklyn. There had been charges that the company had used a succession of low-paid learners.)

"Those Aerovox has been firing each week are people who can't make the efficiency standard," Haish said. "It's just a coincidence that some of those fired were members of the shop organizing committee of the C.I.O."

I was not certain whether there was a half-disclosed sharing of a joke in what he said. But he seemed serious enough about the learners. It was foolish, he declared, to charge the company with trying to run with a succession of learners; a company had a real investment in a trained employee. I wondered about those investments left in Brooklyn.

I asked him again about free space.

"We don't give free space," Haish repeated, "but it is so much less than rents are in New York that sometimes it almost amounts to that. Wages are lower here, but Massachusetts has the highest state minimum-wage laws in the country. Manufacturers are learning that it is good business to get out of the metropolitan areas."

"Away from unions?"

"No, that's not it. When I get a manufacturer who is considering coming here, I say, 'Come on now, let's go see our labor leader.' 'Oh, no!' they generally say. 'A labor leader is the last man I want to see.' 'You don't know our labor leader,' I tell them. 'If you want to run a union shop he'll talk it over with you, or if you want to run an open shop he'll discuss it with you. He's a man of good sense.' " (I wanted to see him, too, but when I was in New Bedford he was in Washington.)

I left Haish, wondering about this procession from the big city. Industries were irresistibly moving, he believed, from New York, Philadelphia, Chicago, even from Boston. They were moving, he hoped, to New Bedford. It was a process, I thought, remarkably like that procession to the South which some New Englanders reported in anger. But it was not only Southern. A committee of the General Court of Massachusetts reported that summer that Maine and New Hampshire were pulling plants out of the Massachusetts to which Mr. Haish was trying to pull them. "In at least one instance," the report said, "trucks bearing the name of a town in a neighboring state were sent to a Massachusetts city to move machinery to a factory building in the town to which the trucks belonged." (New Bedford had only paid for the moving.) Now Rhode Island and Vermont towns were authorized by law to exempt industrial land and buildings from taxation for as much as ten years. There was a flux in industry and a fight in it which was reduced sometimes to the bitter level of a fight for food. New Bedford was losing whales, but it was in the battle for little industrial fish. Sometimes they seemed as rapacious as they were small.

I climbed the steps of the building across the street from the sculptured whaleman. It is an older New England and New Bedford which is represented in the office of the industrial development division of the Board of Commerce. On the walls there were a pair of authentic whaling harpoons and a map of the North Atlantic fishing banks. In twelve years the division had obtained, it reported, new industries which enumerated their employment at 8,002 persons; but it had declined and declined still to meet the competition of other communities "offering ridiculous inducements, tax exemptions, confiscatory rentals, etc." In the room, in his shirt sleeves at a desk which I remember as an old-fashioned roller-top one was a gray Irishman, talkative, imaginative, and with a sense of history, at once lively and sad, in the difficulties of New Bedford. Frank J. Leary looked older than his forty-nine years, years which had carried him as an industrial construction engineer into a good many parts of the world before he came to New Bedford. He ran his hands through his white hair. He hiked up his pants about his paunch. He was the "last gentile," he said, to graduate from Columbia University.

"I'm a mick, see." He loosed his dark tie at his throat. For a rich rambling hour he told me the story, going back deep into the past of the commerce of New Bedford and New England. Mills on the shore grew to provide the goods for the trade of ships on the sea. Industry grows: The copper plant in New Bedford was there because once whaling ships had their bottoms plated against sea borers. Trade change came naturally, too, if disastrously, also.

"There was a woman in here not long ago who kept talking about economic necessity—economic necessity. They were just words in her mouth. I told her what it was. After the war the women all were going to get themselves a man, by golly. They saw the girls in the movies, too, and they were going to show the local boys that they had been looking at the wrong pictures. The women didn't know what 'economic necessity' meant. They hadn't ever heard the words, but they changed the styles as a part of economic necessity. . . . You couldn't iron a lawn dress every night, but you could wash silk, rayon stockings and bloomers. They knew the boss liked for them to look smart in the office, and the boys outside. The change set into motion tremendous forces."

He walked across the room to a hat stand and searched the pockets of his blue coat for a match. He relit his cigar.

"What about the change you Irish brought?" I asked. "They tell me in Boston that one of the troubles in Massachusetts has been the Irish politicians."

He contemplated my question solemnly.

"The Irish elected Saltonstall," he said significantly. "But if you want to understand the Irish politician you've got to know that he grew out of a depression a thousand years long. He had to learn to be a politician or die. The Queen sent many times and got a lot of talk, but she never got the castle. That's what they call Blarney. The Irish had to develop it or die."

That poetic Irish past, it was easy to see, was close to his heart. He talked about the hedgemasters who taught Irish lore when such teaching was punishable with death, of the bright boys who went out in the trade of fish for port wine and were reported dead by the returning boats. But the drowned boys were learning in the universities of Paris and Madrid, and they came back under a load of fish or as a member of a boat crew to carry on the secret teaching of the Irish in the guise of dancing masters or hostlers, or in any humble job in which they could work to keep the old traditions of Ireland alive. Those were the years which bred the Irish politician. The Irish in poverty took their pleasure in hearing great talk. And the Irish—sometimes to their damage —still love a great speaker who will not only entertain them while talking but give them something to think about tomorrow when they won't have to pay for entertainment in remembering.

"A man who is merely a good man can't be a great priest in Ireland," he said.

He stuck out a pugnacious chin. He said again: "I'm a mick. But there's something in the tradition of inherited wealth that you can't laugh off. It means time for something more than scratching for a living."

But that scratching in New Bedford occupied his time and his mind. He did not see the remedy in buying industries for the town. Of some such industries he was afraid. The industrial job of New Bedford, he thought, was not only getting new, stable industries which would come because the community fitted their needs and not because of any subsidy, but in the provision of legal protection for New England against low-wage sections. He did not like to think that some of those low-wage industries might now be at New Bedford's own door, even inside the town and its old mills.

"The New England communities," he said once, "ask no advantage for themselves. They ask that wages in low-wage sections be increased to the standards of New England, in order that all American business shall not go to the low-wage employer."

In a sense, I realized, he wanted the wages and hours law and similar legislation for the sake of a sort of inland tariff to protect New England as old tariffs at the borders had so long been fixed to protect that same industry from foreign competition. The South was in the New England mind in this matter, I knew, and I knew also that the South needed higher wages; but, as Southerner, I remembered that the low-wage poverty of the South had grown while Southerners planted cotton for free world markets and paid out of that cotton price for the price-protected products of New England. The economic morals in the matter were not entirely simple. Now, sections of New England are sad as Southern poverty.

"I saw so many of my friends," Frank Leary said, "—people who had had something—with no jobs or anything that I got so I couldn't digest my food. They call it anemia."

He looked at his watch. It had been a long talking.

"Won't you come have a drink with me?" I asked. He thought it would be a good idea.

At the door of the office building we met his wife and sister-in-law, thin, dark, pretty Irishwomen. In the Spouter Inn, another Irishman, who had come from Boston to make his headquarters in large-scale fish distribution in New Bedford, joined us. He was a shy, squat, dark man with big hands who looked as if his shyness should never be confused with timidity. He could stand—not easily moved, I imagined —between fishermen and truck drivers. In many cases New Bedford was nearer the fishing grounds. Some fishermen did not have to go so far to sell their catches there. That day he had bought mackerel, he said, for half a cent under the Boston price. The New Bedford fish industry had grown from the trucking rackets around the New York piers. But we listened sentimentally while the café musicians played Irish music for us. In my heart I was as Irish as anybody there. Afterwards, we had dinner on the roof. A pair of hopeful and young professional dancers entertained us energetically.

Under the music, the two Irishmen talked of the increasing fishing industry in New Bedford, of the wages of fishermen, of huge Diesel-driven trawlers and little Italian fishers who were still not very different in themselves and their tackle from fishermen long ago on the Sea of Galilee. Far down under the music the whaleman stood still poised.

"A dead whale or a stove boat."

But around him in New Bedford, around the talking Irishmen, the unemployed Portuguese and the old people in the big old houses on the hill, the capital invested in textile mills had fallen from $70,000,000 in 1923 to less than $20,000,000 in 1939. It would take a big catch of little new industries to replace that loss.

Leviathan had died in the streets.

XIII

Descendant's Return

ACROSS BUZZARDS BAY AND NANTUCKET SOUND I read the book about Nantucket with which my aunts had provided me against the day of descendant's returning to the island. With my mother, they had resented my dropping for purposes of brevity the good Quaker name of Worth from the middle of my name. But they forgave my impiety to my ancestors, gave me a book about them, and annotated it out of a genealogical knowledge to which I could not even pretend. There is something about going back to the Quakers like going back to the Old Testament; the *begat's* are necessary in both cases. I opened the book and looked across it at the wide cabin. An old lady with brightly painted cheeks and rimless glasses was sprawled back in her chair for sleep. I read the annals of the island to the first annotation: "Jonathan Daniels is the 11th in descent from Thomas Macy." The old lady in the chair was beginning to snore.

"Jonathan Daniels is 9th in descent from Christopher Hussey." The annotations went on with the history by Edward Starbuck and Tristram Coffin and John Gardner. There was one shotgun notation about my descent from Coffin, Macy, Hussey, Swain, Barnard, Starbuck, Worth, Wyer, Gardner, and Folger.

The ship rolled more, and the sky was grayer. The mouth of the old woman in the chair hung wide open. (I thought

141

how her comic appearance would be horrid if she were dead. It was only funny since she was sleeping.) A little boy ran noisily into the cabin, and her mouth closed. It gradually re-opened. The sound of the sea did not disturb her, nor the mechanical phonograph down the passage which was blaring about "The Umbrella Man." Her snoring came almost perfectly with the rhythm of the ship. But she woke, as if a clock had been set in her brain, when we passed the stubby white lighthouse at Brant Point and Nantucket rose before us gray and green beyond the white summer hotel and the wharves and the little boats to a church dome of dull gold in the gray sky. I was back where my ancestors had hunted the whale. And back, too, where the insulation of water and the preservative of poverty had kept for the man coming back the un-altered picture of the past.

Once, a whaler, returning from a three years' voyage, might fill the water bucket before he went into the house for dinner. Even the dead and gone, I suspected, might walk now up from the wharves to the wide cobbled square under the elms and be puzzled only by the presence of the pharma-cies. In May, even the old lost bustle of the coopers and the sailmakers and harpoon-making smiths was duplicated by the activity of the carpenters and the plumbers and the painters getting ready for the new whale of summertime. The streets run unchanged and sweet by white fences and rose and syringa bushes, between the old, shingled, lean-to houses ("salt-box" in Connecticut), and under the high walks on the mansion roofs from which the old captains looked to sea. The same wind comes in cold off the moors and the tangled bayberry bushes.

The town itself is a better museum than the formal halls where they keep on show the souvenirs of the whale. Indeed, formal museuming even presided over by a genuine, fit-to-be-catalogued whaler sticks out as one of the few modernisms in Nantucket which sits in the Atlantic air as in amber caught forever. I was glad to be there before the girls in shorts, the boys in polo shirts, and the artists in everything. All of them are as welcome now as a "greasy voyage" used to be, and for the same reason. Though a past preserved by poverty now feeds on their summer presence, the streets did not miss them in May.

There was a joke somewhere, and I thought about it irreverently as I shivered in the wind by the pasture-looking place which was the first Quaker cemetery. Down in the poor South, Mr. Rockefeller had built a brand-new Williamsburg to show an old one; but in rich New England poverty had prevailed over progress and had done, I think, a better job. Without benefit of archeologists, the fishing town is truer in persistence than the colonial capital in restoration. There was never any Governor's palace to be rebuilt, but the white doorways open directly to the very rooms the Quakers and whalers filled. There are even some descendants living where the ancestors built with the profits from the casks of oil. Of course, a great many of the beautifully simple houses have been bought for summer occupancy by some of the richest off-islanders; but if they have remodeled for luxury it has been done within. Some of their owners are more tenaciously preservative now than the Nantucketers who had only been caught in poverty which prevented change. A good many of the indigenous in 1939 were themselves being preserved on the WPA.

All of the indigenous in one way or another lived on the change that brought thousands of moderns every year to indulge a preference for the appearance of the past to that of the world which they had made, and in which they made enough money to finance their insular escape. A cow mooed near where the old Quakers were buried without any indulgence in the worldly pretentiousness of gravestones. Some children played a game about the Mad Russian. The wind was cold. I walked back down Main Street by the captains' mansions and the office of *The Inquirer and Mirror* to the square which runs from the old Pacific Bank to the Pacific Club. In a furniture store, featuring a special sale on sheets, a New Bedford man told me about leaving the cotton mill to sell chairs and beds. His Brava janitor sold me some bayberry candles. I stopped in the Spa Café (half of which was shut till summer came) to get a drink. It was there that I met Captain Archibald Cartwright, assistant chief of the fire department, and the Painter and the Plumber and the young bartender who had come to old Nantucket from old Greece.

The Painter and the Plumber wore the work clothes of their trades, and Captain Cartwright in dungarees and his uniform cap was talking to them in a seagoing voice about travel and travel stories. He had traveled himself. He was fifty-six years old now and fixed in Nantucket where he was born, and from which he had run away to sea against the will of a whaler father who wanted his son to stay ashore. (That was a long time ago: now the boy who ran away had a son of his own who was a bosun on a freighter out of Mobile, and another son interested in aviation in Hartford. "Nobody in aviation can pay his board bill," the assistant fire chief said.) Captain Cartwright had gone far off on a sea which led to more fun than profit. He had been whaling in the antarctic. There had been high old times in Montevideo where they put in to reship the whale oil. But between voyages he had stopped for a brief visit in Nantucket, and a crippled fellow had asked him to take his place for a week in dory fishing. He had stayed at it eight years. Then he had become a carpenter in Nantucket. Now he was ashore for good.

"I've got nothing to look forward to." He drank his beer. "I'm too old to outlive and succeed the chief. I'll never be fire chief. I got nothing to look forward to; but I got plenty to look back on, and nobody can take that away from me."

I bought another beer. Captain Cartwright spoke of the superiority of tramp steamers over luxury liners as vehicles for seeing the world.

"It makes a lot of difference whether you see a town with five thousand dollars or three dollars in your pocket." He drank from his mug. "These writers just stir up my memories and don't tell me anything."

I admitted I was one of those writers.

Captain Cartwright considered me and my voice.

"You come from below the Mason and Dixon line, don't you, brother?"

I admitted I did.

"Ever been to Charleston, South Carolina?"

"Yes."

"Ever been to Port Royal, South Carolina?"

I had been.

"Well, I made a voyage from Port Royal to Charleston once. A voyage!"

They were loading lumber on an old ship which was not built for the business, and they were piling it high on her decks. "We were sailing north by Hatteras [Hat-ter-ass]. I was second mate. An old Negro mammy came along the dock where I was working, mumbling to herself. Well, she'd been singing up at the other end of the boat, and the captain went up to her and told her he'd just as leave not hear her sing. She'd better get along. So she came down the dock where I was, mumbling to herself.

" 'Mister,' she said to me, 'de man done run me off, tol' me not to sing. The Lord tol' me to sing. He tol' me to sing for de soldiers in de war, and after de war he tol' me to sing for de sailors. Now de man say he don't want me to sing. It never happen to me but once before, and that ship didn't get north of Hatteras.'

145

"That's the only time I ever was superstitious," Cartwright said. "I told her, 'Look here, mammy, don't put the devil on this ship,' and I reached in my pocket and gave her a quarter; but she went off mumbling to herself."

They loaded the ship to level of the deckhouses and sailed in clean clear weather. Cartwright forgot about the old woman. Then, as they sailed just below the beak of Hatteras, Cartwright was on duty on deck. The captain was forward, leaning against the rail. Suddenly there came a sharp puff of cold wind.

"'Oh, oh!' I said," Cartwright told us. He looked at the captain, and the captain was standing without having moved a muscle. It was not the second mate's place to tell the old man about the weather. Then there came a second gust, sharper and colder. Still the captain did not move. The next gust shook the ship. The captain started. He had been dozing where he stood, and he woke hollering for all hands.

That was the beginning. A big sea tore loose the piled lumber, and a six by four came down across the first mate's legs. The wind took the boat and drove her before it. Seas broke over her; she was caught in troughs between them. The lumber on the deck floated murderously loose. When the wind seemed dying, it roared back again. Finally, twenty-four days after sailing from Port Royal, she made Charleston, just forty-five miles away.

"That was the only time I was ever superstitious," Captain Cartwright repeated, drinking his beer.

"It was a time to be," I said. "That quarter you gave that old woman was probably the best investment you ever made in your life."

"Yes, sir!"

He shook his head and grinned.

"You've got a lot of colored people up here."

(I knew that Nantucket, despite the purity of its old

146

Yankee preservation, had the smallest percentage of white people of any town in New England. It was not a very small percentage. Ninety-two per cent of the population of the town and county of Nantucket was white. Dukes County, which is Martha's Vineyard and the Elizabeth Islands, had the same color ratio. Barnstable on Cape Cod was 93 per cent white. And Newport, Rhode Island, where the slave trade flourished and in 1939 Father Divine threatened, had the lowest white ratio among New England cities with 94 per cent.)

When whaling began the crews of all the ships were Nantucket men; but as the trade and the ships in it increased there were not enough Nantucket seamen to fill the forecastles of all the Nantucket captains. Therefore the Bravas. They had made good seamen, Captain Cartwright said. You got along with them fine if you showed them right off that they could not put anything over on you. He recalled one Brava, a gay and bully black boy, like a lost brother. He had disappeared forever out of the Captain's life when the ship sailed and left the black man in jail in Montevideo. The Portuguese consul, he thought, had sent his shipmate back to the Azores. They were young then. The room in which we drank, somebody said, was called the mahogany room in the summertime when the other half of the café was open. The crowding white visitors filled the room that was shut now; as much as possible the Negroes were shooed into this other room.

"You know Massachusetts is the greatest nigger-loving state in America. They can keep them out of the hotels all right. They just haven't got a room, but they can't keep them out of the cafés. It's not the Bravas who come here but the Negro servants of the summer people."

Not all the off-islanders are summer people. A table in the café filled with a company of men and women most of whom were of the staff of the Great Atlantic & Pacific Tea Company. The Atlantic and the Pacific had always fed Nantucket. Now the A. & P. stores fed not only the three-thousand-odd islanders but the fifteen to twenty thousand people to which the island population swelled in June. It happened that at that time three of the five selectmen were Nantucketers. But times had changed.

"I don't know what brought it about," said Captain Cartwright, "but things have changed most awfully. It happened while I was at sea. I guess it has changed everywhere, even at sea. My father used to say, 'All the right is aft.' There are too many rights forward, now."

He shook his head.

"Nantucket is run now by people we wouldn't have let off the boat in the old days."

Now Nantucket waited the year through for the unloading of the boats. It was busy then preparing for them. Anybody could get a job in Nantucket in May; but, the Plumber said, it was not easy to get workers. They were paying unskilled labor fifty cents an hour. But the WPA made it hard to get men to work. The Painter and the Plumber did not like the WPA. I gathered that a good many people in Nantucket did. It was a long year from the departure of the summer people to the opening and the painting and the plumbing fixing of their houses.

There were men working on the houses the next day, which was Sunday, in the old Quaker town which has no Quakers left. One, working on a house at 2 Cliff Road, was talking with a friend below about his golf game. There were many houses still to be opened wearing signs they had worn through the winter: "This property inspected by the State and Local POLICE. Keep out!" "No Trespassing Under Penalty of Law." Even more interesting than the warnings

148

were the names on the shut summer places: Nirvana, The Rosary, Jettylee, Quiet Corner, Suitsus.

They and the hotels would be filling soon. There would be more people on the island than ever sailed from it for whales. There would be more automobiles on the narrow streets. The boats to New Bedford would be loaded on every voyage. The airplane service would be resumed for those who had to be quick about shuttling between the unchanged town and the changing world. Mr. J. Abazian would open his rug and curio store. Somebody would rent the nine-room cottage on Brant Point entirely furnished with antiques which was advertised in the window of A. L. B. Fisher's antique store. But on that Sunday there were only islanders hanging around the drugstores on Main Street. Five Bravas chatted together on the other side of the cobbles. An old man in boots marched homeward with a basket of clams. In the dining room of the Roberts House, which used to be a Quaker meeting hall, one lady shouted loud enough for a deaf one to hear, ". . . they philandered years ago just as much as they do now." Perhaps there had not been so much human change. There were twenty-seven Coffins listed in the directory, eleven Chases, twelve Folgers. But the only survivor of my own particular Worth branch of the old Quaker and whaler tribe there listed was: "James T. Worth, liquors, 50 Water Street."

He had gone a long way, too, from the rigid discipline of the Quakers, who had been thinned to disappearance on Nantucket by schism and sternness. I went down to see Mr. Worth, but his little bar at the corner of Cambridge and Water streets was closed for the Sabbath day. The Quakers would have liked that, but I was sorry that there was no opportunity for the meeting of their errant children across one of them's bar. The emptiness behind his advertisement of Choice Liquors made me unreasonably sad.

I walked back along the streets by the unchanging houses, thinking about the annual profitable influx of the changed world into my distant relative James Worth's town. Then I thought of some old logbooks young Edouard Stackpole, the Nantucket novelist, had shown me. He had been writing a new book about another Worth, captain of the *Globe,* who had been rather bloodily murdered by a mutinous crew. Bound in sail canvas, the logbooks were still as stout and strong as the men who had written in them and stamped in them the inked images of the whales, seen, caught, and lost, with dies made out of whalebone. One of the old books had been used by a later, softer generation as a scrapbook; in it over the roundly written record of the voyages to the other side of the world little pieces from newspapers had been pasted. You could not tell it from the outside but a good deal of damage had been done within.

XIV

New Tenants

"THE JEWS," HE SAID, "the damned Jews and the women!"

He was a bitter old man, a distinctly unpleasant old man, unshaven, unwashed. He was fat where maybe once he was strong, pasty and habitually inert on the bench in the little triangular park. But I think he put his pudgy finger not on justice but on the change which has taken place in Fall River. There were other men in the park, a good many of them younger and cleaner, filling the benches at an hour when work was going on. For work was going on, Fall River was climbing slowly up out of the depths of the despair which made it not only a place full of French and Portuguese unemployed and old Yankee families poor in a pinched comparison with the rich past, but also a city which had gone bankrupt when the pressure of the poor increased on a wealth which was no longer there.

The men in the little park looked well fed. They were warm in the sun. There seemed no lack of cigarettes among them. They had reading matter of a variety which extended (maybe not a great distance) from *The Daily Racing Form* to Father Coughlin's *Social Justice*. Yet about even the youngest of them there was a capon quality. The workers wanted in most of the new industries were women. In the roughly partitioned-off offices of little industries in huge old mills the new successful operators were not the immaculate, inheriting,

151

young Yankees out of Harvard but the slim or paunchy Jews out of Krakow, Minsk, and the crowded streets of New York. The male and their old masters sat in parks or in old houses which still looked substantial from the street though there might be more heirlooms than income within. Recovery did not seem to lead back to the past.

That week, on the road which ran to the west from the Nantucket boat pier in New Bedford, I passed a sign which announced that practically the entire village of Westport Factory, Massachusetts, would be sold at public auction: the mill, sixteen two-family dwellings, two cottages, and several parcels of land belonging to the company. They had built the first mill there in 1812. The village was a detail between New Bedford and Fall River, not as important, perhaps, as the pickets marching before the filling stations with their placards, "Tydol unfair to striking seamen." Socony, the Fall River pickets reported, was unfair, too.

There was a hideous, huge, green-towered church. A man in a shed was working very calmly with a big hammer on a tombstone. Children were pouring, like happy young bees from a hive, out of the parochial school. Only one little girl was deformed, frail and pitifully pigeon-toed and somehow pigeon-armed. The tenements to which they ran—the little lame girl moved like an old woman—looked clean and in good repair. There was little open evidence of horrid poverty. The big granite mills, rising like cliffs, with high delicate smokestacks, flanging slightly outward at the top, looked from a distance like the very picture of industrial solidity; but I had been riding New England long enough to know the signs of emptiness eager to be filled.

Everywhere they reminded me of my eighth-grade impression, from the days when eighth grades everywhere were fed from a Yankee spoon, of the poem of Dr. Oliver Wendell Holmes of Boston about the chambered nautilus which built vaster and nobler chambers until at last it was free—free as only the dead are. I never to my knowledge saw a nautilus but I am a friend from boyhood of its cousin the conch. And I have found hermit crabs and other creeping sea creatures in magnificent shells abandoned by their builders. In New England, as in the case of the nautilus, other life occupies the abandoned shells even if it does not fill them. That, I hope, is as good anthropology as zoology even if Dr. Holmes, professor of anatomy and physiology in the Harvard Medical School, did not write a poem about it. I doubt if anybody ever will. But there is a poem there: Maybe all of us live in the great halls the past built like little Jewish manufacturers struggling to meet chain-store prices, or like Portuguese girls at sewing machines making over and over the standardized dresses and needing the protection of minimum-wage laws. And some of us are just sitting hating Jews or an equivalent in a park. There's the plot for the poet: It's free.

In the park where the men sat, a former textile worker told me what he thought had happened to him and the others. He didn't take much stock in the talk about the South. He didn't think the Southern workers were as good as the Northern workers were, even if they did work cheaper. The new chain mills that had come in were doing all right. He'd seen what had happened in the mills that failed. They'd let the machinery get out of date. "Old clattery stuff," he said. In some of the mills they were using equipment that hadn't been changed since they were built. "They made plenty," he told me. "But they didn't pay it to us. They didn't buy new machines. What'd they expect?"

He nodded at the old man who had cursed the Jews.

"Of course, now, there's something to what he says. I can't get a job, but I got a daughter working for Schneierson's. Only thing is I don't see how you can blame the Jews. Nobody else around here ever was in business for love." He leaned across me toward the old man. "Name one who was," he dared.

The old man only made a noise which was half a grunt and half a sniff. The textile worker laughed at his muttering, but I doubt whether he silenced it. I am afraid it will not soon be silenced anywhere.

I went beyond muttering to try to get facts. I have a deep prejudice, often placated by individuals, against chamber of commerce secretaries—formed, I suspect, when I was a young reporter. Young reporters being the apprentices of literature, even if they never become its practitioners, share with the masters a preference for murder over the poppycock patriotism of municipal promoters. It is a prejudice I have found generally justified in the search for truth and justice. Pudgy men personally, the worst of their tribe have sometimes conceived it as their duty to organize both the bruising and the bragging of the town, depending only upon whether the recipient of their attentions is the money investor or the labor organizer. Some of the same have treated me to some bad lying about poor causes. Now I have a hope based upon some evidence that such secretaries are decreasing, not because of any general advancing municipal morality in the United States but because of a creeping understanding among the municipal mighty that some brains are necessary if their towns are to survive the increasingly shrewd and ruthless war between the cities which goes on in these United States today.

I think Frank Dunham of Fall River may be one of those better and pleasanter men. At any rate he made me think he was glad to tell me the truth as well as point out to me the merits of his hard-hit town. I hope I'm not guilty of regional partiality, for though he was born in Bristol, Tennessee, his people were Yankee and he was only in the South a little more than long enough to be born. (Maybe there was an old Southern touch in the Fall River promise, "Progress—Prosperity—Peace." Peace in a crowded labor market where people had been hurt seemed a promise like the docility some stupid promoters once promised ignorant industrial itinerants in the South.)

A youngish-looking gray-haired man, Dunham spread across his desk in his long office the statistics of textile pay rolls falling, of empty industrial space, of dollars and people, of space filled, of new industries producing not only the coarse cotton goods of the past but a variety which ran from hats to shoelaces. He told me about the fire which had spread in 1928 from a watchman warming himself to blaze across the town. He remembered the expansive years when mill owners, preferring to pay local taxes rather than big Federal war taxes, had rather acquiesced in increasing assessments on their properties. They had been caught there when prosperity tumbled down. Then he suggested that we go across the street and see the members of the Board of Finance which had been put in like a set of receivers when the town had defaulted on its obligations in 1930.

I stopped him on the curb by the City Hall to look at a granite fountain which was not running any more. Only in the bottom bowl on one side there was a little pool of stagnant water with some trash in it. The granite letters still cried welcome:

Citizens and Strangers
Drink Freely of This
Cooling Stream,
It Will Promote
Temperance, Faith, Hope
And Charity.
The Records of 1882
Deposited Within Will
Rejoice Antiquarians

The fountain had been presented, the granite letters said in a nice distinction, to "citizens and mill operatives," by Henry D. Cogswell, D.D.S., of San Francisco, "who in 1833 as a factory boy marched to the music of the bell." Old Dr. Cogswell, it seemed probable from the date of his boyhood, may have made a killing filling teeth in California at a time when there was plenty of gold for that purpose and other purposes, too. It had been nice of him to remember Fall River, even if Fall River now seemed to have forgotten his fountain. I wondered how well it remembered him when he came back in 1882 to build what amounted to his monument. I think he deserved one even if he bought it for himself: He was the local boy who went off and made good; he was the boy who went to the West when the West was yawning open in promise to the young. For all I know, he was just a tooth puller; but the boy of 1833 was also the man of the past.

Dunham and I went in through an oak-paneled room which seemed in itself a symbol of an earlier time of fine carriage horses and plug hats, of a labor that ought to be grateful and even a management which was still confident that it was wise. In the smaller chambers beyond, elegant also in an outmoded fashion, were the two senior members of the Fall River Board of Finance. The Board, appointed by the Governor and composed at the outset of the solid, scrubbed, and cultured representatives of the Yankee economic aristocracy of Massachusetts, had in a real sense taken over the town in 1930 when the town defaulted on its obligations. But in the nine years its membership had changed. At one side of the ornate old-fashioned table sat little Edmund Coté, the French-Canadian chairman. His skin looked old, his hair was pasted in strands across the tight skin on his skull. His little eyes gleamed behind his modern rimless glasses. At his left was H. William Radovsky, a debonair, bald, middle-aged Jewish lawyer with an 1890 mustache long and a little bushy at the ends. He smoked a pipe like a Britisher or a Bostonian. Dunham introduced me. The other member, an Irish politician, was not in town. We talked about Fall River and finances. Dunham had already told me something about that story before we crossed to the City Hall. The really tough job had been done in the first years after the default in 1930. The Board members then had cut salaries and fired schoolteachers.

"They were called S.O.B.'s by half the town."

Nevertheless they had reduced the net debt of the city from ten to five million dollars. They had even reduced the tax rate in a town in which valuations on mill properties and machinery had come down from $100,000,000 to $12,000,000. They had fed the poor even if, as some of the poor said, "all they give you in Fall River is rotten groceries." (The Board insisted that by the commissary system they saved money for the town and assured a balanced diet for the needy, eliminating the swapping of grocery orders for liquor and the purchase of hops and malt instead of meat and potatoes.) The Board as it aged and changed had less trouble than the original one. The Frenchman, the Jew, and the Irishman had moved away from the fiscal, moneylending guardianship of the National Shawmut and the First National Bank of Boston which had helped the original Board shape its financing. They had been able to get money cheaper elsewhere, Coté said.

"Dey didn't say anything to us," he said of the Boston banks, "but very likely dey didn't like it."

Radovsky made a slip in recounting the history of the Finance Board, and old man Coté corrected him. Afterwards he said, "Hymie ought to learn his lessons."

The old man moved from municipal finances to conditions in Fall River and New England. He talked in an argot which a long living in Fall River had not corrected. I remember his phrase "dose single woman" in his talk about relief. Forty per cent of the people on relief did not need it, he thought. He was sure there were no slums anywhere in New England like those in the South.

"Dose Negroes in de South don't live any better as in Haiti. I know. I went. Nothing like dat here. Nothing."

. I did not argue. Indeed, there is nothing—or very little—in Massachusetts like the apparent poverty of the South. In New England, poverty, like everything else, has to be shut in for the fear of winter. It cannot be seen. But at Harvard, Paul Herman Buck, who won the Pulitzer Prize for *The Road to Reunion,* told me that when he took two fellow professors South in the summer they could not see Southern poverty for the flowers around the cabins. It is not easy not to be blind abroad. But there was poverty in Fall River deep and degraded and some also as proud and as pretending as that of some Southerners who long ago lost their money and their slaves.

When we went out Radovsky put on a jaunty brown hat and slipped into a smart green herringbone overcoat. He looked confident in his world, and so stylish in his dress as to make look almost nondescript an observant man of commerce whom I saw later. He was not fearful of Fall River's future, but he was thoughtful about the change from its past. We talked in his office, we talked looking at its people on its streets, we talked resting in a soda fountain where we had Coca Colas (somehow they are never quite as good in New England as they are in the South).

"We didn't have a damn thing here except cotton mills. We had a worse situation here than they did in Manchester. The whole thing happened at once there, and besides they had a good shoe industry which wasn't involved. But the liquidations began here in 1924. Every time we thought we'd hit bottom, somebody else would blow up."

He considered the causes of the disastrous procession. He named the familiar ones: low Southern wages, wage and hour restrictions, unions, taxes. But there was another reason.

"The old fellows who formed the mills worked up with them; they knew them from the bottom up; they knew the business and the labor. They sent their sons to Harvard and Yale and Dartmouth. Maybe they took law. They were interested in books and music. And yachting and things like that. Though they were the nicest fellows in the world, they did not understand the business as their fathers did. Then there was obsolete equipment, but that comes around to being a management fault."

"The last run of shad?"

"Yes, you can call it that."

"What's happened to them?"

He swung around on his stool at the soda fountain counter and regarded the town beyond the open door.

"Of course, I don't mean to suggest that all our old Yankee stock is run out. It hasn't by any means. Some of it is the best we've got. College hasn't made all of them soft—not by a long shot. But it's pathetic in some cases. Some of the old mill families are now like your old Southern families after the Civil War with big houses but no money. Some of them are having to make a hard struggle to keep up pretenses."

"Cake and wine on the sideboard even if there isn't bread in the pantry," I said.

"Something like that. The old mills that failed were almost altogether family-owned. I think only one moved South. The others failed where they sat. Right here in Fall River something like $75,000,000 was lost in their failure. You can guess what that meant to the people who lost it."

"What about the people who lost the jobs?"

There were relief figures to show some of that. There was the defaulting town in which the need for relief had pressed upon the disappearing wealth to show some of the community situation. Some thousands of people had simply disappeared. (Between 1930 and 1934, 240,000 New Englanders had moved from cities to farms, and a larger proportion had remained there than in the United States as a whole.) He thought—and the figures he showed me made me think so, too—that they had done a pretty good job in filling the 9,000,000 square feet of industrial space which was left idle. (That is almost half again as big a space as the Amoskeag vacancy in Manchester. That is a space big as two hundred football fields.) Some of the space had been filled fairly promptly by branches of chains of mills. But there was a lot of space left: It was filling with the familiar "diversified" industries, principally in the garment business, attracted from New York City and other metropolitan areas by cheap factory space and the hope of abundant labor.

"Sweatshops?"

He looked, I thought, a little sad. "No. First the NRA and now the Massachusetts and the Federal minimum-wage laws prevent that. But Fall River has got about the lowest wage in Massachusetts."

He quoted out of memory the general terms of the state figures. Fall River was at the bottom, but in Massachusetts the state then limited hours in the ladies' garment industry to forty-eight and fixed the minimum wage at thirty-five cents an hour. The Federal law then limited the working time to forty-four hours. Forty-four hours at thirty-five cents equaled $15.40. I knew that would not be considered a low wage in the South.

"The new industries want women workers? "

"That's a trouble," he said. "In the old days here the textile labor was about fifty-fifty, men and women. In the garment factories about 90 per cent of the employees are women. There's a great need for industries employing men."

I told him what the old man on the bench had said about the women and the Jews.

"The Jews seem to be the only people smart enough to take advantage of the chance."

"They work at their business?"

"All the time."

"And they haven't been to Harvard?"

He laughed. "No."

I offered him a cigarette and lit one myself.

"Sometimes I wonder," I said, "if these new Jews aren't more like the old Yankees than the sons of the old Yankees are."

He shook his head. "I don't know. They're the people that are making work in the mills. I don't know what we'd do without them."

"What are you doing with them?"

"What do you mean?"

"Does Fall River like them?"

He considered. "Not very much. I'm afraid that's growing. I think part of it is due to the overenthusiasm of the Jews for displays of racial-religious brotherly love. They're always getting the Protestant minister and the Catholic priest together with the rabbi in some joint service. That does more harm sometimes than good. You know Fall River is 85 per cent Catholic. All the Jewish stores closed when the Pope died. It didn't help."

"Suppose they hadn't closed?"

He laughed. "That might have hurt, too."

"So the old man wasn't just muttering for himself about the women and the Jews."

"I don't think there's any real feeling of resentment among the men over the fact that there are jobs for women and none for them. It's always been the custom here for several in a family to work and together make a good family income. It isn't anything new for the women to work. In the old mill days, as soon as the children were fourteen they were taken out of school and put in the mills. Last year we had the largest high-school class in the town's history despite the fact that the town's 15,000 smaller than it used to be."

He grinned over another puzzle. "But here's another thing. The more educated business-school girls in the garment factory offices make less than the less educated girls at the machines. Of course, there's a social difference between the girls in the offices and the girls in the plants, but some of the girls in the offices are beginning to think it isn't worth the difference in pay."

"A man's strength isn't so important any more—there are more jobs for the girls. Is the schooling important?"

"The children seem to think so."

"I wonder if they do?"

I knew that in the old days when Fall River was prosperous it was one of the most illiterate cities in the United States. Even in 1930 only Charleston in South Carolina among comparable cities had a larger ratio of people who were not able to read and write.

"I hope the children continue to have faith in the schools," I said, "but sometimes they seem to be in the schools only because they can't leave them for jobs. The Yankees went to Harvard and lost the mills, and the Jews didn't go to Harvard and are filling them again."

My Fall River acquaintance smiled slowly.

"You're not talking about Fall River now," he said, "and I'm not a philosopher."

We laughed. But I think I was talking about Fall River and a thousand other American towns as well. I know Fall River may need not only diversified industries but philosophers, also. It may need them most.

"I am and you are," I told him. "Or you'd better be."

And the rest of us, also. It was no simplicity of cause which emptied and silenced the vaster and vaster granite halls of Fall River's mills. There was no simplicity about the life which was creeping back into them. I drove by the little park where the old man had muttered his emotions. Some orators elsewhere were thinking and saying no more. The benches were still full of men. But not all the women were working in the factories. I passed a redheaded woman, pregnant and pushing a baby carriage. There were men working on a sea wall for the WPA near Tiverton, but, on the bridge there, nearly a hundred men were fishing in a pleasanter idleness than I had found in the park. Among the fishers was one middle-aged woman who had just caught a very small fish. Beyond Portsmouth the road became emptier and sweeter: The dandelions were thick and golden in the grass. Behind stone fences a lovely big country house was almost surrounded by jonquils. There were cattle in the fields and a man plowing with a pair of horses. The earth came open in a deep furrow behind the blade of his plow.

XV

Grasshopper's Winter

WHEN YOUNG HENRY ADAMS, who sought learning from all living, went to Newport in 1868 he found it charming, "but it asked for no education and it gave none." What it gave, the young Adams reported when he was older, was much gayer and pleasanter. Friendship in that society was a kind of social partnership. All were doing the same things. "Society seemed founded on the law that all was for the best New Yorkers in the best of Newports, and that all young people were rich if they could waltz. It was," the Adams of Massachusetts thought in his New England, "a new version of the Ant and the Grasshopper."

The symbols of the glutted grasshoppers in a land of laboring (and unemployed) ants remained in Newport when I walked before its palaces in the sun and the dark seventy years after Adams came enjoying and observing. The big houses rose out of their shrubbery as impressively as the brick and stone precipices of the mills rose beside the streets in Manchester and New Bedford and Fall River. In the late spring they were as empty as the unoccupied mills. The old-time halls for labor seemed no more out of date than the old-fashioned halls for play. There had been plenty of pretty girls in those gardens as well as plenty of old women puffing under their paint. But as I trespassed in driveways and stared from the streets I wondered out of my own comparative pov-

erty why anyone ever wanted such public buildings for play-
houses. I suspect that I share one thing with the modern rich.
In general they do not want them, but they can't get rid of
them.

"We have good seasons and bad in Newport," the real
estate man told me. "The rich still occupy their places. If
they try to sell them to clear up an estate or get some cash,
they have to sell them for a lot less than they cost. There
aren't any possible buyers. I understand when young John
Jacob Astor, 3rd, bought Chetwode from Mrs. W. Storr
Wells he got a pretty bargain in terms of what the place cost.
But the taxes are high on such places, and it takes a big staff
in the houses and gardens to run them. The rich may not be
all that some of the professors and the politicians think they
ought to be. But don't think that a good many of them
aren't thrifty with their own money. They are. They want
their money's worth. They move about more than their
mothers and fathers did. If you have a marble palace and
don't use it, the cost runs on just the same."

If you have a marble palace and do use it, I thought, sum-
mering in one in this time must feel like wearing a plug hat
to a picnic. Unfortunately, the people aren't as easily awed
as once they may have been. There may still be people who
are acutely conscious that they rank at least 401 in the 400.
That must be sad. But to most of us who rank up in the millions, it seems also a little ridiculous. The ostentatious waste
of the palace builders by this time seems like paying too
much for the privilege of looking ridiculously like a monkey
in a ruin even when the ruins of an attitude are kept in good
repair at great expense.

"Yes," said the merry and shrewd young woman who had
given intelligent service to the modern rich and found them
good companions, too, "I should say definitely that wealthy

people are finding such places more of a burden than a pleasure."

She explained the palaces: "They were built when the barons wanted to throw out their chests, but I think the younger generation hates the idea of marble 'alls. It wants more charm or sport and less gossip and the boredom that is Newport personified."

She shook her head. "And what misery and tragedies have taken place in these palaces! No, they are not of this time."

Still, if you have inherited one, you have a good chance to keep it. John Jacob Astor, 3rd, does not come along every day shopping for a palace. But the tax collector comes promptly every year. And the tourists come every day in the summertime gawking down Bellevue and Ocean avenues, wisecracking about the rich who have increasingly fewer facilities for play which are not possessed also by the poorer. Envy comes down the street undoubtedly. Sometimes anger comes. In recent years the desperately poor in Massachusetts and Rhode Island have not been very far from the architecturally ostentatious rich. I do not think the rich behind the beaches need have any fear of the pikes of the proletarians. But Newport's palaces might go down like the walls of Jericho if their occupants could hear some of the modern laughter which goes down the streets between them.

XVI

The State of Hope

THE ROOM I LIKED BEST IN THE OLD, sprawling plants by the greasy Woonasquatucket River was the quiet wood-smelling room where long in advance of the assembly of the sleek steel machine tools men drew plans and cut models out of mahogany, cherry, or cork pine. There was a skill there which Samuel McIntire could have used long ago in Salem, but the woodwork the men made in Providence would decorate no mansions. It was delicately cut to the fraction of an inch to make imprints in sand. The sand took liquid iron, and from the castings under other men's hands grew the machine tools which in other factories everywhere turn out the products bought by the people.

Chief ingredient in the whole process is the Yankee's pride in the Yankee's skill. It is the first line of New England's defense against encircling competition from new industrial regions. Other regions may make textiles. Other regions might take shoes. But Mark Twain's Connecticut Yankee and Eli Whitney himself had been New Englanders. Everywhere I went men spoke to me about that with a conviction that was like patriotism. Sometimes men spoke of skill as I had heard some Southerners speak of blood and honor. It was, as they spoke it, an absolute in the region like coal or iron under the ground. They depended upon it. The officer of the company who put on a battered and yellowing straw hat to show me through the oily and smoky shops and foundries talked about skill as we saw it and about skill as they tried to create it in the apprentice system of the company. He himself had come through the various shops of the plant. I remember he told me that for a long time the foreman of the pattern-making shop had kept a plan he had made.

"Every time I complained about anything, he'd take that plan out and show it to me. It took me a long time to get it away from him."

Such lapses in the young have not interrupted the tradition. Brown & Sharpe had been depending on skill for a great many years. Eli Whitney was only eight years dead when the company was founded in 1833 by David Brown. Samuel Slater, who slipped out of England with Arkwright's patents in his head to start the American textile industry in Pawtucket, was still alive. Lucian Sharpe had come into the business in 1853, and his son, Henry D. Sharpe, who is power in Providence for promoting skilled labor and opposing organized labor, has been with the company himself since 1894. His place in Providence is almost as eminent as in his own plants. With the two elderly Metcalfs—ex-Senator Jesse H., who married Sharpe's sister, and old man Stephen Olney—Sharpe helps run the big Rhode Island Hospital Trust Company, the two Providence newspapers, Brown University, the Metal Trades Association (which handles with a stern shrewdness such things as unions and strikes), and the Rhode Island School of Design.

The combination is a design in itself beautifully patterned to keep Rhode Island and its new polyglot populations safe in the shape of power at the top and skill at the bottom. It may not be a beautiful design, but it has worked to preserve the Unitarian plutocrats at the top of the human hierarchy in the foreign and Catholic City State. It is a practical pattern in a practical state, in which, as elsewhere, the Americanizing aliens seize upon Yankee traditions even when the Yankees sometimes feel themselves assailed. Every year one of the great in power pays for the painting of the white First Baptist Meetinghouse, but the tradition of Roger Williams' town continues not only from religious liberty but also from rum and molasses and niggers for sale.

The Irish and the French and the Italians have not broken the continuity of Rhode Island. They share it, even if not in opulence, in the little commonwealth which is only fifty miles across in its widest distance from Watch Hill to Woonsocket. The poor seek the skill the rich want in the state with the least natural resources in the New England region, which has nowhere any resources except the people who are present and the money that has been preserved out of the past. So I went across the capital from the big plants where skill is employed to the School of Design where skill is taught. It is taught now not only in the old designs for machinery and jewelry and textiles but also in interior decorating, costume designing, and the fine and graphic arts as well. The school full of eager young people deserves the tribute of their eagerness.

Briefly, Dr. Royal Farnum told me about the school which he has headed since 1929. There are standards for admission, a high-school education, no color blindness, a series of drawing tests. There are problems with graduates: It is difficult to place Jewish graduates even in jewelry except in New York; it is impossible to place them in the textile industry even in mills financed by Jews. The Negro graduates cannot be placed anywhere except as teachers in Negro schools. So skill is not always enough. They had, he said, trained some boys in textile design who had gone to the South. I was interested. It seemed a new aspect of a New England part in the movement South which included also money and machinery. I had seen banks in Boston which lend money to finance mills in the South while their officers cried out against Southern competition, and I had seen machinery companies eagerly seeking orders from plants far off which would use the machinery to compete with plants close at hand. It was perhaps an inevitable situation in a free world. Here was training in New England for Southern competitors, but it was matched in some degree in the South, I knew, by New Bedford boys in the textile school of the North Carolina State College. Some of them would be coming back. As Rhode Island should have learned when Slater slipped in from England, skill is a commodity which cannot be kept at home.

"Mr. Fales can tell you about that," Farnum said.

He took me into an adjoining building and introduced me to William D. Fales of the department of textiles and clothing, a thin, small man with firmly fixed ideas about the superior skill of New England labor. Dr. Farnum was wrong, he said: their graduates weren't going South.

"He mentioned the McKelweys, I think it was," I said.

"Well, yes, that's a special case. One brother had a job down there, and the others just went where he was. But they're an exception."

"Are many more mills going?"

"No. The workers aren't as good in the South even if they do get less. I'm not afraid that many more mills are going. We've got the best labor up here. I'm not talking only about the boys in the school. I teach not only regular students but a night school of textile workers, trying to improve themselves. They come from all around. They're the equal of any workers I've seen in any industry anywhere. The labor up here is the best in the world."

"What about the management? What about nepotism in the mills?"

He swung his thin body forward in a gesture of emphasis. "That's the whole story—the one big cause of loss in the whole industry. There's no trouble with the labor."

"And you think it's better than the labor in the mills in the South?"

"I know it." It was an announcement without qualification. "Why, I went South and saw the Southern workers." He shook his head in a memoried disgust. "When the mountaineers give out it will be all over. I never saw such poor people. I saw them around Asheville traveling in overalls, and their overalls were all they had. They'll work for anything. But when they begin to feel as our workers do, that electric refrigerators and things like that are necessities of life, the differences in the wages will disappear. I'm not disturbed by the South. The textile industry will either go on to Brazil or come back to New England."

I wished I had more time to talk to him. He had the most complete faith in the superiority of the New England worker in general and the textile worker in particular that I encountered north of Long Island Sound. It was complete and, I thought, complacent. He knew more than I did, certainly, about the New England workers, but I felt that he pushed the Southern operatives down to a Tobacco Road level. Some of them had been close to that level in the past, but a good many of them since had learned about electric refrigerators and Fords and Chevrolets and permanent waves. The comparative desire, I knew, was in the South. The question I sought without getting any absolute answer was that of the comparative skill.

But I had an engagement to go to a plant which not only utilizes skill. It advertises it. Across the years and the magazine pages I had seen the photographs of the Gorham silver craftsmen working on the priceless chalice and the rich man's plate as well as the bride's flat silver. In the pictures they were old men, most of them, clear-eyed gray men with steady, delicate hands. I wanted to see them at work and the bowls and plates and knives and forks and spoons they made. So I drove through the center of Providence and out to Earl Street near Reservoir Avenue, where the Gorham Manufacturing Company makes more sterling silverware and more ecclesiastical articles than any other plant in the world. (The last reminded me that another time as I drove in Massachusetts by Attleboro there was a sign: "Crucifixes—rosary beads —sold at factory prices.") I asked for the president of the company, Mr. Edmund C. Mayo. He was expecting me.

He was a little man and gray, and he received me with such a brusque directness as startled me. The New Englander, properly approached, is at his worst polite. There is sometimes an arrogance which makes a Southerner feel like saying, "Well, anyhow one rebel can lick ten Yankees." Even so, the executive in his office is invariably polite. But Mr. Mayo set upon me in a manner which gentlemen preserve for housebreakers or friends. What was I doing there, what did I want? I told him unenthusiastically. Then, suddenly, he told me a joke. He asked about my father and recalled seeing him once in a sleeping car in an old-fashioned nightshirt (something I have never seen him in). I realized what I should have known, that he was a Virginian. It was my ignorance—stupidity even—because the names of Edmund and Mayo would only be put together in the Old Dominion. When Mayo came back from college he found, he said, that in Richmond most of the men of his generation were just sitting on their bottoms drinking in the Westmoreland Club. It was very pleasant but not quite so productive as pleasant, so he had left the capital of the Confederacy and had moved by degrees to Relay, Maryland, to Worcester, to Bridgeport, to Providence. He had been in New England for twenty-five years. He thought he knew the Yankees.

In Providence I told him I was interested in the skilled craftsmen of New England, I had heard so much about them.

I had been to the machine-tool factory, and the School of Design, and I thought that in his plants—

Mr. Mayo snorted. It was all a lot of tommyrot, he suggested. He had heard the talk, too, twenty-five years of it. It was not true. The New England worker is not especially skilled.

"I made a speech about it some years ago," he said. "I've got a whole bookful of the clippings of the storm I stirred. My! My!"

"What did you say?"

He grinned, remembering. "I said it was not true. I showed them that a long time ago, in the time of Eli Whitney and after, a great percentage of the patents in America came from New England, more than the size of the region justified. There was ingenuity then and skill, too. But that's not true any more. The greatest percentage of the patents now come from the Middle West. There was a time when, if you drew a median line through the machine-tool business in the United States, it would run somewhere near Lowell, Massachusetts. Now it would come nearer Cleveland, Ohio. Of course, there are skilled workmen here, excellent ones; but there's not anything peculiar to this region about their skill."

He leaned back in his chair. "That speech got me criticized all over. *The Providence Journal* jumped on me, and the Boston papers. I didn't know what I was talking about, they said. I think the storm I raised was one of the causes of the organization of the New England Council. New Englanders didn't like what I said, but it's true. It's still true."

He sent me through his plants. There were skilled men in them cutting the dies that would smash the spoons and the forks and the plates out of sheets of silver. There were other master craftsmen working out, with hammer and hand and chasing tools, the elaborate designs in plates and cups and bowls. Some of the old men in the photographs of the craftsmen had gone to the good craftsman's Heaven. Not even in the making of silver are all workers highly skilled. Machines stamp out the sterling just as other machines in other plants stamp out pieces of brass and steel. There are men and women who tend machines and check their stamped pieces who seem rather the machines' assistants than their masters. But in a high-windowed room a young man who had little pictorial value as craftsman was working the hand-chased design into a set of plates which when completed would cost about $1,350 a dozen. It takes skill to make them and luck to be able to buy them.

It was late in the afternoon when with another Southerner, Sevellon Brown, who runs the Providence newspapers for old Henry Sharpe and the Metcalfs who run the town, I climbed the steep hill which leads up from the town to the Hope Club. Brown is a good newspaperman and a delightful gentleman. I doubt that we agree about many things, but he is a hospitable man who behind a giggling laugh (almost the echo of that of Oscar Johnston who runs the biggest cotton plantation in the world down in Mississippi) keeps a headful of wisdom enlightened by humor. The Hope Club is what the politicians (of the Irish and Democratic persuasion generally) talk about when they talk in the halls of the Statehouse about the plutocrats—I suspect, with considerable accuracy. ("Hope" is the important word in Rhode Island. It sits alone on the state seal. It is the name of a street in Providence. Hope was the name of old Nicholas Brown's furnace in which cannons were cast for the Continentals. Hope is what keeps the horses running at Narragansett Park. It is not only the name of the club on Prospect Hill but the power in the heart of the Italians on Federal Hill across the town.) The club is an old-fashioned place designed in terms of old-fashioned masculine elegance. There were not many people in it when we checked our coats, but Colonel G. Edward

Buxton, textile man with mills from Rhode Island to Maine, was waiting for us. (Later in the year the Colonel resigned his textile command because, financial gossip said, of disagreements with the controlling First National Bank of Boston over selling policies.) We sat in big chairs in a corner of the club, and the Colonel ordered Scotch.

He is an immediately interesting individual. He wore, I remember, a rather loud-checked, tight-cut suit. He is a talker whose conversation runs from textile economics to war corresponding in 1914, to Harvard days with Felix Frankfurter and a lively son of Ambassador Walter Hines Page, to a train ride up from Washington with Sidney Hillman of the C.I.O. on which they discussed Ortega's *The Revolt of the Masses.* He had just come up from Florida, where with Georgians he had been sailing and fishing on Noah's Ark. (My brother Frank had been out with Captain Noah and his black crew, all of whom bait a hook or mix a drink with equal dexterity.) Before that fishing voyage he had been in Washington as an employer representative on the wages and hours committee which fixed the textile wage which was fought by the manufacturers in the South. He talked about the North-South competition between the mills.

He went over the points which he thought were significant in the migration of mills South and in the competition between the Southern mills and the mills that remained in New England. (In 1905 there were 14,000,000 active cotton spindles in New England; in 1938 there were 4,780,000.)

Power rates were not important, he thought, if they were not higher than one cent per kilowatt hour in ultimate costs.

Heating the mills in the North.

There were more holidays in the North.

Proximity to raw material. ("That may change as we make yarns out of goo instead of cotton.")

Wages: He cited figures which showed that the average

wages at that time were about 44½ cents in the North and 36 cents in the South—a 22 per cent differential. "At the present price of cotton, labor cost is 30 to 45 per cent of the cost of the product (40 per cent in a normal fine-goods mill). That means 6 per cent difference in the cost of goods—a ruinous differential when we are all selling the same goods in the same market."

He shook his head over the disturbing facts.

"But aren't there some other causes, also? What about the management of third-generation owners in the mills?"

"I never believed ability was inheritable," he said.

Of course, there had been other difficulties. He told a story about a cotton salesman who always had to add a commission for a brother-in-law to the cotton price when he sold to a mill. He was aware that family owners had used devices to cheat minority stockholders. He did not think such practices were limited to New England. He had heard about them in the South, also, as had I. New England might have had a longer time to grow its weaker generations in control. That was all.

He was a pessimist, but a good-natured one. It explained a good deal later when I discovered that this Yankee was born in Missouri. Pessimism is more humorous, it seems to me, when the troubles it expresses are older and escape from them most uncertain. The Irish and the Southerners have such a sense of the ridiculous about the things that plague them though both can be also humorlessly rhetorical. There is some of the same laughter in trouble on the rocky farms of Vermont. But I did not expect to find it in the Hope Club in Providence.

By some quirk of circumstance Colonel Buxton's regiment in the World War had had a large Georgia element in its personnel. A number of his friends, therefore, are Southern, and a good many of them are in the textile business. They invited the Yankee manufacturer to come South for the

Southern Cotton Manufacturers Association. He decided to make the trip a leisurely and restful drive. In Durham, North Carolina, he stopped long enough to telephone his regards to Kemp Lewis, who operates the big Erwin Cotton Mills. The phone call turned into a party. When he got to Fort Mill, South Carolina, where Elliott Springs lives in the midst of a whole group of mills in almost feudal towns, there were not only more parties but modern mills to be shown the visiting Yankee. Springs called another textile manufacturer, Benjamin B. Gossett, over from Charlotte to help him show Buxton all the new machinery and new processes in the Springs mills. Colonel Buxton looked—from new process to new device, thinking of the poor comparison some of his old New England mills would make. He stood the showing as long as he could.

"Come outside, you fellows," he said then. "I want to tell you something. Fifty years from now we'll all be dead. Only our descendants will be living then. By that time Rhode Island will be a state that does nothing but raise Angora goats in the wintertime and serve as a watering place for rich Southern textile manufacturers in the summer. Some summer the Gossetts and the Springs will be enjoying themselves at Narragansett Pier, and they'll get telegrams from down here in the Carolinas about labor troubles and sit-down strikes and flying squadrons. They are going to be mighty sad. They'll be out worrying and riding around Rhode Island and they'll come on a tumble-down cabin just surrounded by little half-naked, runny-nosed children without shirts to cover their bottoms. Every one of them will be named Buxton. And a Gossett is going to say to a Springs, 'Why in the hell don't we start a cotton mill up here? These bastards will work for anything!' "

It will take a long time for that wheel to go all the way round. The present Buxton looked prosperous enough when

I left him. There was nothing about him to promise such a prospect for his progeny. And it will take some time to clear the crowded hills of Rhode Island of the people to make room for the Angora goats. I walked from the Hope Club in the late afternoon to Federal Hill. It is an Italian hill town with many times as many Italians in it as Assisi where St. Francis chose the life of poverty. The Italians in Providence have taken no vow about it, but they have some poverty just the same. In the dusk on Atwells Avenue the streets were crowded with groups of men chatting in Italian. Some were serious. One was noisy in the universal language of laughter. But a little boy said something was "lousy," and another punctuated his English with the expletive of "Jesus Christ."

"We're going to get thrown out anyway," a slim adolescent said to his companion.

The Columbus National Bank advertised on its windows that it maintained a special foreign department to handle drafts and checks to Europe. The windows of the Adriatic Food Stores were piled with sausages like coconuts, olive oil, an amazing variety of spaghetti, macaroni, vermicelli, and all their kind. In other windows there were round loaves and long loaves of hard bread. There were wines. There was music coming from A. Polililli's Music Company. Outside in the music a hunchback Italian was leaning on a banjo big as he was while he talked seriously with a dark man in working clothes. In the increasing darkness children were playing on the steps of the Holy Ghost Church. I passed the Federal Hill Baptist Church with its church notice printed in Italian. (Pastor John Di Tiberio said: "One cannot speak of movement, but rather of individuals, who, disgusted with religious formalism, crossed the threshold of a Presbyterian, Methodist, or Baptist Mission or Church.") In a pharmacy on Knight Street a beautiful Italian woman was sitting in a soda fountain chair waiting for a prescription to be filled. A crowd of

dark, mischievous-looking boys were singing in a vacant door-
way. Under the light on the corner boys were meeting girls.
Two young girls passed me in the dark, and one said, "You
take me—we'll go to Plainfield, and I don't give a darn what
it is." I ate in a little restaurant decorated with much bead
and paper drapery. But the *scaloppini con funghi* was excellent and the Chianti wine was good—and cheap.

My waiter looked like Victor Emmanuel III. He was not
less old and only a little taller. I asked him about the excited
conversation across the room. One man was talking in a Lat-
inized English, and the eyes of all the others were glittering.

"He was there," said the waiter. "He saw them get the
money."

"What money?"

The old waiter, who looked like a frayed version of an old
king, regarded my ignorance in surprise.

"At Narragansett they had a nice double. Six tickets had
it. Very nice. Two dollar double tickets pay two thousand
dollar. Very nice. Six had 'em."

He shook his head and brought me some Parmesan cheese.

"But not me," he said. "Never me."

He left me and went back to the group that was listening
with glittering eyes. Dark heads moved. And hands beneath
them. In the dim light a traveler could see that even on Federal Hill, Rhode Island was still the State of Hope. I wondered over my coffee if the human chance there was as long
a shot as had been the thrilling and profitable combination
of Ground Oak's win in the first race and Miss Martis' victory in the second. Each was a long shot; their conjunction in
winning was a miracle. It was also a fact.

"It will not happen again tomorrow," said the old waiter.
"But sometime again, maybe. Why not?"

I went back down the dark hill to the center of the town.

XVII

By Vanderbilt to Galilee

"I GO TO BANQUETS," the newspaperman said. "The Irish and Italians and the French are always having banquets. I go, and generally I'm the only white man there unless the Vanderbilts are there. They're smart and they're nice, and I think she's a better politician than he is. And that's good."

But it was a phenomenon, I considered, remembering both Newport and Federal Hill. As a plebeian by preference, I wondered if the Irish and Italian and French banquets in Providence were not at least as much fun as the parties in the big old houses of the millionaires. I did not belong to the tribe. Governor William H. Vanderbilt's cousin had married the Duke of Marlborough, and back in the 1880's a girl named Alva Murray Smith of Mobile, Alabama, had as the wife of William K. Vanderbilt helped the Vanderbilts into Newport society where, before, the Astors and Ward McAllister, the Georgia boy who invented the Four Hundred, did not approve of them. The Governor had been born safe inside the sacred precincts. But since his father's time they had become precincts almost like an Indian reservation. For him the problem was not to get in but to get out. He did.

Henry Adams, great-grandson of President John, wrote in his big book that the great-great-grandfather of Governor William H. "lacked social charm." Fortunately for the Governor of Rhode Island, while the money has come down the

deficiency has not. In his office in the big white classic Statehouse of the State of Hope, the young Governor sat undisturbed while his general assembly hurried through the last
day of its session. The Governor was thirty-seven that summer, a dark, slim, pleasant young man. He smoked a pipe.
Outside in the marble halls and corridors (327,000 cubic
feet of marble from Georgia), a harried House was in session,
senators were assembling, lobbyists were watching; but in his
big office in the columned Capitol, the Governor was as composed as he would be on a peaceful day on his Oakland Farm
at Newport. He had indicated in his first message that he
knew as a former legislator that almost anything could happen in confused final legislative days and nights. But what
the legislators might do that last day did not appear to have
him worried, and as a Newport boy he was naturally at home
in the midst of McKim, Mead & White architecture.

Republicans around him in Providence had spoken of the
young administration of this young rich man as if the state
had been rescued from the wild wantons of Democracy. As
a hereditary Democrat myself I could not be expected to be
immediately enthusiastic about this report from the hereditary Republicans. The Governor had presented a program to
his legislature which was safely Republican for the first time
in years. Some of it looked good to a stranger. He had secured
state reorganization, he had initiated civil service though
with some Republican pain (the Democrat on the commission was John Nicholas Brown, who as one who had grown
up from being the "richest baby in the world" could not be
expected to be a roaring radical), but he had not secured the
life tenure for judges which he had asked, nor a state labor
relations board. The Governor's pipe and the Italian's cigarette were both going to be taxed to help balance the
budget. The Republican utilities were going to have to pay
more taxes, too. Outside his office on that day anything might

be happening in the legislative halls. The Governor seemed as philosophic as his first message: ". . . administrations come and go; men flourish in power for a little while, either to the benefit or to the sorrow of the state. . . ."

In his office, beyond the anteroom where a dogmatic Irishman had been explaining a piece of legislation to a quiet, listening Jew, I apologized to the Governor for intrusion on such a day. He was hospitable, unhurried. He considered New England beyond the immediate pressures of Rhode Island politicians.

"No. I'm no pessimist about New England."

There was the important question of the loss of industries. It was being faced, he thought.

There were national questions which involved the state. "I'm not altogether against the New Deal." But he thought that relief should take the form of grants in aid to the states.

I had heard so many good Republicans speak of the elections of Republican Governors like Vanderbilt in Rhode Island and Saltonstall in Massachusetts as if they represented escape from political skulduggery that I asked him about it. If bad Governors came back to succeed good Governors, as they might, what would happen to relief if it were turned over to the states?

Governor Vanderbilt bit the stem of his pipe. He took it out of his mouth. The Federal government would have to supervise, he said. That would be necessary.

He looked very young, but very self-composed. He was better-looking than the rich, aristocratic Governor of Massachusetts, not as pretty as the beautiful young Irishman who is Mayor of Boston. I thought, looking at him, that politics must be a more exciting sport for a rich man than breeding horses. And it could be a more productive one. Money may be potent in politics in Rhode Island, but I am sure young Vanderbilt brought more than his checkbook to the Statehouse. He seemed to me to be, with or without his money, a hardheaded, honest young man, aware that problems cannot be solved by head-cracking or calling the police. It was significant, I thought, that in Rhode Island the conservative Republican party's man said, "The principle of collective bargaining is so well established and recognized that it is almost superfluous to speak of it." If that means anything, it means a lot in Rhode Island.

Ralph E. Bailey, publicity man for the Republican party in Rhode Island, showed me about the marble Statehouse. He took me into the House of Representatives and introduced me to the very busy Speaker. That gentleman paused to deliver the appalling invitation that I take a seat on the dais, but I politely and quickly declined. A member shouted for recognition, and I am sure the Speaker was as glad as I was to have the courtesies quickly dispensed with. Bailey and I left the House's oratory and routine and looked at the empty Senate chamber. It would be full soon, he said. Then he took me into the Senate cloakroom, found us comfortable overstuffed leather chairs and began to talk. The Republican party, he said with some solemnity, had become the true liberal party in Rhode Island. Governor Vanderbilt and the other younger men in the party, who were enthusiastically behind the Governor, were not interested in reaction. They pushed a program which would push the state. It was needed. (Elsewhere they said Rhode Island, like Maine, would not cooperate with the other New England states in advertising New England. The Assembly had refused to allow a Stuart portrait of Washington to go to the World's Fair. The World's Fair Committee for Rhode Island was complaining of financial starvation. The Governor said: "Establishment of a stable economic and efficient government will, of itself, be one of the best methods of advertising Rhode Island.")

"We've lost so many industries," Bailey said, "that if normal employment returned in the still operating companies, only three out of four Rhode Island workers could get jobs."

It was a long story, he told me. Rhode Island had suffered from nepotism in industry. Too often management had gone to sons or sons-in-law whether they were able or not. In the whole state the new racial groups had not been given the consideration they were entitled to. Several politicians of a physical appearance which somehow marks the tribe everywhere and in every party in the United States passed by our chairs. One or two of them stopped to speak.

"What about labor leadership?" I asked.

"Labor leaders in Rhode Island," one said as if he were spitting out a fact, "can all be bought on the hoof."

Even in so small a state as Rhode Island, that seemed a pretty broad statement. But I knew that, if it did not represent the facts, it demonstrated an attitude in Rhode Island which is a fact.

"One day," a tool manufacturer told me, "the foreman in the foundry came in and told me the men had stopped working."

He shook his head over the memory of it.

"I didn't want to talk to them as a group. When you do, some fellow is liable to holler 'Horse manure!' So I went out and picked me out one man. That old fellow over there." He pointed to a fat and aging Italian who was sweeping the floors as a sort of work pension beyond his productive years.

" 'Come on,' I said to him. 'Won't you work for me? Don't you want to work for me?'

"He hesitated. And then he said: 'Yes.' The whole business was over then. The next man was easier, and so I got them all back to work."

Now the old man had a job for life. His employers and other employers did not ever forget the possibility that other younger men under him might get strike or union ideas in their heads. There was contagion abroad in the land. Garage mechanics were striking in Rhode Island when I was there. The memory remained of the time when the late Robert Fechner, as executive officer of the International Association of Machinists, undertook to introduce collective bargaining into the metal trades in Providence. He failed.

There has not been much forgiveness on either side. The story of organized labor's efforts to build up a strong trade-union movement in New England, Fechner told me, is long and complicated. He stated the main handicaps:

"(1) A closely knit and generously financed organization of employers for the sole purpose of preventing trade-union organization of their workers." He named men, big and rich, representing old New England companies and new huge national corporations with branches in New England, who openly boasted, he said, of their determination to prevent their own and, as far as possible, any other workers in the region from organizing.

"(2) The heavy foreign percentage of workers or the new generation born in New England who were completely dominated by old-country practices and traditions. Not so many years ago it was common practice for employers to advertise, when help was needed, for specific racial groups; and individuals of other racial groups had no opportunity of being employed. This policy kept the workers divided and made them easily subject to spreading and maintaining racial prejudices. Religious prejudices also were frequently promoted.

"(3) Probably no other area in the United States was subjected to such harassment by labor spies and similar activities as have been the New England states. It has been and still is a common practice for employers to bribe or otherwise influence individuals with leadership abilities to betray their fellow workers. This policy is so well known that almost every representative of a labor organization working in New Eng-

185

land is constantly confronted with the difficult task of retaining the confidence of the membership of his organization."

In one respect Fechner was unique. In the South I have heard the Piedmont resound with indignant denunciation of Yankee labor agitators in the same communities where new Yankee-owned mills were welcomed with bands. The labor organizer from the North has been dressed in the frightening habiliments of the carpetbagger. Sometimes Southern industrialists did not hesitate to say that the organizers were sicked on them by their Northern competitors. But Fechner, as a union organizer in the North who came from the South, was no more warmly welcomed by many industrialists in New England though the Harvard School of Business Administration got him to lecture to its students. I hope they profited by it.

"Providence and Rhode Island have been completely dominated for many years by a certain company," Mr. Fechner said. "This is true, both industrially and politically. Almost without exception this company and its antiunion associates have been able to control or secure the wholehearted support of state, county, and city authorities in their campaign of opposition to trade unionism. All of this has been such a severe handicap that for the past forty years the employees have been afraid to make a move."

That night in Providence the legislators had a merry time as they adjourned. That is a custom not restricted to Rhode Island. But the lawyers I had lunch with in the high Turk's Head Club the next day were pleased with the Assembly's product, which is not always a good sign, and relieved by its adjournment. (Providence is blessed with clubs. The Turk's Head is not exclusive, but in a feudal state there is said to be a nice arrangement of the tables by the rank of the sitters. The Agawam Hunt Club, which has not had a hunt in forty years, is proud of its grass tennis courts and of the select company of the players.) The lawyers at lunch moved on from the legislature to the world. One of them hazarded the opinion that it looked this time as if there might actually be a war. But the hurricane of the past fall was a reality worn smooth by conversation. I heard one fresh thing about it in Providence: Even the conservative agreed that the WPA had done a good job.

"They knew they weren't raking leaves then," one said. "I suspect they aren't fooled when they are."

I went down one of the roads they had cleared, toward Narragansett Pier and Point Judith. There were potted petunias for sale: five cents each. Children by the road were selling violets for a nickel and a dime a bunch. Down the road farther the rich smell of manure on the fields met the smell of the sea. There was a painted sign:

What shall it profit a man if he shall gain the whole world and lose his own soul?

It gave chapter and verse. Even a lost soul would stir at the view across Narragansett Bay and big Conanicut Island, white house and blue sky and green grass and blue bay. No wonder the millionaires came. And not only the millionaires. I got lost on the road to Point Judith, and a little city Jew came out of an unpretentious house and told me how to get to Galilee where South County fishermen that year were having almost as much trouble fishing as the disciples did before Jesus came to tell them where to drop their nets. It was evening when I passed Mystic. It was night in New London. I rode in the dark close to the Sound to New Haven.

XVIII

Shadow Under a Torch

I LAY IN BED IN NEW HAVEN and read the paper. There was
a lot of New England news in it. Lydia Pinkham's daughter
was dead in Marblehead. The Mayor of Waterbury was being tried for participating in a million-dollar pilfering. (I remembered, reading that, that the presidents of the power
companies in both Hartford and New Haven had not long
before gone to jail.) A steer from the rodeo playing at the
arena had run loose across the New Haven Green. The town
of Stratford, Connecticut, home of Governor Raymond E.
Baldwin, had issued a pamphlet describing itself as "historical
. . . most advantageously located in all New England . . .
stately elms" in order to advertise the auction of 172 lots that
had been taken by the town for tax defaults. There were
going to be only two G.A.R. veterans in the Memorial Day
parade.

Much had happened in Connecticut, I thought, since the
guiding hand of J. Henry Roraback, utility man and Republican boss, had relaxed in self-imposed death. I laughed
in bed, not in disrespect for the late Mr. Roraback who
picked governors and dictated policies for so long, but at the
story about one of those governors he had picked who denounced an editor for his editorial criticism. And the editor
replied, "I have just as much right to my opinion as you have
to J. Henry Roraback's." Even in the morning in bed that

188

reply seemed neat. I had let my coffee get cold. I lit a cigarette an obliging manufacturer who advertised by sample
had sent up with my tray. Outside over New Haven the
towers of Yale stuck up beyond the Green.

Old Eli had grown mightily with the money of Harkness
and Sterling. It had more than five thousand students, and
it paid professors five and a half million dollars to teach them
everything from early Assyrian to advanced otolaryngology.
Its Gothic architecture spread from the slums to the Green.
Its Harkness Tower rose to the points of its crown beneath
the sky. I had gone beneath it with the best guide in New
Haven, Dr. James Rowland Angell, the first non-Yale man
to be the president of Yale and the man under whom the
old university had grown most in stone and dollars and
students since its beginning.

I got such a guide by Southern luck: the scholar from Burlington, Vermont, who had come to the presidency of old Eli
from the University of Chicago and who was the President
Emeritus, had had the wisdom to marry a lovely lady from
North Carolina. She sent me welcome to New Haven. When
I came she was away on some good works she was doing;
but Dr. Angell gave me good sherry, good luncheon, and
good talk in the house on Blake Road which seems secluded
in the center of a suburban block like a house in a forest.
After luncheon he took me to see the great new brick and
stone body of the old university. The former president, who
was educated in Michigan, and the rich Harknesses from
Ohio, and James Gamble Rogers, the architect from Kentucky, had built wisely in New England for both learning
and beauty.

A greater Yale had to be built. Dr. Angell came with the
wave of boys who followed the war into the colleges. The
great American middle class, Dr. Angell told me, had seen
that in the World War only the college boys got into the

189

officers' training camps. That taught a lesson that was multi-
tudinously learned. Since it is the essence of American democracy that everybody who has enough to eat wants to be an
officer, the young cramped campuses everywhere. Yale was
swollen with students who taxed its treasury and it walls. So
the detail of the cathedral, the line of the château, the spirit
of the early Congregational Church grew in New Haven beside the old brick buildings to make a remarkable congruity.
The lady of a famous librarian planted shrubs shrewdly
about new buildings to soften the appearance of swiftness in
their emergence. Endowment went up like the Harkness
Tower. And though young Stover of Yale, who now must be
an old man in the pages of his adventures, probably would
not approve, the story of the elders is that youth has grown
more serious in New Haven and less collegiate. Say it softly:
Even Skull and Bones and Wolf's Head and Scroll and Key,
like the old gray mule, ain't what they used to be.

We went first to the beautiful Sterling Divinity Quadrangle, within the Georgian Colonial bounds of which it
ought not to be difficult for anybody to be religious. The
open court within the buildings of brick with white trim
looked like a cloister for Congregationalists. It is not necessary now to be a Congregationalist to walk its ways. I wondered what the Christian purpose was in requiring a recent
photograph of applicants for admission, but I did not wonder
very much. I remember that, as we walked in the cloistered
quadrangle, there was a woman's hairpin on the ground.
Girls can become Bachelors of Divinity, too.

I did not like the Sterling Law Buildings so well. There
is an ecclesiastical opulence about its brick and limestone
Gothic which the satirical lunettes of lawyers do not quite
offset. Though I knew that some of the conservative members
of the Yale Corporation did not delight in the high New Deal
content of the Yale Law School, it seemed odd to expect

liberalism to flourish where so much wealth had accumulated around the boys and the books. We went on past the big gym that looks like a cathedral and the old chapel which looks like a barn, out to the monument to our times which is the Yale Bowl. Then we came back through the streets where the new undergraduate colleges are and to the old campus and the old buildings beyond the grass and the trees which, perversely perhaps, I liked best. Also I remember the pleasant court in the great Sterling Library where in the fountain bronze boys held between their legs fishes from which the water comes. The effect at a little distance for a nearsighted man is interesting. And I think the effect for anybody is an indication that the Puritan tradition has not been altogether lost.

The great university all together is lovely in the sun; but it seemed warmer and truer at night with the lights on in the windows where the boys were studying (and where I noticed that there were pennants on the walls, despite the report that the collegiate attitude is passing; I suspect that if I could have looked closer I should have seen pictures of movie stars). But Yale is not New Haven by day or by night. It is not quite true, as one New England newspaperman told me, that New Haven is "three-fourths slum and one-fourth Yale." There is, nevertheless, a hunger in New Haven which Yale does not fill. And, though it seems a little sad, the University, grown to wealth and greatness in New Haven, not long ago felt impelled to present its case in print to New Haven taxpayers and taxgatherers and quote a local tool manufacturer, educated at Iowa State College, to the effect that the University is a "going concern."

As much as Fall River does, or Manchester, New Haven wants to add new industries to the corset manufacturing on Derby Avenue (I wondered later if corset styles that Paris decreed that summer helped), to Winchester arms, to hardware, and to clocks. This is natural, but I am afraid it indicates what seemed indicated elsewhere, that New England in general is not aware that the education business is one of the best industries of New England. (A few years ago a Boston University professor counted that 23,813 students came to New England colleges, universities, and preparatory schools from other sections of the country and paid for the privilege $27,-731,000. New England boys and girls who went outside to school spent $6,321,654. Net "balance of trade" for New England, around $20,000,000. I think he was conservative.)

Yale looked so big and bountifully solvent that there was some sentiment in the town around it to make it pay a big share of the town's taxes. The movement was serious enough for the University to print a little book about it which showed that Yale and its officers and business agencies were already paying a million dollars in scholarships and aids to New Haven students and direct contributions to the city. Furthermore, it had an annual pay roll of $5,508,000; it had spent an average of $3,600,000 for fifteen years in building operations; it was buying every year $2,695,000 in supplies. It estimated that its students and their friends spent $2,721,-000 a year in the town. It added up its direct and indirect contributions to New Haven to a grand total of $15,383,-375.69 a year. The total is probably more now. (The pay roll of big Amoskeag Mills in Manchester, New Hampshire, approximated $15,000,000 in prosperous 1920.) Also Yale said, among other things, it kept, for the people of New Haven to see, the first dinosaur to be mounted in America. Maybe it was a symbol; the big fish of Yale was caught in Mr. Rogers' brick and stone; but with all New England, New Haven was fishing mightily for new, if smaller, industrial fish.

I went to see Oscar Monrad who directs the fishing as secretary of New Haven's Chamber of Commerce, which is not so very much younger than Yale itself. They thought about commerce as well as education a long time ago in Connecticut. Mr. Monrad was a native of New Haven, but he had gone serving organized commerce to the Middle West and to New York State. He had come home with some ideas in his head. He disagreed with the statement of an eminent business man in a new high business tower in New Haven that garment factories were undesirable business citizens.

They were not sweatshops. "This town is unionized in garments. Girls working on dresses to sell for $2.75 and less get $21 minimums under their contracts. On higher-grade stuff they get more. I can take you into watch plants and show you girls getting less. The only trouble with the dress business is that it's seasonal."

The phone on his desk rang. He listened, then he said: "He's got everything in hock but his shirt. He needs help, but they won't put a thin dime in while he's there."

The trouble in New Haven was not the yawning space of Fall River and Manchester but lack of space. He pulled out a thick book full of pictures and descriptions of industrial properties for rent.

Scornfully he said, "They call that industrial space!"

It was not pretty; most of it was not very new. None of it offered to industry any industrial housing comparable to that which Mr. Rogers had built with Mr. Harkness' money to hold the boys and the professors in the system of new colleges within the University. But, though smaller and composed of more second-story space, the industrial room for rent in the book did not look vastly different from some of that emptied space which energetic—sometimes almost desperate—citizens were trying to fill in other cities. (Dudley Harmon, active director of the New England Council, had told me: "Too large a proportion of the buildings now being offered to industries seeking to locate in New England are not in suitable condition to be offered to prospects. They look at it and go somewhere else. And you can't blame them.") Some of Monrad's buildings were certainly in such condition. I had seen a good many such for rent in other towns. I said so.

"Why, some of those old buildings," Monrad said, "are worth less than if they were just vacant land."

"What are you going to do?"

I had turned my question straight up his alley. He was a man with an idea, an idea which he had put to work, I think, in New York State, and which had grown first in Great Britain where the problem of unemployed men and empty old industrial space was not unlike the problem of New England. He got out a pamphlet about the Scottish Industrial Estate at Hillington, near Glasgow. There, under subsidy from the Crown, modern plants, never occupied before, had been provided to furnish place for such new diversified industries as some New England towns were coaxing into old and emptied mills. That ought to be the American plan, too, he thought.

"Isn't that something like the RFC lending money to move industries?"

"Yes," he admitted. "There's a similarity."

"How do the old sections in Britain like it, and the owners of the old properties?"

"They don't," he said. "But it gives industry a chance to live."

And people a chance to get jobs maybe, I thought. That was what New Haven wanted, and New England—and were not getting. For valuable as Yale is to New Haven, and even though its staff goes down in its big housing and feeding job to cooks and chambermaids and cops, it is above and beyond a body of the people who hope for wages without aspiring to learning. (The Federal wages and hours law that spring provided a minimum wage of $11 a week. If the worker was employed every week, that would be $572 a year. But not all workers worked every week. Too many did not work at all. Many made more.) Yale told its prospective students: "With respect to total costs, $1,000 a year is probably a minimum; the average for boys who are working a substantial part of their way is $1,200 and the average for boys who receive all of their expenses from home is $1,600. These figures do not include travel or vacation expenses." There were then in New Haven, Homer Borst, head of the Community Chest, told me, as many unemployed young men and women between the ages of sixteen and twenty-five as the whole number of the students at Yale. Undoubtedly from a national point of view they are not as important as the young in the colleges being trained, as Yale says, for leadership. Yale is now cosmopolitan, and seeking to be more so with special scholarships for the best students from distant states. New Haven is polyglot with 40,000 Italians, 30,000 Jews, 20,000 first and second generation Irishmen, 5,000 Negroes, Poles, other peoples. The young in New Haven sought jobs, not leadership; but they sought jobs and did not find them in a city in which leadership had been a professed product since the college came from Saybrook in 1716.

The same process has been going on in Cambridge since Harvard was set up not far from the wilderness in 1636. Some wilderness remains. I remember how close I was to both one afternoon while we sat over cocktails in a pleasant room in a house on DeWolfe Street. There were lilacs at the door. The Charles River was only a little way off across Memorial Drive. The house had stood there for a long time. A learned but laughing Harvard professor quarreled in good nature with our hostess because the room in which we sat in the old house was what the decorators call modern in its furnishings. As old-time Yankee, he protested over his glass against the new room behind the old door and the lilacs and the little yard. She smiled, slowly and not disturbed.

We came to other contrast by and by. That was the evening Paul Herman Buck spoke of the difficulty of some of his Harvard colleagues in seeing poverty in the South for the flowers around the cabins. And I said something about the difficulty for a Southerner in seeing the different poverty of the North. Merle Fainsod, political scientist who had invited me to speak later in the evening to some students in Leverett House, looked at the wall in his house opposite that in which the modern room opened upon the old House's façade.

"In the next house," he said, "is a family of eleven living in two rooms. The father makes about $25 a week as a truck driver."

That was not little pay as Congressmen and industrialists, even labor leaders, debate minimum wages to prevent profit based upon distress. But $25 divided among food for eleven mouths and clothes for eleven backs and shelter for eleven heads would be precious little. Behind Fainsod's wall you could think of the woman in that family dividing that money with the possibility of more children in her head as she counted, maybe even in her womb as she walked to the store. And around Harvard, which has been spreading knowledge for three centuries, it was still a legal question in Massachusetts as to whether a doctor who taught such a woman how to limit her babies to her bread was a criminal.

It is almost a brutal little distance from that woman to Leverett House which sits with the other "New Houses" in the glittering Georgian Colonial array along the Charles River shore. We ate well in the big dining room and afterwards Harvard masters and students and this stranger talked about the distant and disturbing poverty of the South. They were a good company. As far as I was able to discover on that night and others the Harvard man of supercilious and per-

nicious legend is as legendary as that mythical Rinehart
whose name is shouted from the windows by recurrent generations of Harvard men in each recurring spring. But Harvard
is no more Cambridge than Yale is New Haven. There are a
good many other things than learned men and learning boys
in both.

When I went into the New Haven Community Chest
office, Mr. Borst was talking on the phone, and I remember
that he told the receiver, "The unmarried mother problem
has been quiet for several months." He is a gray-haired,
middle-aged man, a little distrustful, I think, of itinerant
writers and questioners, and probably no more so than he
ought to be. But he told me the striking comparison between
the learning young and the unemployed young. I wanted to
find out about them and their mothers and fathers and sisters
and brothers. What was the sum of relief that supported
them in a city like New Haven: What did the Community
Chest plus municipal relief expenditures plus WPA plus
other forms of relief add up to?

Mr. Borst considered my question in an approximation of
amazement which it may have deserved. If I would stay there
a month, he said, I could work it up. He was not very hopeful of my making any sense in less time than that. They had
the statistics, they had a statistician. But they had not tabu-
lated them. What good were they untabulated, I wondered.
He explained to me very patiently that I was asking the impossible, and he took me back to let the lady statistician explain. I am sure they must have been right. I remembered
that when I came back from Europe in the middle of the depression to work on *Fortune,* all the big businesses in down-
town New York had huge statistical departments. They had
all the facts, but these did not add up to anything. Maybe the
expansion of knowledge in continuing confusion applied

even to the bigger Yale. Mr. Borst gave me copies of his annual reports. They seemed admirable, particularly a statement in the last one: "To state that $602,709 was subscribed in the last campaign does not say anything. We need to see this sum in perspective." I still think that's right.

Outside on Elm Street a policeman had been putting tickets on too long parked cars and singing, "Sweetheart of mine, I love you." Now as I came out there was brassier music coming from under the elms across the Green. Before Center Church the listening, looking crowds were already lined up to see part of the pageantry in which Benedict Arnold (still in the role of hero) was to demand for the 164th time the keys to the Powder House. The Yale boys and the Negroes, the Italians and the Poles and the Irish in the crowds knew he would get them from the selectmen, but they waited in expectancy while the notes of "Onward, Christian Soldiers" roared up the Green from the horns of the band of the Governor's Footguards. The big clock in the church tower belled three. Then came the police of New Haven on motorcycles and marching with their clubs held like sabers. They took their places on each side of an elderly clergyman in red-caped black gown who waited on the church steps. The Governor in shining top hat came in a limousine. Then the Governor's Footguards came marching under their hot, foot-high bearskin shakos (I think that is the name). The Footguards were gentlemen in an age in which most gentlemen are sedentary. As soldiers they did not look very formidable. I remember one man who still looked like a professor peering nearsightedly through his pince-nez glasses as he marched in determination under his tall fur hat. All of them in their old-fashioned uniforms looked less like soldiers than like well-to-do middle-aged men whose wives had gotten them into costumes for a ball. But they marched. A bugle blew.

"Christ," said a plebeian behind me in the crowd, "some gob would 'a' done better than that."

"They ought to go to camp for about six weeks."

"What the hell! It's more of a social gathering than anything else."

The Footguards halted. A plumed officer grinned at his men.

"He ought to laugh," said another of the commentators in the crowd. "The Boy Scouts do better than that."

The officer, a florid man in a cocked hat with blue and white feathers, got a cigarette out of his colonial uniform and lit it. He dragged on it gratefully. A command came from his superior on the church steps. He threw his cigarette down and echoed the command. The clergyman and the Governor, the Footguards and the policemen all moved into the church with the flags bringing up the rear. Only the Yale field artillery unit of the R.O.T.C., remained outside. They took, grinning, the taunts of other unmilitary Yale boys. But the regular army sergeant kept his eyes on his fieldpieces, unamused and grim.

The crowd dispersed slowly, and I went on to the Taft Bar to meet a friend who told me about the teachers' union in Yale. Not even all the learned felt secure. Later he sent me a clipping about the union at Harvard which contained a union statement that "teachers are not fungible goods." "Fungible" is a learned legal word meaning, I gather, interchangeable. It is true, and not only true of teachers. Just north of where we sat drinking, Eli Whitney, who fixed the economy of the South with his cotton gin, had profoundly altered even Connecticut with his use of interchangeable parts in manufacturing which is the basis of mass production. North and South, even within the limits of New Haven, people persisted in being infinitely different and diverse. One professor of paleontology was better than another one; on

199

Derby Avenue one woman was more skilled than another at making corsets. But there are hungers and fears which run through them all, through the neurophysiologist as well as the needleworker. Yale rises in New England and helps light the world, but there remain dark places close to its edges in the town, maybe even in the Gothic corners of its own halls. There may be a shadow even under a torch.

XIX

Skill Before War

THE BELL WAS CONTINUALLY RINGING. A determinedly gay man in his late forties, paunchy and vacant-faced, kept pulling the string that rang the bell on the automobile costumed as a French locomotive and cab which sat parked on Asylum Street. He grinned at passers-by mechanically and went on ringing his bell mechanically. I recognized him and his train before I read the sign: "Quarantee Hommes et Huit Chevaux." My older brother had been one of the Horses and Men, and I knew the uniform. The veterans were gathering for meeting in Hartford. At the door of the Bond Hotel, two uniformed men were worrying out loud about the late arrival of the band. There were more veterans in the hotel in uniform, and with them one strikingly handsome man in a wheel chair. It was easy to see that he was important. Two very pretty women came across the lobby to speak to him. As I passed them I noticed that the handsome man in the chair had no legs at all.

I had come into Hartford by Farmington, a lovely town at a lovely time. The dogwood was in bloom and the magnolia, and a stand beside the road advertised not only fresh-cut asparagus and broilers but pie: apple or lemon. There was one apple tree lying on the ground where the wind had blown it, but nevertheless in full white bloom; and, being never wholly the aesthete, I wondered if its beautiful blossoms would ever grow to fruit and pie. Grand fat cattle munched the grass in that combination of steady activity and complete leisure which seems possible only in cows. There were lilacs. An old sleigh stood in the green yard of an antique shop. As I came into Farmington I met a company of horseback riders, among them a blonde girl wearing green breeches and a yellow coat. The picket fences were white, and there were ancient dates on the houses. In a field in the midst of the old houses were more cattle, and in another field two boys, with model airplanes almost as big as themselves, were preparing for a flight. In the old town kept sweet for the secure in the present, they were, I knew, part of the same Connecticut tradition which builds and tests the roaring airplane engines and bright aluminum propellers beyond the capital in East Hartford.

There was no war then. The nagging threat of it was no sharper than it had been in the months before; but the world was moving to war, and Frederick B. Rentschler, chairman of the board of the United Aircraft Corporation, spoke from the facts when he indulged in the prophecy "that 1939 shipments will be the largest in our history." In 1938 the shipments had risen to $36,800,000 from beginning in a tobacco warehouse without any orders in 1925. It was not the war that interested me then. A good deal of man's modern movement had begun in Connecticut. The bicycle had begun in America in Hartford. Automobiles had been made there. Both rolled in possibility upon Charles Goodyear's invention of the process of vulcanizing rubber not far from Hartford in Naugatuck, just a hundred years before I rolled on his invention into Hartford and across the Connecticut River to the United Aircraft plants. But in recent years the bicycle had been left behind. The automobile had moved West. Aviation was something new and precious in the tradition in which they began. Aviation plants in East Hartford and

Bridgeport are counted as details of national power by the generals and the statesmen; but in New England before war they meant a new industry in a region which was clinging, precariously sometimes, to old ones. They meant, also, tribute to the New England faith in the New England skill, and jobs which even in fortunate Hartford have been as welcome as needed.

"During a little less than fifteen years," said Mr. Rentschler, who was born in Ohio, "we have grown steadily to a point where our original personnel has been expanded into an average force of between 5,000 and 6,000 people, with a pay roll approaching a million dollars monthly. We have given employment to the very finest type of mechanics and skilled workmen, at highest wages. We have always been extremely satisfied with our location in New England, and particularly in Hartford, principally because of the availability there of the skilled labor which is so necessary for our operations, as well as the facilities which it offers for the procurement of materials and even manufacturing assistance from many of the other skilled workshops of New England. We believe that we must have been a considerable factor against unemployment in Hartford and Connecticut, particularly during the last five or six years."

The offices of the plant in East Hartford sit behind a green lawn in an unimpressive-looking building. I went to them with a telegram from President Donald Brown (born in Wisconsin), saying I was welcome to come and see. The little anteroom at the door was crowded with people who looked like salesmen hoping to sell and job hunters hoping to get bought. I waited while the telephone operator called, and at last, a slim, pleasant young man in white linens came out. He was E. L. Eveleth. He gave me passes to sign. I had to be an American citizen. (Foreigners could only get in with the help of the air attachés of their embassies and the approval of the War, State, and Navy departments.) I was No. B24049 on a blue pass to the Pratt & Whitney engine factory and No. 10971 on a red pass to the Hamilton Standard Propeller factory.

"If I was a spy," I asked Eveleth, "have you got any secrets that I could get?"

He laughed. "Well, Jane says—" He looked unsuccessfully for the statement he wanted in the authoritative reference book on the air forces of the world.

I gathered that Mr. Jane (or rather those who still write under the name of the British gentleman more than twenty years dead) did not think that there were many secrets which some nations held from other ones. Nevertheless, not even I, who should not recognize a secret if I saw one, nor any other of the rank and file of the citizenship could go even with the red and blue passes into the experimental department of the factories. (A large part of United Aircraft's business has been abroad. It sold planes and engines wherever it could. It in effect swapped Peru planes for guano. From 1933 it did a big business with Germany and, with pretty clear understanding that Germany was rearming, gave the Bayerische Motoren Werke in Munich a license to make its planes and engines from United's plans and patents. On a royalty basis the German B.M.W. manufactured at first, then, when Germany did not care to report the number of planes it was producing, on a fixed annual fee basis. All of this, of course, was done under license from the United States government which presumably was allowing no marvel secrets to get loose. Airplane makers everywhere then competed with other plane makers in other countries, and so none could be far behind the researches of experimental departments anywhere.)

Eveleth took me out through a garage and a locked door into the engine factory. I wore my pass on my coat. We moved past guards in a huge room. In a real sense it was an

204

assembly plant since most of the engine parts were forged and cast elsewhere and shipped in. But the mass production lines of the automobile plants are not duplicated. More care is necessary, more skill. If a Ford breaks down south of Cincinnati it can be pulled into a garage. If an airplane engine stops turning above Saarbrücken, or on an air-line route in Colorado, it may be a different and sadder story. Certainly the men finishing and assembling the engine parts looked liked skilled workmen doing skilled work. (Women were used only for packing small spare parts and for inspection in which they have a reputation for a patience superior to men's.)

"There's millions' worth of machine tools in this plant," Eveleth said. They came from Worcester, Providence, Hartford (United Aircraft grew from the combination of the spare money and spare space of the Niles Bement & Pond Company, Pratt & Whitney division, the old Hartford machine tool makers. It grew also around Rentschler, Brown, and George J. Mead, the one New Englander of the trio, who had seceded from the Wright Aeronautical Corporation in New Jersey to form a company of their own.) There were tools from the Middle West. I particularly remember one beautiful gear cutter made by a Middle Western firm which bore the name of a woman who had designed the machine.

One man assembles a whole engine: That means both responsibility and skill. But certainly he does not do a one-man job. There is as vast and varied an assistance behind him as behind the single aviator who takes the controls of the strong, clean, completed plane. He only stands at the bottleneck of tools and foundries and laboratories putting together the products of a technical civilization for such a roaring mechanism of power as means speed or fury. The product he puts together costs something like $12 to $15 per horsepower, and there are plenty of 1,000 horsepower engines with more power in one of them than the whole company of the settlers of Hartford had in themselves and their stock when they came over from Cambridge, Massachusetts, in 1635.

And they roar: We went out big doors to the noisy space before the thundering testing rooms. In each room engines were set up and running, and despite the heavy brick walls and big thick wooden doors about them, the noise was terrific. They made a power which was designed to fling wings across the sky, but all their monster droning there was for men behind plate-glass windows who, with rubber guards against the roar in their ears, watched the motors hours long, watched dials, and recorded every reading on every phase of performance on special sheets by five- or ten-minute intervals. Afterward the movement of a man's hand would make all their power silent. Men would take them all apart again and then put them together for final tests. In big boxes they go to Bridgeport where in the Vought-Sikorsky plane plant of the company they provide the power that rides the sky.

Propellers might seem an anticlimax after engines. They did not seem so to me. Next door to the engine factory the Hamilton Standard Propeller plant occupies the whole space the Chance-Vought Airplane Company used before it moved to Bridgeport. ("The army couldn't wait on bricks and mortar," the explaining secretary of Hartford's Chamber of Commerce said of its departure.) I was aware that propellers were no longer the mere revolving wooden blades they had been when flying began; but I did not know that hundreds of parts are required in a propeller alone, and that one propeller may cost $3,000. They are beautiful things which emerge from the raw, rough-shaped slabs of aluminum alloy almost as a statue comes out of the stone. Indeed, I had the feeling that what workmen did with aluminum and steel in these plants was more aesthetic as well as more precise and utilitarian than what I had seen other skilled men doing with silver in Providence.

They were making beautiful things, even if, as some men said, the arms makers were the war makers. It is, I think, too simple an indictment: Mr. F. H. Love, of the United Aircraft Exports, Inc., remarked in September of 1933 that "conditions in China so far as they affect our business are very good." That might be very bad. Somebody told me that the big Colt factories across the river in Hartford were manufacturing a variety of things besides arms; but the melodramatic reports of their agents in South America (the curious may read them in the report of the Senate Munitions Industry Investigations, 74th Congress, 2nd session) did not suggest they had gone all the way to the scriptural injunction about swords and plowshares when they began to make plastics as well as pistols.

Still, I suspect that we are all munitions makers in a time when all goods and services may be quickly turned to the uses of war. I know that cotton farmers and tobacco growers and shipyard workers may rejoice as much in war profits as steel or plane or gun makers. A plane may be as innocent as a bale of cotton and not much more quickly be turned into a weapon to destroy. But if plane making is more vicious than cotton growing or cotton spinning, it is a villainy which runs from East Hartford to include all the changing individuals who have composed the 6,000 workers who have grown from the original 30 in the tobacco warehouse plant in 1925 (17 of them were still working for the company), and all the steel and parts and aluminum and machine-tool and construction people and workers across a civilization.

The danger, I thought, lies not in the villainy but in the spreading dependence which may grow around plants whose products are necessary to war. Shoes are as necessary to war as ships, and I thought about the sadness in such shoe towns as Haverhill. War might make spindles turn again in Fall River. Maybe nothing less than war would fill all the vacant space in the big empty factories in New England. War trade could put a rich end to New England's difficulties. Good people, hating war, would be blessed by the filling of factories and the reappearance of jobs for them. But I had been by Amoskeag, and I remembered that it was never so rich as the war made it just before it began beyond war to die. Maybe nothing but another war boom would make jobs in New England for all the boys and girls and men and women who needed them that year in New England. One had made them rich before and left them poor, too. What after the next one?

All that is beside the point for United Aircraft and America. Specific and important, it is one of the efficient units in aircraft production which provide the basis for the faith of the admirals and the generals that the United States can out-build any other nation on the earth, and the government's millions in that building provide the certain promise that United's machine tools will not rust. The United States was seventh among the nations in its air force in 1939 with 3,900 planes; but before war in Europe it had appropriated $300,-000,000 for the Air Corps alone, not counting the Navy and Marine Corps aviation. The present industry, they say, could build 1,000 planes of varied types a month. In a war, with both skilled workers and essential materials available, airmen believe that the present aviation industry could be expanded and quickened to produce 36,000 planes a year. That would mean at least a multiplication by three in plants and machines and materials and men. And the men will still be most important if the American planes are to continue to be among the best.

The present company of workers look excellent certainly. By no means all of them are descended from the Connecticut Yankee. The skilled trades of New England depend, as the

unskilled trades do, upon all the complexity of immigrant
stocks which have come in; but I wondered, remembering
the father that had spoken of a son in aviation, if the Nantucket whaler's son's boy was in one of the big halls shaping
the twist of a propeller, assembling the parts to make an engine's power, standing at a window and watching the im-
prisoned roar of 1,000 horsepower in a testing room. Here
was work for men in a New England in which jobs for men
were less and less available in the cities where the garment
factories and novelty companies had come to fill emptiness.
Here was needed the old combination of strength and skill.

And of youth. The old man of United, Chairman Frederick Rentschler, brother of a machinery manufacturer in Ohio
and of the president of the National City Bank of New York,
was only fifty-one. President Brown was forty-nine. George
Mead, the third of the technical trio who began the industry in Hartford, was forty-seven. There has been no time for
old workers to grow around them. I remember young and
very young-looking John Burridge, whose regular job is keeping air-line maintenance men acquainted with factory
methods. He went with us through the propeller plants. His
young interest in the air was as bright and certain as the
blades of the propellers he showed us.

There are more like him in New England. They count
with even more enthusiasm than their fathers the new planes
in the Yankee sky and wait with less patience for the development of such a huge flying center for defense and attack over
the Atlantic as the Army sought that summer. Wings may be
more important to tight little New England even than they
are to the wider spaces of the West. If there turned out to be
a moving validity in the argument that airplane plants should
be farther away from the seaboard and the bombs of possible
enemy planes, New England would lose something more
precious even than jobs. Aviation provides a new enthusiasm

to turn hands to skill, heads to ingenuity. It might be the last industrial youth in an old region. If it departed it would leave more behind than space to fill.

I rode into town, from the newest New England to the oldest, to talk to a farmer who tells other farmers how to farm. He was disturbed over the temporary trouble of drought. The late spring had delayed the planting, and the lack of rain kept the seeds from sprouting. There were troubles beyond that spring. Connecticut farming had suffered long ago when the Erie Canal poured cheap food in from the West. Then the automobile had made part-time farming possible, and now the absence of horses in an automotive land made manure precious when manure was needed on the steadily cropped truck farms. The dairy farms needed their own manure. Taxes were high in the crowded land. The young Italians did not want to work on the farms.

Up the Connecticut valley there were human problems on the tobacco farms: The weed is usually grown as a one-crop specialty. The little one-family home-living New England farm is giving way, under demands for large amounts of capital and labor required to produce shade tobacco (whole fields look tented), to corporate farms. Cigar manufacturing companies own and operate their own huge places. Labor is often brought out by the truckload from Hartford. The independent yeoman was not having it easy in Connecticut.

In the late afternoon at Main Street and Central Row I looked up beyond the Travelers Insurance tower to a plane in the sky. None of the armies of insurance company clerks around me paid it any attention. They were headed like pigeons home to the suburbs, which have grown faster than the town. The aviator up there in the Connecticut sky, I thought, was independent. A whole technical civilization was behind him, rules surrounded him. But he was up there free with tremendous power under his hand. That would, of course, be an illusion: the power did not belong to him; his right to be a free man or a fool was more strictly limited than a Ford driver's. But the illusion was a great deal in a crowded world, more than a man can have working tobacco under a tent, or a woman sewing leaves on laths to be hung in the long barns. Maybe more than a clerk can have in an insurance tower. A woman bumped into me and told me to look where I was going. She was right, and so I took my eyes out of the sky.

I kept them on Hartford. I walked down Main Street and listened to street preaching to the street poor, "We are all sinners of Adam's race." I went back by the Bond Hotel and past it, following the sound of a carnival's calliope to a midway by the New York, New Haven & Hartford tracks and under the illumined dome of the Capitol. In the flaring midway the biggest crowd of Connecticut Yankees were gathered before the suggestive gyrating of the Creole Belles, some very unattractive yellow colored girls. I followed the crowd in and sat down beside a big cripple who waited in contented lechery for the show.

"I always come the first night," he told me, "because they do things then to get the word around. There was a carnival over in East Hartford, and a girl had her tit out. I always go the first night. They do things then to get the word around."

I went back to the hotel. The Forty and Eight train was still at the door. There were veterans in the lobby. I looked among them but did not see again the clean, handsome man in the wheel chair. Later in my room, as I tried to go to sleep, the bell of the toy train kept sounding. I wondered if several rang it, or if it were rung so often by a never wearying hand. There was music around it, dance music which went on, scarcely ever stopping, for such veterans as still had legs.

XX

White-Collar World

THERE HAS BEEN CHANGE IN HARTFORD. The Morgan family which produced the J. Pierponts and built the pink granite Morgan Memorial museum will no longer sell you a cup of coffee, though it was around their cups in their coffee house that the insurance business began. They have moved away and done very well. Mark Twain, who complained that the Hartford city government had done him many a mean trick in sixteen years, is dead, and the reverent show his house, forgetting that he also said that irreverence is the champion of liberty and its only sure defense. Anne Royall is dead, too. She was an early journalist who worked under the name of Paul Pry. She came from Alabama to Hartford and reported: "The ladies of Hartford have a slight tinge of melancholy in their countenance; it is softened by a shade of placid tranquillity." Of all the dead I wish most that she could come back and see the ladies pouring into the insurance buildings in the mornings and out again at night.

Hartford, the patriotic there will tell you now, is the insurance capital of America. It is a good deal more than that. Actually it is the white-collar capital of the world which is more often than not better symbolized by a white and feminine throat. It is not only insurance which gives employment to armies of women in towers in Hartford as well as soft-handed gentlemen and swift-fingered girls across a continent.

Hartford is the capital of those insurance agents everywhere who once were spoken of with no more kindness than still goes to Congressmen. In Hartford, also, more typewriters are made than anywhere else on earth. It is the machine upon which women everywhere rode to freedom or labor—I am not sure which. He was a neat Yankee god or one liking to make his caprice called progress very clear who put the clerical industry of insurance and the clerical engine of the typewriter side by side in the same Connecticut town.

The result is not a feminine town. There were, the last census said, more women than men in Connecticut. But the old Yankee surplus of Yankee spinsters disappeared before women went to work in such large numbers in the office buildings and the factories. In four New England states there were more women than men, there were also more women than men in six Southern states, and nowhere else in America. This may mean that the men are still leaving the older regions. I don't know. I do know that in Hartford the women work, and that in working in one way or another their activities touch lives all across the land. I went up Asylum Street toward Main early in the morning to see the girls gathering.

All of them were hurried, and some of them were pretty. There were two men walking in no hurry at all up and down before a shop with signs which charged that the proprietor was unfair to organized window cleaners. The women were washing windows no more. But they were pouring into the doors of the Travelers Insurance Company at 700 Main Street, the Aetna Fire at 670 Main. They would be filling doors, too, I knew, on Pearl and Elm and Cogswell and Trumbull streets. Out on Farmington Avenue they would be crowding the parking lots around the biggest colonial building in the world. Not all the women who came in from the spreading suburbs filed the papers on the risks and answered the letters of the agents. In a city in which one out of every seven humans is a woman working for her living, they also made typewriters at which other women would work, inspected arms with which men would kill, worked for Connecticut in the Capitol, and in season labored for the big corporate tobacco growers. Up Main Street, a woman ran the biggest store in Connecticut, G. Fox & Company, established 1847; Beatrice Auerbach ran it during a time of change which was putting women to work but also in which the coming together of the new Jews and Catholics made an emotional violence under the economic prosperity. And where there was pinch there was hate.

There is pinch. Occasionally it is dramatically displayed. I remember when I walked up the steps to the granite-columned porch of the beautiful building of *The Hartford Times* the view on my right held in the foreground the back porches of tenements not lovely to behold. On the porch of the templelike newspaper plant the architect had put, "News is an immortal bubble." And poverty, I thought, looking back at the tenements, is immortal even in the midst of prosperity. Where it exists, it ought not to be surprising if a priest in Michigan can stir anger in Connecticut. Just as in the South there is more than a casual connection between hunger and lynchings, so in New England anti-Semitism is economic, also.

In New England as in the South, the well-to-do of the old American stock are safe above the darker furies. They are even more remote, I think, in New England. The Yankees who rule the banks and the insurance companies and the mills are in large measure a race above and apart. The angry gentiles are themselves, at least in the cities, people of the immigrant stocks. The ancient Jews are a new people, too. In Hartford in recent years they multiplied around the few old Jewish families until the city had proportionately a larger

214

number of Jews than any American community except New York or Atlantic City. In the same years the old group of full native American parentage decreased to scarcely more than a quarter of the people.

Still at the top the tradition of the Yankee goes on. It is a tradition full of charm, if also one based upon hardheadedness. For instance there is Morgan Brainard, president of the Aetna Life, whose place in the bright office beneath the tower which James Gamble Rogers designed for him depends upon his own lively intelligence, but who stands, nevertheless, in the blood line of the founder of the big company. Quiet, hospitable Charles C. Hemenway, editor of *The Times,* took me to see him. A tall man, gray and merry, Brainard rose to greet us. He took us out on the green roof garden beyond the wrought-iron porch at his office door. We could look back at the center of the city and down at the tennis courts of clay and of grass. I think there was also a bowling green. He told us a story about old Yankee Hartford. Appleton Hillyer rushed home to lunch and hurried through it in order to be sure to catch the horsecar on the line which his father owned.

"Son," said the father, "it costs five cents to ride the horsecar. Don't you realize that five cents is the interest on a dollar for a year?"

That was only Act One of the joke.

"The really funny thing," said Mr. Brainard, "is that not long ago I told that story to one of my old friends. He didn't laugh. He said, 'Yes, I can remember when savings banks paid 5 per cent.'"

We saw the table where the Aetna directors sit, which Aetna publicity says belonged to Thomas Jefferson. Mr. Brainard expressed a doubt that Jefferson ever saw it. He showed us an interesting old chime clock, an old-time lithograph of a very uplifting nonalcoholic barroom. He laughed,

"All the really nice things here belong to me, not the company." Down in the city I knew the business man with a sense of both history and humor had given the Avery Memorial museum the collection of old Connecticut inn signs which hang on its walls.

The hospitable Mr. Hemenway took me back to town to meet some of Hartford's men at the Hartford Club. I was anxious to go there because, when I had been in the town before, a Southerner who had retained a very Southern sense of humor in the insurance business in Hartford had depicted it in pleasant mockery. He had asked me to lunch there, and I could not go.

"You should see it," he said; "it represents the stiffness of Hartford. I told a friend the other day, 'The most amazing thing happened to me today.'

" 'What was that?'

" 'I was in the club, and a gentleman spoke to me.' "

He laughed.

"It's true," he said. "It's true. And they don't want women in it. Women can't go into but one room. It doesn't change even if Hartford does."

I found the club and the company friendly and pleasant enough. Graham Anthony from North Carolina was there in his proper person as a Hartford manufacturer. Berkeley Cox, who taught me in prep school, was there as a counsel of the Aetna Life. The others might have been more awesome: two bank presidents, an insurance company president, the president of the big Niles Bement & Pond Company, a typewriter manufacturer, a big printer, Maurice S. Sherman, editor of the venerable *Hartford Courant,* a couple of other manufacturers, and the manager of the employment bureau of the Manufacturers Association of Hartford County. Altogether they made a powerful party. There were plenty of feet at which an inquisitive itinerant might sit and secure information. There were too many of them, and if they were not of clay, they were still feet to stand upon a common American earth. Above them the stories went around, masculine and hearty. If there is a rivet in the neck of the masters of Hartford, it has a hinge in it for laughter.

"I was thinking afterwards," my host, Hemenway, said, "that while this group was not the only one which could be assembled of which the same thing could be said, nevertheless it did typify what might be called the old school of Hartford philosophy about as well as any that could be gathered. Yet at least eight of the fourteen present came here from outside the state as mature men, most of them within twenty years or less. So the community impinges on the consciousness of those who come here from elsewhere to have part in managing affairs."

But, if old Hartford puts its pattern on the men at the top, men and women at the bottom are subject to influence from outside. The newspapers found that out when they casually criticized Father Coughlin. It was like setting off a storm. Whatever may have been the intentions of the pastor of the Shrine of the Little Flower, he stirred a storm which came in general from the Catholics in the direction of the Jews. The Catholics? Well, that is hardly fair. There are in Hartford, as elsewhere, a great many Catholics who are as tolerant as any Protestants—many, indeed, who know that Catholics themselves have suffered from the sharp end of intolerance. (The old fatuous Know-Nothing party flourished in New England; in Boston a convent was burned.) The truth is that North and South—and everywhere else—intolerance is most often the unintelligent or misled expression of the exasperation of the poor. It happens that, in New England in general, the poor are Catholic. Coughlin stirs them only as Tom Watson, a Catholic baiter, stirred the violent intolerance of the poor Georgia Protestant whites. The poor who hate seem to me as sad as the pitiful who are hated. It is the seashore and schoolhouse anti-Semites who make me sick.

In Hartford the thing swelled up out of a secrecy in which it had spread from little mind to little mind. It rose in an avalanche of letters, anonymous and otherwise. The phones rang and rang and rang in the newspaper offices. An angry Irishman, someone told me, called up Maurice Sherman, editor of *The Courant,* and told him he could not pretend to be anything but "a damned Jew" with that name. (Sherman is a Congregationalist, a Son of the American Revolution, and was born in Yankee Hanover, New Hampshire.) More menacing, as its growth had been more secret, a movement of petitions began to come in from rural Windham County, from schoolteachers and farmers, protesting against the firing of gentile girls and replacing them with Jews in such big stores as Fox's. The petitioners had been lied to. No such thing had happened. Beatrice Auerbach, who is generally regarded not only as the Number One merchant of Connecticut but also as one of its best citizens, had the pay-roll sheets to show it. Sometimes the truth runs a poor race with a lie. Even when fury quiets, nobody knows how widespread intolerance remains. It begins in the dark. It works there. Its explosion waits for a spark.

The white-collar capital and the white-collar suburbs around it might be tinder for it. That white-collar mind extends to skilled workers in factories from their sisters in the offices. They certainly do not make any familiar proletariat. The unions had not made much headway in Hartford among the office workers. The tool makers and airplane makers were still unorganized. The real estate men and the chamber of commerce urged home ownership: 22 per cent of the people owned their own homes in Hartford. They needed very little urging to buy automobiles. It is the business of *The Hartford Courant* to know what the little folk of Connecticut want.

It understood that they were afraid of death, even of being buried in one of those unobtrusive bits of meadow which Hendrik Willem van Loon reports, as new resident and new patriot, to be the most pleasant cemeteries in the world. I suspect *The Courant*, which has been reporting the news in Connecticut since October in 1764, understands it better than the dearly loving Dutchman. At any rate it announced, during the summer I was in and out of Hartford, that "although it may be depriving its readers of a bit of information which they have been accustomed to find in the press, THE COURANT is now omitting to mention in its obituary columns the nature of the disease or ailment to which death was attributable . . . If we can make through the policy here announced a small contribution to the peace of mind of those who foster gloomy predictions we shall be well satisfied . . ." All day in offices the women work on the risks and rates of death from all its causes. Men make planes and pistols that conceivably may kill. Afterwards they run home to the suburbs. They have reason to know even better than the rest of us do that, no matter how long or how often the big insurance companies call it life insurance, this big item of Hartford's business remains death insurance just the same, and nothing else.

The state around their fears does look as sweetly tolerant as the appreciative Mr. van Loon, whose first faith is tolerance, sees it from his house under the elms in the Connecticut to which he, like a great many other authors and artists, has come from New York. (And besides, as Lily Pons and Peggy Wood said, the taxes are gentler on the artists.) Mr. van Loon said: "It may be the landscape that has made the people of this state a little more tolerant." In Hartford all the public patterns are tolerant. The schools are open for all—that is, the public schools (but many of the Catholic children do not attend them). Even the Negroes can get such an education in Hartford as not even a white child (who gets the lion's share of the school advantages) could get in the South. But beyond the schools: Relatively few Jews are employed by most of the big insurance companies in Hartford. There is "no prohibition as to race or creed"; neither are there many Jews. Negroes are rarely employed in any business operated by white people except as porters or messengers. (I remembered that I had been told in Providence that Negro graduates of the Rhode Island School of Design could only be placed as teachers in Negro schools to teach more Negroes who have no chance of employment except as teachers of other Negroes to . . . If there ever was an example of what the colloquial call the "run around," here, it seemed to me, was it.)

Hartford is a pleasant city as well as a prosperous one. In the afternoon the big office buildings pour out their contented office workers. In the factories the typewriter makers stop preparing for more white-collar and white-throat workers in Hartford and far away. The insurance premium income pours into the town by the millions. The airplanes and the typewriters go out. The late-afternoon sun hits the gold leaf on the dome of the ugly Capitol. Hartford rests in content and confidence that it knows the risk on almost every aspect of American life and will not lose on any of them.

"Your South," an executive told me in the Bond Bar, "used to be the most incendiary region and the poorest risk in fire insurance; it's better now."

"That's good," I said. Through a wide door I watched young Hartford dancing in the next room. The boys and girls seemed both decorous and gay. But, looking at them, I wished someone in a city of actuaries could work out the risks to decency in their democracy from the bitterness and the fear that were out there somewhere still working in the dark.

XXI

Noah's Book

Yan′kee (yăng′kê), *n*. [Often derived, through an early *Yengee(s)*, fr. Am. Ind. corrupt. of *English*, or F. *Anglais*, but prob. fr. a D. dim. of *Jan* John, as applied by the Dutch of N. Y. to the English of Conn.] A nickname for a native of New England, or, by extension, of the northern part of the United States; also, as sometimes used by foreigners, any inhabitant of the United States. —*adj*. Of, pert. to, or characteristic of, the Yankees; loosely, *Brit.*, American.

thrift (thrĭft), *n*. [ON. *thrift, thrif*.] 1. *Obs*. A thriving condition; prosperity. 2. Economical management; frugality. 3. *Now Scot.* Work. 4. Vigorous growth, as of a plant. 5. Any of a genus (*Statice*, family Plumbaginaceae) of tufted acaulescent herbs; esp. one, a scapose herb *(S. armeria)* with pink or white flower heads.

skill (skĭl), *n*. [ON. *skil* a distinction, discernment.] 1. *Obs*. **a** Understanding; judgment. **b** Reason or ground for doing, saying, etc. 2. The ability to use one's knowledge effectively; technical proficiency. 3. A particular art or science; now, a developed or acquired ability.

in′dus-try (ĭn′dŭs-trĭ), *n.; pl.* -TRIES (-trĭz). F. *industrie*, fr. L. *industria*.] 1. *Obs*. Skill; ingenuity. 2. Habitual diligence in any employment or pursuit; steady attention to business; assiduity. 3. Any department or branch of art, occupation, or business; esp., one which employs much labor and capital and is a distinct branch of trade; as, the sugar *industry*. 4. *Econ*. Systematic labor or habitual employment.

I read them in the leather-bound copy of Noah Webster's book, which President Robert C. Munroe of the G. & C.

Merriam Co., had given me, over my dinner in the Town Hall Grill. Ingham Baker in almost herculean hospitality had offered to entertain me that evening though I knew his family was leaving in the morning for Honolulu or some such place. I declined and ate alone. I closed Webster's book and watched a pretty young waitress badger an elderly bartender who was mixing cocktails for her customers.

"Oh, you can be had," she said. "I'm not trying to make you today. But you're just a push-over."

She was pretty, and the old man grinned as he set the cocktails on her tray. I thought that language, even in Springfield, had been moving since Webster died and went to the lexicographers' heaven long ago. But his book lived and grew. I think I like the men who keep it in wise commerce as an educational institution not much, if any, inferior to Harvard, better than I should have liked the old man who wrote it or at least left his name to be put on the front of it. The last Southern traveler who described him—Anne Royall, who wrote in 1826 before his big *American Dictionary of the English Language* appeared—did not like him at all:

"I knocked at the door with more than common enthusiasm," wrote Mrs. Royall, who was noted for her sharp tongue, "for though we back-woods folks are not learned ourselves, we have a warm liking for learning. In a few minutes a low, chubby man, with a haughty air, stepped into the room; his face was round and red, and by no means literary looking. He was dressed in black broadcloth, in dandy style; in short, he comes nearer the description of a London cockney than any character I can think of; he eyed me with ineffable scorn, and scarcely deigned to speak at all. I am sorry for his sake I ever saw the man, as it gave me infinite pain to rescind an opinion I had long entertained of him."

If the lady scorned didn't like him, some millions of others since have nevertheless revered his name—which must be the most valuable name in the whole history of the written and printed word in America. I don't think the Merriams ever saw him; I am sure the Bakers never did. But when the young Merriams, booksellers of Springfield, bought for $3,000 in 1843 the publishers' remainders of his big book and the right to reprint his books, including the famous *Speller,* they bought a bargain and began a business which, beyond every difficulty and the millions it has made, still remains rich and enriching in Massachusetts. Of course, the process was not so simple as that sounds nor quite so cheap. They later paid the Webster family a quarter of a million for copyright renewal.

Before the company grew to its present safety in its big book's present preeminence, it had to fight the War of the Dictionaries, Webster *vs.* Worcester. Old Noah said before he died at the beginning of the fifty years' fight that Joseph Emerson Worcester was a plagiarist, but there were plenty of the fastidious who preferred Worcester's book. Today the Merriam Company may report that in those days the Merriams, grateful for the competition which made them produce a better and better book, used to get down on their knees and "Thank God for Worcester!" Maybe so. I suspect that the victor counting his spoils can get more satisfaction out of saying his prayers.

I came to the old Myrick Building on Broadway, where Noah's erudite and profitable tradition persists, over the short pleasant road from Hartford. The road led past the Fuller Brush factory—and I remembered that it had not been many years since Fuller Brushes were as well-known for the foot-in-the-door persistence of their salesmen as for the excellence of their products. A Connecticut countryman who had sold all but one of the Boston terrier pups he advertised had pinned a piece of brown paper over the *s* on "pups."

There was tobacco growing under its tented shade and beautiful lettuce and tomatoes in the fields. The drought did not seem quite as dire as it had been described. Beside the road an R.F.D. carrier was conversing with the proprietor of a farm which advertised duck eggs. A girl in shorts was helping her mother and father pick vegetables in Suffield. Florists and tobacco buyers were in business close to the highway. A hitch-hiker wanting a ride undertook to make himself momentarily and almost indecently attractive like a grimacing prostitute. Men like ants were laboring on levees to keep back the floods which too often come up out of the long and beautiful Connecticut.

The Myrick Building on Broadway was a worn, even weary-looking, old building in which to expect alert specialists to be catching the precise meanings of the last words for people everywhere. An old-fashioned elevator in it took me up to the floor where, beyond cases full of Websteriana—from copies of Noah's *Speller* which sold 70,000,000 copies to the last and richest full leather, seal grain, India paper copy of the *New International Dictionary*—a switchboard girl let me into the office of Robert C. Munroe.

At fifty-nine President Munroe had been with the Merriam Company for more than forty years. He had come from birth in Holyoke and high school in Springfield to a clerkship among the dictionaries when he was eighteen years old. He had never been far from the trade in definitions since. At twenty-four he was the company's advertising manager. Before he was forty he was a director and the clerk of the company—which is the New England equivalent of the secretary of the corporation. He had become president in 1934. Man with a long nose and sharp eyes, he looked, I thought, as a city Yankee ought to look back of the British-tailored influence of Boston in the cities in the country and not on the sea.

He talked with dry humor and practical philosophy. He

contemplated the New England past and future with calmness but not without pride and not without hope. He was a rooted man, and chain stores did not please him. He was, I felt, typical of his place and position without being tagged with it. He lived in suburban Longmeadow, which is a rich man's town (82 per cent of the inhabitants own their homes, 202 people out of a thousand file income-tax returns, the highest in both cases in New England). He was not only the expected Congregationalist, Republican, Rotarian, he had also been president of the Longmeadow Historical Society which has filled the old Storrs Parsonage with a fine collection of colonial furniture. In the Merriam Company, he stood on his own hard heels as president, not being connected with either the tribe of the three Merriam brothers, or the newer tribe of the three Baker generations.

Mr. Munroe, who had been expecting me, took me into an old-fashioned paneled board room. There under a portrait of the over-all-presiding Noah (another, better picture had been sent to a world's fair), he introduced me to Ingham C. Baker and Lewis L. McShane. By Merriam hundred-year standards Mr. McShane, a well upholstered pleasant gentleman, is a newcomer from Kansas—out of education, I think—into the book-building tradition which has extended from Webster to Dr. William Allan Neilson, president of Smith College and editor-in-chief of the newest big dictionary. Baker is, like Mr. Munroe, on the book selling side. He is the grandson of that Orlando M. Baker who came from the West to enter the company in the 1870's (president, 1904–19), and the son of Asa George Baker (president, 1922–34), who is now chairman of the board. He has a cousin, Harris W. Baker, also grandson of Orlando, who is now clerk of the corporation. There is not a Merriam in the company now; there never was a Webster. But some of the Merriam descendants still own stock.

We talked about the business, its history, its size. The main thing I felt about its strength was the belief in the book. They turn out books by the thousands and deal in words by the hundred thousand. But there is a sense of responsibility about each word and a determination to assume that responsibility cost what it may in technical specialists, in scholars, in the search for citations. Printing and so publishing may be the true grandparent of mass production. But the quality of the product, about which more and more New Englanders are talking in a competitively difficult mass production age, is nowhere in New England given greater emphasis nor more profound faith than I found in the old Myrick Building in Springfield.

Today Webster is a name and not very much more. From it Merriam provided the productive continuity in understanding that no product is ever perfect. When they called in Chauncey Goodrich to supervise the first Merriam-Webster Dictionary—which appeared in 1847, four years after Webster died—he was not merely Webster's son-in-law. Even so early in New England, businesses were probably suffering from the presence in them of men who were just sons-in-law. Goodrich was a scholar in his own head. Dr. Noah Porter, who made the book better after him, was scholar, too, sufficiently able to be called to the Presidency of Yale. The procession of scholars, who have steadily built new and better dictionaries under Webster's name, down to Dr. William Allan Neilson and all the specialists in diverse fields who helped make the latest dictionary, were called by men of commerce who realized from the beginning that the best business was the best book. Such men may be more important than the scholars in New England. At a time when the pressures in many industries are for cheaper, cheaper goods, rather than better, better ones, success in the commerce of the dictionary may be at least a symbol.

Of course, it is simpler as well as wiser for a company with a product that is an accepted standard to keep its quality high and higher than it is for a maker of textiles or shoes or anything else in a fierce industrial competition related chiefly to price. It is all right to talk about quality, but if the chain stores demand price in purchases the quality has got to come down or the plant will have to shut down. Ralph Waldo Emerson, whom the Merriam Company likes to quote about the world beating a road to the house of a man who made better chairs or knives, crucibles or church organs, had never seen a chain store. Sadder or better, in recent years the world has been going to cluttered counters which sell cheaper chairs or knives, crucibles or church organs. Drugstores have been selling a good part of them between the prescription counter and the soda fountain. But quality remains in New England factories as well as in the dictionary offices where scholarship is steadily spurred to make a better product for a world-wide sale.

Not only does quality remain: Around it also in New England there persists the character which is the basis of quality. Upon it, free from the fear of quick cheaters in a fly-by-night world, the Merriam Company rests some of the important economic continuities in its business which are almost as old as the book it makes. For instance, since 1861 or 1863, The Riverside Press in Cambridge has printed the great bulk of the Merriam-Webster books. As old as Merriam and still as successful, The Riverside Press, close to Harvard in Cambridge, printed long ago the blossoms of New England's literary flowering. It still prints—even more books—now that the flowering is past.

"There never has been any formal contract about the printing," Mr. Munroe said, "never anything but gentlemen's agreements. We never ask for bids though, of course"

—and the Yankee smiled—"we do watch printing costs, we confer about prices and so forth."

Since 1870 Merriam has bought its paper from S. D. Warren Company of Boston, which makes it in Cumberland Mills, Maine (where it has been making paper since 1852). Between these companies and Merriam there are no financial connections. There are not even, Mr. Munroe said, any close personal friendships between the officers of the companies involved. There is a good deal of respect based on long and satisfactory dealings.

Later Benjamin S. Van Wyck, director of Warren and salesman who handles the Merriam account, told me: "It is possible that you may have gained the impression that because we, the supplier, happen to be of New England, we received the Merriam business. That is not the case. Several experiences with the Merriam Company have called for considerable technical supervision, the settlement of some complex and technical requirements, and the study of printing and bookmaking processes in cooperation with the The Riverside Press, Merriam's chief printer.

"Interestingly enough, we can point to at least ten or twelve relationships with publishers—some of fairly recent origin and some as old as the Merriam relationship—that have been handled in what many people outside of New England term 'the peculiar method of doing business that obtains only in New England.' This 'method of doing business,' in my estimation, came about not by New Englanders being smarter than those of other sections, but rather that New Englanders painstakingly try to know every phase of their respective callings. The industrialists try to keep up with or surpass the respective technologies of competitive industries in or out of New England. I truly believe it is one of the important reasons why many New England industries have survived."

And the reverse, I thought, may be the reason why some have not.

The past in such a company as that the Merriams began went back straight and stalwart and successful. But there was not a Noah Webster's Dictionary to be picked up by energetic young Yankees every day in the past or the present.

"No," Mr. Munroe said. "But there are other things. I think there are young fellows starting things all over New England now just as there always have been. Al Fuller started the Fuller Brush Company in the cellar of his sister's house over in Somerville. There was the man who started Absorbine, Jr. It was a horse liniment; he diluted it for human use and made a great business out of it."

(Somebody in Boston told me that the neighbors so teased the young fellow who started the Absorbine business that he himself sent out the first cases with the letters P.D.F. stamped on them: "Papa's Damn Fool." I hope not, but the story is probably entirely apocryphal. It indicates, however, both the irreverence of neighbors and the disregard of it which in New England sometimes exist side by side.)

There were other such cases, Mr. Munroe said. He thought there always would be. He spoke of a Buxton keytainer company which had grown recently from small beginnings in Springfield.

"And in New Bedford . . . there are some interesting facts about a certain Portuguese or Italian fisherman who has, within a very short time, on his own initiative, developed a large commission fresh-fish business with New Bedford as the base of operations."

There are thousands more. I knew that up the Connecticut River in Brattleboro, Vermont, young John Hooper and his wife had not long before begun in the Stephen Daye Press a publishing enterprise shaped in the flavor of the region which was already successful by national standards. Down in Stonington, Connecticut, Henry R. Palmer, Jr., who got bored in the brokerage business after Brown '36 ("I'm no mental ball of fire"), had begun a boat business in an abandoned shipyard which in a little while had multiplied itself by ten. There was young James H. Prentice, of Massachusetts, who could find nothing but an office boy's job after college but later found that people were willing to buy in increasing numbers the electric games he began to manufacture (like Fuller of the brushes, first in a cellar), from 600 games in 1935 to 35,000 by 1939.

Up in Maine, Eric Kelley had bought a bog at Jonesport for six cents an acre and was selling it successfully as peat moss by the bale. I talked to young H. O. Robinson of Medford who began selling oranges in an abandoned blacksmith shop in Cambridge and had reached the point where he was worrying about the bookkeeping on his employees' unemployment compensation and social security. ("You almost wish you had stayed small.") Even on the land Douglas Forrest of Bantam, Connecticut, had discovered that there was opportunity in the quality about which New Englanders talk so much and so wisely but perhaps to too little effect. Forrest had a herd of fifty pure-bred, registered Ayrshires, but in all New England, he said, "only slightly more than one per cent of our cattle are pure-bred registered." The field of quality was not crowded. ("We figure to make a profit of about 30 per cent on the investment.")

Whatever may be happening in cellars in Somerville and on the fish piers in New Bedford, everywhere new words are being added to the language. Waitresses in cafés, scientists in laboratories, the advertisers and copyrighters of new products, inventors, discoverers, musicians, politicians, physicians, and thieves are adding constantly to the oral language; and it is a rare word in the oral language which does not soon reach the printed page and beyond it quickly in accumulation in the new-word file which Merriam keeps for Webster. When old Noah Webster published his big dictionary in 1828 he put 12,000 words into it that had never been listed and defined before. All his words totaled 70,000. In the *Webster's New International Dictionary, Second Edition,* which cost $1,300,000 to prepare, there are, Merriam says, 600,000 entries and 122,000 more words than in any other dictionary. And the words are still growing everywhere. They have been growing for a long time.

I went down in the old elevator to the street and from an Italian boy bought one of the four newspapers which are printed in Springfield (two Democratic; two Republican), by the descendants of old, forthright Samuel Bowles who founded *The Springfield Republican* in 1824. (Despite its name *The Republican* is a Democratic paper and a good one.) There had been improvement in Springfield. Mr. A. R. Tullock, of the Employers' Association of Western Massachusetts, said that day that reports from the large industries in the greater Springfield area showed a pleasing improvement in man-hours. Noah Webster did not know what a man-hour was, but in his name it is defined in his new book: "A unit of work performed by one man in one hour." There were still more men and hours in Springfield than were being put together in a process which meant old-fashioned work-wages.

Springfield that afternoon was hoping that the army would establish its new New England air base up the Connecticut at Chicopee Falls. The Westinghouse Industrial Union of the C.I.O. was hoping that it could get John L. Lewis to come and speak at the convention of the United Electrical, Radio & Machine Workers of America. A mail clerk testified in probate court that day that he didn't like the way his wife had been dancing with an aviator. Mayor Roger Putnam was worrying about the tax rate at a time when his doctor had ordered him to stop smoking his pipe. Members of the trolleymen's union were hoping to get a penny-an-hour increase in their wages.

I rode out State Street to Federal to see the site upon which the Merriam Company was preparing to build a home more in keeping with the dignity of Webster and the success of Merriam than the dusty old offices down in the town. The city was giving them permission to consolidate lot numbers to make its address 47 Federal Street in commemoration of 1847 when the first Merriam-Webster dictionary, edited by Webster's son-in-law, Chauncey Goodrich, appeared in Springfield to spread over the world. On the way I passed the wide properties of the United States Armory. Rifles were an older story in Springfield than words. George Washington had helped select the site when it was established by Congress in 1794. Charles Sumner, the abolitionist, had visited it in 1843, the year the Merriams bought the Webster books, and had made a speech to the guide about how much better it would be if the government spent the money on books instead of rifles. But in the war Sumner helped to make, the armory turned out a thousand rifles a day. It was operating at accelerated rate turning out arms in 1939.

"It's nice, steady work," a street-corner citizen told me, "and it's a big help to the town."

At dinner I looked over my Merriam material. I had a lot of it. In the word business the company not only gets out its big dictionaries and smaller ones, it has also produced (as a little part of spending the most money ever spent to advertise one book) some tiny ones quoting the great in praise of words. In small type William Cowper sang of:

Philologists who chase
A panting syllable through time and space,
Start it at home, and hunt it in the dark
To Gaul, to Greece, and into Noah's Ark.

Most of the rest of us go instead to one or the other of the editions of Noah's book. I wonder sometimes what good it does us. The difference between the right word and the almost right word may be, as Mark Twain said, the difference between lightning and the lightning bug. But that summer the more, the constantly more words in the bigger and bigger Webster book seemed almost like the bales in the cotton surplus, the money which the bankers said was just resting in the banks, the more idle men in the bigger American population. Noah Webster's first big dictionary had 70,000 words in it and sold for $20. In the *New International* you could get 600,000 entries for as little as $20. Words were cheaper, maybe better. But nobody was putting them together that summer to make much more sense.

That may be sad for America but beside the point for Merriam. The important thing seemed to me that Merriam was doing its job and doing it well. It could not be held responsible for the failure of men in the use of the more ideas expressed by the more words which it patiently, persistently, in the pursuit of perfection, collected. Indeed, I thought that as capitalism goes in New England and America, the wisdom in the combination of commerce and skill in the old-fashioned offices provided a basis for a definition of quality which may be more important than any definition in its book. Of course, there is no real conflict between cheapness and quality. A cheap dress may be the best dress for millions of women who can afford no other. There is need in this world for both silk and sacking. The real meaning of quality is honesty.

233

Even in a hurried and hungry world I think the demand for it exists. More than that: Sometimes it seems a field in which the competition is no more crowding than young Douglas Forrest, of Bantam, found it in pure-bred cows. Or the Merriams in big thick books.

XXII

By Brattleboro

You cross more than the Massachusetts line on the road north into Vermont. There are two New Englands, and from Newburyport to Williamstown the northern boundary of the Bay State cuts them apart in a division almost as distinct as that of town and country. (More distinct than town and country in New England where the country may be in the middle of the town.) Below the line is the crowded industrial south, above it the comparatively empty rural north. Mason and Dixon did not draw the Massachusetts line, but the region falls apart along it in a difference at least as clear as the nation separates along the line they did draw.

In Vermont the native American stock is the purest in New England. In Vermont, New Hampshire, and Maine more people own their homes but fewer people pay income taxes than in the three states below them. Old patterns persist, and there are more old people in them than in any other states in America. In the forests and on the steep hills there is less money, but no less desire for it. The Yankees there will not like it, but there is a conservatism in their old-fashioned Republicanism which only differs in voting from a similar states' rights Democratic conservatism in the South.

Indeed, in this ultimate North which sent its sons by the thousands to fight against the right of states to withdraw from the Union there is a fiercer faith in states' rights, I think, than in the states that fought for them. Massachusetts, Connecticut, and Rhode Island do not like it, but there is an industrial pull on their industries by these rural, lower wage, less unionized states which differs from that so much discussed pull from the South only in that, being nearer at hand, they have probably done more damage.

I went a roundabout way north from Calvin Coolidge's Massachusetts town to the state where he was born and where they buried him. And where somehow he has failed to become the folk hero he might have been expected to become. "You don't find as many people inquiring about it as you used to," the little rotund gray man in a straw hat, who may have been a Northampton professor or a Northampton groceryman, told me when I asked the way to the simple double house in which the most recent Yankee President had lived. Indeed, the only mark of memory that I thought I found in the town itself was the Calvin Theatre and the adjoining Calvin Candy Shoppe. There is also a Calvin Beauty Parlor. Even these, a lady who should know told me, perpetuate not the memory of the President but of a French-Canadian tribe whose name is the Gallic Calvin, the final syllable of which is pronounced with a different nasal sound from that which Coolidge customarily used. But I crossed the impressive Coolidge Memorial Bridge on the way to Amherst by the big greenhouses and the onion fields, patches of tented tobacco and white cows.

In Amherst where once upon a time, at least, the Smith College girls made a nice distinction between the boys at Amherst College and those at the agricultural Massachusetts State, I remembered the lines:

> It is not very pleasant
> To go with a peasant;
> An Amherst man I'll marry
> And go in so-sigh-o-tee . . .

236

The song went on beyond my memory. Near the Amherst campus I stopped to give a ride to three young Massachusetts Yankees, Alex Karpinski, Edmund Adamski, and Michael Palembas. Poland was already lost to them. They were American boys going home from school.

"What are you boys going to do this afternoon?"

"Weed onions," Michael Palembas said.

I asked about machines on the farms.

"Somebody better hurry and invent a machine," Alex Karpinski declared, "or I won't have any hands."

We passed the onion storage barns. They used little outside labor on the farms, the boys said. At harvest time, they pulled the onions up, left them on the ground for a couple of days, stored them through the winter and sold them for fifty cents (tragedy), or two to three dollars (joy), a hundred pounds. All of them were tired of weeding onions. None of them wanted to be a farmer. Maybe one of them will be another President educated in Amherst. Or a senator or a poet or a preacher.

They got out in Sunderland and waved me goodbye. My road ran west by Conway and Adams. The country spaciousness began in Massachusetts. There were lovely unproductive hills beside the road and magnificent fields of white and yellow and orange and lavender wild flowers beside it. Outside the Connecticut valley the towns were farther apart. They clustered again in the northwestern corner of the state. In Adams the sign on the Catholic Church said: "Bingo Friday 8:30." Beyond the town was a row of old brick tenements, ugly and squat, but interesting items in industrial archaeology. Down the road a church had been turned into a tavern. There was a pond of a blue as hard and bright as postcard seas and lakes; it was colored, the man at the grocery said, by the waste from the lime plants. Fish would not live in it. On the road into Williamstown big boys, naked to the waist and beautifully muscled, were digging a great ditch for a sewer. It seemed strange that in the cooler North workmen in the summer strip to the waist while in the South big black boys keep their clothes on under the hottest sun. I am not sure whether the difference lies in blisters or Puritanism.

I crossed the line that splits New England. Beyond it up the tourist-serving road I came to a picture which is one of the reasons why I like Vermont: Mrs. Thatcher (I'm not sure that it is spelled with a "t"), sitting slim and gray-haired in a wash dress just out of the sunlight in the one open door of the old Congregational Church in Old Bennington. She was knitting from a maroon-colored ball of wool.

I had come on a genealogical mission. I told her about it. She went with me into the old churchyard armed with an index of the graves prepared by the sometimes useful as well as patriotic and decorative ladies of the D.A.R. The sun poured down, hot on the graves, and even in the churchyard a stranger could feel that that other stranger, Rudyard Kipling, was right when he said that there is creole blood in the veins of the Vermont summer. We found the tomb of my wife's ancestor, Major Samuel Billing, who departed this life on the 23rd of June, 1789, in the fifty-first year of his age. Beside him, his wife Beulah—or the stone cutter—had added an s to the name to make it Billings. When the dead played little tricks like that, I said, they put some sport into genealogy. The Thatchers had some similar trouble with the t, she told me. She told me, also, that modern Bennington had grown from the manufacture of long woolen underwear. It was not so much in demand as it once had been.

"In the South we think all you Vermonters wear them."

She smiled. Even in Boston, where her daughter was taking nurse's training, they shiver at the idea of 20 degrees below zero, she said. It did not seem a strange shivering to me. But it did seem far and cold to think on that warm day that sometimes the thermometer in Vermont goes down to 41 below. I thanked her and rode after her directions in the sun to "what we call the big mill." It was shut and very silent in the green-shaded yard behind the high mesh fences. Even the stag on its weathervane was still against the windless sky.

Brattleboro, across the whole state, was only forty miles away. I got there in the late afternoon when the lights were just coming on in the electric sign in the marquee stuck onto the Brattleboro Town Hall in which long ago the quarrel between Kipling and his brother-in-law, Beatty Balestier, over a little bit of boundary line had come to trial. That must have been a better, if also a sadder, show than the "Woman Doctor" which was advertised in lights when I came to town. I got a big room with a bathroom almost as big in the old Brooks Hotel. The only man I knew in Brattleboro, Howard Rice, editor and publisher of *The Reformer,* was at a dinner downstairs. He and other gentlemen of the town were engaged in the consumption of a salmon which Harold W. Mason, Brattleboro's wealthiest citizen and the Republican National Committeeman from Vermont, had sent down from his fishing in Newfoundland. I met them all later, and later still had a bedtime Scotch and soda with some of them on the pleasant piazza of a house high on a hill above the town.

I like Vermont. I did not feel like an outlander in it. Indeed, I suspect that any Southerner who goes there in anything but Confederate uniform must find it a land like the greener parts of the South. The small-town men in it who make organs and pull teeth and publish newspapers may seem quaintly early American and pleasantly rural to people from Manhattan who only touch the earth in the summertime, but they seemed like men out of my own world to me. I am by chance and choice a small-town man myself. I am a Rotarian, a Democrat, and a Methodist in North Carolina. It is a condition not vastly different from that of a Rotarian, a Republican, and a Congregationalist in Vermont. Indeed, I suspect that in most things the difference between Vermont and North Carolina and the people in them (excepting for purposes of comparison the new foreign stocks and our venerable black one) is a good deal less than the difference between either of them and the summer visitors from the city who now have a house on every other hill.

In steep old Brattleboro, Howard Rice is as native as they make them in Vermont. Hard-working, hardheaded, conservative, he has been successful enough as publisher and editor to have the house that sits highest up on the hill in town, to be able to take time off for hospitality as well as public service. He was sixty, which is practically infancy among the Green Mountain gaffers. His hand is close to Republican politics in Vermont, he knows a good business deal, and he appreciates a good Irish terrier. Better still for me as I followed him, he has not only a wide streak of sentimental love for the green hills of his old state but a warm, witty knowledge about its places and people from Ralph Flanders, boy from little Barnet whose big tool plants in Springfield, Vermont, look more like Connecticut, to blue-cheeked old farmers scratching the hills.

As we rode in Windham County once, he grinned at wise little Mrs. Rice over a joke they shared.

"Over there," he told me, "Mrs. Rice's great-grandfather and my great-grandfather are buried in the same grave. How's that for Yankee thrift?"

"Don't let him pull my leg, Mrs. Rice."

She laughed. "It's true. The 'two' great-grandfathers were the same man."

He took me first to the offices of *The Reformer* which sit close to the bank of the Connecticut River. I was admiring the view outside the editorial windows on the Connecticut River which in more ways than one is New England's Mississippi.

"You have a grand view of the river," I said.

"And the gas house," said *The Reformer's* managing editor.

The big familiar tank does sit there on the shore. But it did not deface the picture for me. One thing I like about Vermont views is that they grow so. The fields were fixed for pasture not for prettiness. I suspect that managing editor. He wrote a book about the covered bridges of Vermont and declared in it that they are not structures of beauty. That's a very real aesthetic question. Maybe not in him, but in some of his fellow citizens there is a thick skin of brusqueness over appreciation of beauty. The Vermonter knows that gush may be greeted by grunts from neighbors who are no less appreciative than he is but distrustful of display. Reticence, also, may come in reaction from hearing lady tourists exclaim or city-writer residents report on their adopted land. The new patriot everywhere is more articulate than the old one. Just as I know that there are no Southerners quite so Southern as Northerners who have bought plantations, I gather that the Yankee may be more articulately Yankee in direct proportion to the distance he comes from outside. I think covered bridges are beautiful, and I am not otherwise persuaded by the fact that their builders allowed them "to be plastered with circus bills and posters for spavin cure, soap and an endless variety of nostrums." I like even circus posters, and the view from *The Reformer* offices across the river is grand.

Young John Hooper took me away from it, not against my will, to the offices of the Stephen Daye Press, where in the name of the oldest printer in America some young New Englanders in Brattleboro have done as much, I think, to serve the best New England regionalism as any other people in those states. Hooper is not from Vermont, he came from Maine; but he and his wife, Marion Rice Hooper, Howard Rice's daughter, had in little more than half a dozen years made the Stephen Daye Press which publishes only books about New England a nationally known institution. They did not do it alone, of course; there were other young zealots about books in this state which with Maine and New Hampshire has more old people in it than any state in America. Ruth Hard, daughter of Walter Hard who deserted his drugstore in Manchester, Vermont, for bookselling and poetry, is office manager—which, as she says, includes everything from public relations to emptying the waste-paper baskets. Samuel Lincoln, who once trucked milk, and Richard Sherwin sell the books. Mr. Lincoln is the old man of the organization; that summer he was thirty-four.

Hooper took me to the Press' pleasant office and introduced me round. Marion Hooper, the editor and book designer, who had just written the text for the best-selling and beautifully prepared *Life Along the Connecticut River,* was down in Boston waiting for the arrival of John Rice Hooper, who will probably cut his teeth on bookbindings and designing boards. But the then potential father in Brattleboro told me about the Press.

Although he had some early urge to medicine, Hooper got book publishing into his head, I think, before he graduated from Wesleyan in 1928. Right after that, at any rate, he was selling books, and a lot of what he was selling seemed to him what the Yankees along with the rest of us call "tripe." If bad books would sell, he had the idea that good books might. This certainly does not mean that his books are the earnest and exalting books which maybe people ought to read but will not. They have been as lively as skiing, which was the subject of one of his continuing best sellers. But they have been books published around an idea: the increasing consciousness of New England among New Englanders. John and Marion Hooper went to work to make the Press in Brattleboro in 1932. No capital was put in to start with; its only assets were their brains and credit extended by Ephraim Crane of the Vermont Printing Company. It was important that they were young, but it is also significant, I think, that the older business man who took the chance in Vermont was named Ephraim.

"We started out," Hooper said, "to specialize in the New England field. We feel that if there is anything we know, or at least have a right to feel that we know, it is the New England subjects. So we built a fence around our Press. All the booksellers and jobbers told me that we were crazy to build a fence around ourselves, that we ought to get into the general publishing business and take a gamble on the best sellers and so forth."

He shook his head.

"My feeling was that it was much more important to take something which the larger houses were overlooking, and to concentrate on that field to the extent that we at least were specialists in one phase of something which probably is the craziest business in existence. Well, instead of throttling ourselves by putting a fence around our enterprise and publishing nothing but New England books, which we have been doing ten a year for the last six and a half or seven years, we did pretty well. Seven years ago, when we started, you couldn't find on any publisher's list a book on contemporary New England. Today you can find a book about contemporary New England—or several of them—on practically every publisher's list."

He smiled.

"As a matter of fact, while we have produced sixty-five books, the other houses have produced, along with us, about sixty-five books. New England is a tremendously varied and interesting subject, not only to New Englanders, but to people all over the country."

"I hope so," I said, being in the business myself.

I took the Vermonter across the street for Coca-Cola before we went back to meet his father-in-law at *The Reformer*. Mr. Rice had his Lincoln Zephyr parked in the alley, and with Mrs. Rice we went out to see the highroads and the back roads of Windham County. We went first, I remember, to Kipling's house, Naulahka, where the Englishman was so productive and at the last so unhappy. Cabot Holbrook, whose aunt bought the place from Kipling, showed us through it, showed us where Mrs. Kipling sat as watchdog against intruders before the room in which Kipling wrote, and the room itself with the legend across the mantel, "The Night Cometh When No Man Can Work." (Maybe that line, which has been used in the advertising copy of the National Life Insurance Company of Vermont, has been more useful to Vermont than any line Kipling himself wrote.)

It was hard for me to realize that the man who had worked under the goad of that legend, already rich and famous, was only twenty-seven years old when he came to Brattleboro, only thirty-one when he went away without a very good opinion of Vermonters. If he thought the "New England peasants" watched secretively, Vermonters still make no secret of their memory of the spectacle which the rich, famous Britisher and his horses and coachmen and footmen made. Howard Rice remembered, as a boy who was going into the newspaper business, his special excitement over the metropolitan newspaper reporters who came to cover the Kipling-Balestier case trial in the Town Hall.

If Kipling shook the dust, the slush, and the snow of Vermont forever from his feet, he certainly did not frighten other writers off. Indeed, the writers and the retired are as much an industry in Vermont as in Florida. There is room for them. In the afternoon we drove up the bank of the West River to Newfane, where there is not only a beautiful four-columned courthouse but one building which houses both an inn and the jail. On the green square also are a white town hall and Congregational church. The town seemed empty un-der its elms. Indeed, the census only counted 159 people in it. Perhaps because there are so few people, some sections of Windham County provide the best deer hunting in the state. The deer thrive on the abandoned orchards which men left behind when they went West or to more hopeful towns long ago.

Both the deer and the people are coming back. It is not surprising that they went. The "famine year" of 1816 ("eight-een hundred and froze to death") accelerated the movement West. There was a foot of snow that year in June, more snow in July and August and a killing frost in September. There was little harvest, and the stock died. There was no WPA, but there was the West. People moved then and after-wards. They left the orchards and the cellar holes and some of their sisters and brothers behind. But there were scarcely any deer left in the 1870's. Closed seasons and short seasons have brought them back. Men have come back to grow short stories and novels and elevating essays for city readers about life on the land in the old houses on the old hills. Sometimes they see deer in the yard.

The road to old Dover went up steep past a cemetery. There must be more dead men under stones in the town than walking on their feet. But the lovely place men once walked remains. Someone told me that in the 1840's and '50's the town had 700 people, but that today there are only about 150 and some of the human stock that remains is by no means the best in Vermont. High up the road was the place where the story began about Lemuel Osgood falling off his farm. It is by no means a ridiculous story about an impossible feat. College professors and retired professional men like such precipitate slopes. They have become almost the only industry left for the remaining people. Sometimes these summer folk are so easy they take the joy out of bargaining: There was for instance the wife of the Yale professor who was remodeling her old place in sophisticated semblance of a utilitarian barn. She went about offering farmers brand-new boards for the old weathered boards in their barns. They took the lady's lumber; that was gain but there wasn't any sport in the trade.

It was interesting to come down from such almost empty hills and read in *The Reformer* about Governor Aiken—whose home and wild-flower farm was not far off at Putney—talking down in New Jersey of a back-to-the-farm movement which ought to include five million families. (Some Vermonters who had supported him for Governor thought he was talking too much outside the state and thinking too much about what people and politicians outside of the state thought of him. But after all Calvin Coolidge, born in Plymouth, Vermont, had been nominated for the Vice Presidency. Any Governor can hope.) In New Jersey he said, "If we could get these folks out of the congested centers of population, we could put them back in the hills where growing children would get the bottoms of their feet tickled by real green grass . . ." There were endless possibilities in the idea, and he enumerated some. But the people did not leave Dover because they were merely restless. Not everybody fell off his farm as Lemuel Osgood is reported to have done. But a good many of them are steep and stony.

We drove back to Brattleboro. In Prospect Hill there, one of the most famous of those boys who went off and made good—or bad—is buried. Jim Fisk, who got control of the Erie, fought Jay Gould for a corner on the gold market, and was killed over one of his girls, is not exactly typical of Vermont; but he had some Yankee horse sense in his head nevertheless. Long before he was buried at Prospect Hill, the Brattleboro boy was asked to contribute toward the cost of a fence around the cemetery. He declined: "Nobody in it can get out, and nobody outside wants to get in."

So Mr. Fisk failed to make an investment which might have served him later. They brought him home to bury him, and over his grave an elaborate memorial rose with four nude female figures on it.

"I can imagine that conservative Vermonters were more or less shocked by it," Howard Rice said.

It was not the shocked but the souvenir hunters who got to Jim Fisk's monument. It is not only toeless now, it is also nippleless. The hills are green everywhere around the broken stone. The winters are not warmer, but there is sport in the snow. The Yankee in the land of milk and maple syrup still labors on his steep hills, but like all men everywhere who work hard and long for not very much he has a warm heart and a lighting humor. Both may be kept almost like a secret. But it does not take even a stranger long to know that they are there. If I had a house in Vermont I should not be afraid, even as Southerner, of inhospitality; but I should watch and carefully for the laughter which is always sharpest where there is burn in the sun or sting in the snow and life is not easy under either.

XXIII

Wild-Flower Man

"BOYS," SAID OLD MAN DWIGHT DWINELL, sergeant-at-arms of
the Capitol of Vermont, "if you'll make the body I'll carve
the head."

He did. When I came to Montpelier a new statue of Ceres
stood safe on the golden dome high over the destinies of the
agriculture of Vermont. Whittling is not only an art attached to the art of argument in the Green Mountain State.
It is also part of the general craft which is thriftiness among
the rocks and the snow, part of the necessity that any man
turn his hand to anything from repairing a plow to providing
a new lady of heroic proportions for the pinnacle of the
Statehouse.

Mr. Dwinell was nearing ninety. He was the oldest man, I
think, in the Capitol which seemed to be full of gray and
aging men. The statue of Ceres, which John Henkel of
Brattleboro carved from the design of Larkin Mead in 1857,
had been in Vermont almost as long as he had been. Possibly he felt an affinity in age for the "old lady" of Montpelier. At any rate when the engineers reported that the
long exposed and much patched statue ought to be removed
for safety's sake, Mr. Dwinell, with the approval of the wild-
flower grower who is Governor and with the help of younger ·
Deane Bancroft and Gordon Yeaton, undertook to replace
her. There she stands now high above the classic granite Cap-

itol beyond the green lawn between the old Pavilion Hotel
and the National Life Insurance Company of Vermont. Even
if she does look, as young sprightly Jean Douglas, secretary
to the Governor, said, like that new Vermont citizeness
Dorothy Thompson with a *Herald Tribune* under her arm,
she stands serene. As *The Brattleboro Reformer* declared,
"Vermont agriculture still needs a goddess."

Dorothy Canfield Fisher, who is under no illusions about
the prettiness of poverty in Vermont, points a virtue in the
willingness of Vermonters to live within their incomes small
as they may be, to get along very happily with a homemade
statue or homemade clothes; but it is a virtue from which
most Vermonters like most Mississippians (who may not be
so thrifty) would gladly escape. Indeed, the summer I was
there a member of what is probably the first family of the
state stressed that poverty as emphasis for necessity to escape from it. Three of the marble-quarrying tribe of Proctors have been Governors of Vermont; they say Mortimer
Proctor would like to be. He knows that he or any other
Governor must confront the uncomfortable trinity of low
per capita income, decreasing population, and debt-loaded
towns. The per capita income for Vermont in 1938, he said,
was $378 as compared with a range from $420 to $642 in the
other New England states.

"You have to go as far south as Virginia and as far west
as Nebraska before you will find a state with per capita income as low as Vermont's."

I had come north from Brattleboro by his town of Proctor, by some of the little hill towns which the Vermont Agricultural Experiment Station in Burlington had studied because of the special difficulties of their problems. Calvin
Coolidge's Plymouth was one of them. Maybe Coolidge was
one of those better educated boys who are leaving the hills
at a faster rate than the less well educated ones. Most of the

farms on the hills about his grave were found to be abandoned when the study was made. In the whole state of Vermont between 1900 and 1930 the number of farms decreased
almost 25 per cent. During the same period, the acreage of
land in farms decreased about 18 per cent. Within the past
thirty years, there had been a decrease of over 8,000 farms
and of 828,000 acres in farms in the little state. (There are
29,000 farmers in Vermont.)

Along the highway there were magnificent barns with high
white silos and beautiful cattle (there are more cows than
people in Vermont), knee-deep in the green grass. Nothing
looks more like agricultural prosperity than a big and beautiful Morgan horse. But back of the big highways on the little
roads, as the old people died, the young were letting the
trees have the farms if the professors and the writers would
not buy them. Even on the main traveled roads the "For
Sale" signs on farms and houses make an impression even
more depressing than the whole book of homes and farms
for sale which the state gets out as a service for its selling
citizens once a year.

There is money in marble, or there has been. Certainly
there is no sign of poverty in the town of Proctor from which
Mortimer Proctor came as politician to talk about poverty in
Vermont. But there is an ironic sadness about it nevertheless: It grew in deliberate determination to avoid the pains
of absentee ownership. All the Proctors moved there soon
after old Senator Redfield Proctor left the law for the quarries
and began to build the biggest marble business in the world.
The Proctors live there still. In warm-hearted honesty, I
think, if also in paternalism, they tried to make it a model
town. Not even marble walls could keep the serpent or enlightenment, whichever it was, out of Eden. There was a
strike in 1904. There was a longer and sadder one not many
years ago. But around school and library and hospital and

marble exhibit, the town of the Proctors and the Italians, the Swedes and the Poles seemed that summer serene and green as the cemetery in which is not only the marble temple of the Proctor tomb but also a simpler stone over a stonecutter, "nato in Carrara." He had died a long way from the quarries out of which Leonardo and the Medici took their stone. I wondered how he had liked the winters in Vermont.

(I remember another like it in the granite town of Barre. The stone figure of the little Italian there sat above his grave: He had curly hair, handlebar mustaches, a bow tie, and his hand lay against his cheek. "He was a carver himself," the fat Yankee cemetery attendant said, "and a good one. I knew him. It looks just like him. He was shot in a fight between the anarchists and the socialists down on Granite Street." And that was a good while ago, too.)

The road ran north to the city of Burlington, which served for both the study and the simile of Elin Anderson, who (*We Americans,* Harvard University Press, 1937) looked at the melting pot in Vermont and found it was instead a stair step which ran up from the slums on the shore of Lake Champlain to decorous residences of the old Yankees on the hill by the university. Not only are the Yankees separate from the slums; also, in a precisely arranged democracy the Jews and the French, the Irish and the Italians have their separate site and status. In sympathy sometimes the Yankees are not much further from the Italians than the Irish are from the French. I asked my waitress, a big rawboned Irish girl about it.

"I live with a French girl," she said. "She talks with an accent, but she can't stand the French. It riles me to hear people talking French just as it did my father."

Her father would have been a wild Irishman in Winooski, which is not Polish for anything but Indian for Onion. Its French-Canadian population is proud of the fact that it is the most Democratic city north of the Mason and Dixon

Line. I felt a duty as a Democrat from below that line to examine it before I drove on up the same Onion River (the name of which Vermonters changed in self-consciousness back to its Indian equivalent), on which school children for generations learned was the Yankee Republican capital of Montpelier. The French-Canadian town clerk showed me the figures. They would have been satisfactory in Georgia even if they do not make a very big dent in the surrounding Republicanism of Vermont. Also he told me that in the mill town of Winooski a man can park his car as long as he likes. I did not park long. I looked at the mill, I looked at the church, I drank a Coca-Cola which was no better because the town was Democratic. Then I went out past a filling station where a sign said they spoke French and by fields warmed with wild flowers to see the wild-flower grower who ruled the state.

I went into the Capitol past Larkin Mead's marble figure of Ethan Allen which has lasted better than his Ceres, into the lobby where other heroes are remembered. They are not only such big heroes as the national Lincoln and the local Dewey, but also, there are in big frames galleries of little photographs of the officers of the regiments which went off when Vermont sent for its size more soldiers than any other state to save the Union. Some of their pictures are missing and little American flags substitute for Vermont faces. Some of their faces are strange, even a little pathetic: The pictures of a good many lieutenants, who must have been youths when they went off to war, are of old men grown beardy and broken, old men and fat. It is not only war which does things to the slim, stirring soldier. Vermont in its Capitol has made a monument to the villainy of time.

Governor George David Aiken is the wild-flower man who not only became the Governor of Vermont (two terms), but also and with almost equal impartiality denounced as Gov-

ernor "the erratic wanderings of the New Deal" and "the
self-satisfied smugness of Old Guard Republicanism." In a
precarious prominence between the two, he had erected in
speeches around the land the image of the independent,
thrifty, natively wise, hard-working American who looked
very much like George David Aiken of Putney, Vermont.
Some New Englanders thought he had the lightning rod up
for nothing less than the Vice Presidency. Some Vermonters
thought national attention had gone to his head. He has his
share of vanity, I suspect, as also his share of shyness. But he
seemed to me at heart even in his office in the Capitol one
of those strange mixtures of the poetic and the practical
which are by no means rare on the hilly farms of Vermont.
He himself told a story once which illustrates that combination. It was about the farmer who had been across the road
to do his milking (such a location of the barn cuts down the
snow shoveling when the road is cleared), and he came out
with the pails in his hands and faced the first night of spring.
Above him the stars shone like little lights coming through
the sieve of heaven. There was the faintest rustling in the
leaves. Off somewhere the first brush fire scented the air. He
carried his pails into the house and set them down.

"Wife," he said, "it's too beautiful a night to stay in the
house: I think I'll go out and kill a hog."

There's a poet under the politician in the Governor of
Vermont. He wrote some of it in the preface to his *Pioneering with Wildflowers*. There are flashes of it in his speeches
(and I don't believe any ghost writer put them there). Like
some other possible poets born on small Vermont farms, he
has had little time for poetry. The big world opened suddenly for him in Montpelier. He not only began to speak in
a wide land; he has begun to fly in an uncrowded sky. He
goes over to Burlington for lessons. But his feet remain on
the earth in poetry and politics. Here are his Republicans:

"Men whose families slept in beds of straw, which were renewed each year at threshing time; men who rose before daylight to cradle buckwheat while the dew was on so that it would not shell and waste the precious grain; men who wielded the axe or followed the plow until darkness fell and who after supper, by the dim light of a candle lantern, did the chores and made preparations for the morrow, until weariness overcame them." They do not sound like members of the National Committee. They do sound like the men in the darkness around that oil lamp in Plymouth by which Coolidge took the oath as President of the United States. Aiken was out there. In the simpleness of strong country muscles and shrewd country minds there remains appeal.

"I don't know as much about labor as I would like to," the Vermont Governor said once. "I never worked in a factory. I never owned a share of stock or had anything to say about the management of a corporation. The first money I ever earned was weeding gardens at five cents an hour. The most I ever earned was last year, thanks to my salary of five thousand dollars as Governor of Vermont."

Vermont does not deal opulently with its Governor. It provides him no mansion. When Aiken stays in Montpelier, he lives in a furnished room. His family remains in Putney where the Aiken nursery, the wild flowers, and the fruit and the berries are. Mrs. Aiken has no servant, only a neighbor to come in and help her with the work. (The absence of servants in the spare living of Vermont is interesting in comparison with the prevalence of servants in the even poorer South. The colored folks are thick as chocolate around every Governor in the South—and around a lot of other, poorer white people, too. Whatever the characteristics of the white man and the colored man may separately be in the South, combined they do not equal thrift. Where there are servants

in Vermont, except in the rare instances of the rich who
sometimes put on city manners with country money, the relationship of master and servant is gently tempered by a democracy which contains a real sense of equality. They often sit
at the same table and talk across no chasm of class. But democracy does not keep either the dishes from getting washed
or the wages from being paid.)

In 1912, when he was twenty years old, the Governor began with a small fruit farm. Now he has five hundred acres
under cultivation and sells, he reports, in all parts of the
world. That still does not mean as rich a business as it sounds.
He started the cultivation of wild flowers in 1926. Four years
later he started in politics as a member of the legislature. He
became speaker and wrote *Pioneering with Wildflowers* in
1933. In 1936, the year he was elected Governor, he added
Pioneering with Fruits and Berries. Even when he is in Montpelier the flowers and fruits in Putney are not much more
than two hours away.

He is a square-looking man with a thick thatch of gray
hair. He talked slowly, and there was about him a deceptive
appearance of sleepiness. That summer he was forty-seven,
but he looked older. He had been having trouble with his
gall bladder. But he grinned with a warm, even boyish
humor at an unsteady elephant of knitted gray wool on his
wide desk. It did not look very strong.

"No," he said. "The legs are the National Committee.
But the back is strong—it's the rank and file of the party."

There was also a tiny white elephant, maybe of ivory,
which he said had been given him by WPA workers. I wondered if its size indicated the support among them of the
independence-preaching, work-praising Vermonter. I remembered that the whole front of the floor where I slept in the
old Pavilion Hotel (which had been holding legislators longer

than this Capitol had) had been occupied by WPA writers. There were WPA projects in progress in the surrounding hills.

"I spoke in Pittsburgh on Lincoln's birthday with the senior Senator from South Carolina," Governor Aiken said. "What's his name?"

"Cotton Ed Smith."

"Yes. I didn't bring Lincoln in. He had troubles of his own without being pulled into ours. But I thought that indicated that the War was over."

I had been hearing, I told him, that because of his fight with the Federal government over letting it take Vermont lands in connection with its flood control—and power—policies he had become a sort of Calhoun of New England fighting for States' rights again.

He did not seem to like the historical simile.

"I'm just trying to maintain the balance between the State and Federal governments. The South seems to agree with me."

He had stated his position: "The rank and file of the Republican party is not opposed to Federal leadership. The country needs it. We want it. We cannot tolerate Republican lip-service to the slogan of States' rights simply to cover up abuses that backward states or backward Big Business refuses to exterminate. The states have rights—vital rights. As Governor of Vermont I have fought to preserve them for the people. To preserve these rights I have at times had to fight the public utilities. At the present time I am having to fight the Federal government. Far apart as these two forces are, I find the palms of both have the itch for acquisition."

I think there is more than talk to that statement. One New Dealer who thought Aiken was serving the power companies told me: "Aiken's attitude seems to be, 'Let the floods come and be damned—but not on Vermont soil.' Massachusetts and

Connecticut bear the brunt of the floods anyway." But I also found in Vermont, power company supporters losing enthusiasm for their man Aiken, if he ever was their man.

Furthermore, he was not by any means opposed to the whole program of the New Deal, he said. But some of it, he thought, looked silly in Vermont: "Wallace sent a man up here from Nebraska to tell Vermont farmers to plow around hills, not up and down them. We'd been doing that for a hundred years." Solemn Vermonters have turned their unsolemn humor upon other aspects of Federal activities. They reported the fury of Dorothy Thompson—who, being able to live anywhere, had chosen Vermont—when she learned that by Rural Resettlement standards her place was uninhabitable. They reported that the Rural Resettlement insisted that the farmers must be moved from the hills while the United States Engineers, working on flood control, insisted that they must be taken out of the valleys. There are few other places in Vermont. The stories may be entirely fabulous, but they are true to the spirit of the unexpected rifling ridicule of Vermont.

The agricultural satire, however, is the satire of an agricultural state. Neither Vermont nor its Governor shares the brittle city hostility to any Federal or other efforts to help the farmers. There are too many of them there, and they need help too much. Governor Aiken told me about things being done in the state. He quoted, with a facility which seemed to me to indicate their frequent use on the stump and at the banquet, figures on the large percentage of business done in the state by co-operatives, in the handling of milk, in insurance, in all sales and purchases.

I asked him about the "For Sale" signs on the roads and the book about farms and homes for sale, published by the state, which included places for thousands of dollars and others for a few hundred. I had noticed one hundred-acre

257

farm with house and barn, good hunting and fishing, put up for sale for $400, and that was the asking price. It was located in Eden, Vermont. A hundred acres of Eden for $400 seemed cheap enough.

"We want permanent residents, not tourists so much," the Governor said.

He walked with me to the door. In the afternoon he asked me to go with him to the ceremonies in connection with the formal dedication of a community refrigerator in which each farm family around it was to have a locker. Such things help on the difficult land. But the Governor was not under any illusions about any real back-to-the-farm movement in America in which not only could the growing children get the bottoms of their feet tickled by the grass, but children and parents, too, could learn the lessons of nature first hand and not from books—on the earth of Vermont "where independence is no myth."

On the land, he said later, a dispersed people "would require lumber, stoves, wire, refrigerators, trucks, paint, rubber boots, sheepskin coats, and a thousand other items that the city fellow doesn't have to buy and doesn't know how to use. This all sounds like an easy solution. But the catch comes not in the surety that these people would not have to buy all these things, but in the fact that they would not, under present conditions, have money to buy them with. We need to decentralize the population, if we are going to maintain individual independence in America. But to do this we would have to decentralize industry also."

And that, I thought, is exactly what Massachusetts and Rhode Island and Connecticut are fearing.

The people may not be coming back to the land, but more children are born on it. The birth rate in rural Vermont is 17 per 1,000 people; in Connecticut and Massachusetts it is 13 and less. For a long time the children moved to the jobs, now also the jobs are moving to the children, to the rural areas where many young people are, and where rural standards of wages and of "independence" prevail. Governor Aiken is not the only man in Vermont who has had "little experience with labor organization." Not only Governor Aiken is waiting for the decentralization of industry to Vermont. There is a boy or girl waiting, and on every hill. They wait in a patience and order which make terrifying by contrast the so-called docility in the homicidal South.

In "unspoiled Vermont" the peaceful poverty is one of the prime characteristics of the pastoral state. Crime is rare. We talked about the comparison with the rural South as I rode with Vermonters around Montpelier, up to the Wrightsville Dam which the CCC boys built to protect the capital in its tight valley from the floods, and to Hubbard Park which sits back of the town and above the gold dome of the Capitol. There were two French-Canadian women, one man said, who came down many years ago from whom are descended a large part of the criminal and insane of the state. We talked about sterilizing the unfit, I remember, as we stood under the unfinished rock tower in the park high over Montpelier. Another man shrugged and pointed with his toe: There was an item of childless city civilization discarded in the grass. The country is taking more things than factories from the towns.

XXIV

To John Greenleaf's House

"You mustn't drive up there, Mr. Bickford," Mrs. Dickinson said. On the way home from learning as a woman how to save pennies by making her own clothes she spoke a language precise as the schoolhouse. "The road's so bad you can't make it. The road commissioner hasn't made the effort to do anything about it yet. I suppose we ought to have had some cider to offer him, but we didn't. I've got to stop at the store anyhow."

So we let her out at Vershire, a grim, limited little village with hardly more than a post office and the store. It was difficult to believe that, fifty years before, copper mines near by had kept 2,000 miners busy. But the mining had ended abruptly: Three hundred workers in the declining mines had gone to war to collect $25,000 in back pay. There would be money or dynamite, they said. But the National Guard had come and fought the bloodless Ely War (they were the Ely Copper Mines). The miners lost the "strike." There was only $4,000 in the company to pay them $25,000 with, and the mines never operated again. The farmers who dig the hills around have also gotten less and less out of the earth. Orange County is, indeed, one of those Vermont regions which have been set aside as a "depressed agricultural area," and, as such, I had come to see it.

Paul Bickford and I had ridden down the highway close

to the Connecticut River from Bradford where he has his office in the Inn to Fairlee. He drove and talked, as he drove, pointing sometimes with his thumbless left hand, about the crops of the Orange County farmers with whom he was working as a Rural Rehabilitation supervisor of the Federal Farm Security Administration. He did not look like a farm supervisor. Instead, in his brown herringbone suit with brown tie and blue shirt, he looked like a city man. His hair was as smooth as a banker's. But he knew the land and the people. Before he had come across the line in Vermont to work with the little farmers who were trying to make a go of it with the government's money and aid, he had been for eight years one of the three selectmen in the town of Tamworth in New Hampshire; and he knew not only the ways of the big out-of-state taxpayers in the resort area but the little native farmers as well. Yankee Democrat by inheritance and conviction, he had been elected and re-elected steadily in the Republican town. He had taken his agricultural training at New Hampshire State College. At thirty-three he knew what would grow out of the New England earth and the farmers who undertook to make it grow.

We talked about potatoes and blue Hubbard squash and the Bradford strawberries, long grown in the region, which customarily bring twenty cents on a fifteen-cent strawberry market; then, as we turned away from the river to the hills and the trees, about maple sugar: a tree twelve inches in diameter can have only one spile (or spout), which once was whittled out of wood, now is all metal. We passed a sap house, a small building with a ventilator at the top. A year or so before, a lot of the sugar had been thrown out because there were traces of lead in the sugar; so the farmers were covering the solder on their buckets with aluminum paint. The big factor in maple sugar is the Cary Maple Sugar Company of St. Johnsbury (Maple Grove candies, sugar for cigarettes, syrup). The Cary who used to run it, he said, lost out a few years ago and then died; New York bankers run it now. Other dealers wait for and follow the Cary price.

That spring following the hurricane, the crop had been less than the crop of the year before; but the price had been lower, too. Dealers give farmers fifty-gallon steel drums into which to put their sugar, which practically obligates the farmer to sell to the dealer who owns his drums. But a maple sugar co-operative (which handles more things than sugar) is selling much of it now. For Vermont it is an important cash crop, but even in a good year it amounts only to about 3 per cent of the total value of the state's agricultural products. The Vermonter cannot live on sugar alone.

We found Pearly Norris, a thin, gray-pompadoured man, in the field cultivating his potatoes, on his little place in West Fairlee, but he seemed glad enough to stop for rest by the rusty barbed-wire fence along the road. He wore the standard uniform: blue denim trousers and a lighter blue shirt. He carried a tin of tobacco in his shirt pocket and another tin of big red-headed matches. He had been South, he told me; he had served in Norfolk during the war, and he had been thinking more than one time about a story some people there told him about the Confederates sinking a big boat full of stone to stop a channel in that even more distant war. He was not sure about the story, but he liked Norfolk and the people who told him that story. Now he was content with his potatoes but troubled about his squash. They had been planted two weeks and had not come up. Also he was glad to see Bickford because he had received some postcards from the poultry people about the pullets for Mrs. Norris' laying flock.

"I thought the price was a little dear," he said.

"What does Mrs. Norris think?"

"She hasn't seen them—she's up to Brook's."

"I'll look into it," Bickford promised.

We went on up the road toward the farm of John Brook, where Marjorie Taylor, one of Uncle Sam's home management supervisors and a pretty one, had all the wives of the Rural Rehabilitation borrowers gathered in a dressmaking session. New England women, I learned later, keep their craft about canning and the like; but the chain stores have been luring them away from dressmaking. As if to prove this growth of town desire we overtook John Brook's teen-age daughter and stopped on the dusty road to give her a ride. She was wearing silver slippers without any self-consciousness in the dust.

And there was drama as well as dressmaking at Brook's. Marjorie Taylor ran out to tell it to Paul Bickford where none of the gathered farm wives could hear, though every one of them knew it. It was a matter for gentle handling. One of the government's borrowers had gotten drunk and been arrested for that or for disturbing the peace. Whichever it was, justice in the matter had cost him $17. It was a tragedy and a fortune. Bickford would have to see him. He agreed.

"You don't look like God," I said, "but I begin to suspect that you are."

He laughed. Mrs. Taylor went back into the house to the women. John Brook, followed by his progeny, came across the road from the barn toward his undecorative but substantial house. He had been getting ready for the whitewashers, he said. He wore denims like Norris and, in addition, a cloth cap.

"How are your squash?" Bickford asked. "Pearly Norris is worried about his."

"They're up fine, but there's a bug eating the back of the leaves. I'm going to dust them."

We went across the road to see. There was a scarecrow with a good deal of red in his costume down the field. Bickford knelt and examined the leaves. He thought the dusting would be a good idea. The women had finished not only their dressmaking but their cleaning up as well, and we went back to give a ride home to Mrs. Dickinson who stopped in Vershire and Mrs. Gordon Wright and her youngest. The boys had stayed at home with their father. We rode in an empty country on dirt roads. Mrs. Wright entertained us as we moved with detailed recital of the disappearance of two guinea hens on Sunday while they were away from home.

"They're hard to catch, they are," she said by way of emphasizing the mystery of their disappearance.

A big house and a big barn stood close to the road. Both needed paint. Hard times had come knocking at the bighouse door, too, and not only in Kentucky. Farther down the lane we passed an abandoned country schoolhouse which was occupied as a home.

"Who's living there?" Bickford asked.

Mrs. Wright looked at the dilapidated building and the children around it.

"I'm sorry, I just don't know. They moved in a little time ago."

She went back to the mystery of the guinea hens.

"You know what I think," she both said and asked. "I think it was a horse jockey who tried to sell us a horse last week. He was eyeing them. We wouldn't have bought a horse from him if we had wanted one. Maybe it was him. That's what I told Gordon."

The hill of the Wright farm ran almost precipitately up from the road. The house and barn and pigpen and chicken houses were clustered close together. Wright greeted us with something like a whoop. He was a lively man with graying hair. There was the dust of fertilizer on his spectacles. He was tanned almost as dark as an Indian, and I noticed a dagger tattooed on his right forearm and some other design on the other. Not all of his life had been spent farming in Vermont. He had been born on a farm there, I think; but he had been in the Navy and then for a number of years had worked in the Fairbanks Scale factory in St. Johnsbury. He was one of those who had come with the depression and city unemployment back to the farm. He had bought this place, around 100 acres, for about $500. But he was in bad shape ekeing out an existence on whatver jobs he could get until the Farm Security Administration began to help him a year before I came. Then, as if nothing could stop his hard luck, the hurricane had blown down his barn. The Red Cross had given him $100 with which to rebuild.

But he seemed as independent as any man I ever saw on earth, gay on the land and joking. He grabbed Bickford's arm (the young supervisor was the well liked, familiarly treated god of agriculture) and took him up the hill to show him his heifers. We could hear their bells in the woods, and Wright shouted to his two boys—one a freckled blond, one a brunette wearing spectacles which made him seem solemn— to go run them in.

"They're up there where I cut the pulp," he hollered.

The two youngsters set out. They made a noise in the brush, and then the cowbells rang sharply as they moved. Behind them a young boy's voice sounded clear, "Get on, you dirty bitches."

On the hilltop Wright laughed. "Listen to him. That fellow," he said, indicating the man who would have been the hired man if he had gotten anything but his board, "he comes from Leominster, Mass. He said if they were his he'd hammer them. But I said, 'I won't beat them for what I do myself. Would you?'"

He laughed again. "You ought to have heard that youngest one in the hurricane. It blew out the downstairs windows, then the upstairs windows and half the roof, then the basement windows; and you could feel the house being lifted and dropped on the foundations. I went out in the yard to get a piece of sheet iron, and the wind carried me and the sheet iron two yards before I dropped. I found the iron a quarter-mile over there in the woods the other day. Well, anyhow the oldest boy began to whimper, and the youngest one got after him for crying. I'll never forget he stood there in the floor and said, 'What the hell, dad, let her blow!' I can't whip them for what I do myself."

The heifers came down with the boys behind them, and Paul Bickford went with Wright to give them professional examination. Then he went to look at the pigs. Wright's were fat. There were two runtier thinner ones which belonged to the "hired" man. Wright regarded them and winked at me.

"I think they are New Hampshire hogs," he said.

Bickford of New Hampshire considered. "Then they must have jumped over the line."

There were chickens and a calf and a little white steer for which they were hoping to find a mate. Mrs. Wright patted the ponderous forehead of one of the two tan steers which were lying resting in the yard. The best loved one worked the hardest, she said; but she thought that the other could pull the most if he would. The whole family gathered before the house with the steers and the heifers and the pigs and the chickens behind them to wave us goodbye. Financially they were close to poverty maybe—certainly poverty was not far behind them; but, by some standards I had seen, these children of Uncle Sam looked not only well off but gay. I said as much.

"They were pretty bad off last year," Bickford said. "I think they are going to do all right."

"They are certainly not taciturn."

Bickford grinned. "I've heard about how tight-mouthed

we Yankees are. These Vermonters are supposed to be especially so. But I notice that when we make a loan the news spreads quickly to neighbors who know every detail of the transaction. And it may not be long before the neighbors come in with an application, too."

The road ran up steeper into the hills. The dirt road over which we moved in greater care of the springs was impassable in winter, Bickford said. We reached a turn so sharp that he had to twist and back to get around it. A slim unshaven man in denims on the roof of a house beside the turn shouted to us.

"They told me when they came down by to tell anybody that they had gone over to West Fairlee."

Bickford shouted his thanks, but we proceeded nevertheless up and up over a road so bad that the tracks turned out of the road into the better grassy field beside it. We moved slowly in low gear up the side of the mountainous slope through timothy and clover and witch grass and patches of devil's-paintbrush to John Greenleaf's house, which sits on rotting beams on a magnificent eminence. The pasture went down steep to the wood, and the wood rose beyond in another long hill which ran to the sky. I never saw a fairer place for a house for a man who wanted peace. But in the front yard, not far to go on a winter's night, sat an old-fashioned backhouse. And James Whitcomb Riley, who lamented the old institution's passing, was himself twenty-three years dead.

Behind the little house in the yard the farmhouse itself was not very pleasant to behold. If a professor bought it (John Greenleaf had paid $300 for the farm), he would want to spend money quickly on the main beams which supported it. The place represented undoubted poverty, and a poverty unapproachable in winter. Except in summer Bickford has to walk to see most of his so-called clients. (That is the government word for them, and it may be a good one. Uncle Sam is the moneylender and the leader, but in many cases he and his representatives stand *in loco parentis*.) But there was a radio aerial above the old house. There was a strong sense of property and possession, for everything was locked up tight with new cheap padlocks. John Greenleaf had no cow but owned a horse. He had a pig and a dog. We peeped through the locked windows, and then I looked off at the wide green stretch of Vermont around us. I tried to think of it white with snow and the wind coming up across the hill. In that cold any deeper poverty would be death.

It was growing dark as we came down the steep dirt roads to the surfaced state highway. I thought as we rode that the main thing the government was lending these farmers was not money but trained direction. In the state in which Governor Aiken had said "independence is no myth," it was not quite clear to me whether the government was teaching and helping these people to a greater independence, or whether it was helping them to succeed on the land by substituting directed farming for independent farming. Certainly the independent farmers we had seen seemed to take Bickford as a welcome and special blessing. But if such a system was good for farmers so poor—who had failed because of the quality of their heads or their lands—that they had to have the financial assistance of the government, should not such trained direction somehow be made available in similar measure to those farmers who had not failed, but who might with similar detailed technical direction succeed in even greater measure? The limited number of county agents, of course, could not give all farmers the management services Bickford was giving this limited group of men and Mrs. Taylor was giving their wives. I said something of the sort to Bickford. He did not pretend to have the answers.

He stopped the car at a summer camp (it would be called a cottage in the South) on the shore of Lake Morey which he shared with Mr. and Mrs. Taylor and Miss Mary Lewis Hoey, who is secretary to the Farm Security office in Bradford. All around the lake, above which a nice moon hung that night, summer people have cottages. Vermont was very quiet there. A boat went up the lake and left behind it little waves which lapped against the shore. The moon would be lighting John Greenleaf's hill.

"How does it feel," I asked, "to be god, to be making people's lives ever nearer to perfection?"

"What we do is far enough from that, I'll tell you," Mrs. Taylor said. "I wish you could see sometimes—"

Then she laughed, and Bickford laughed, too.

They were doing a good job, I thought, as a part of a job that was being done and needed to be done everywhere in America. Nevertheless I doubted that it had anything to do with the little independent farmers with whom the whole program professed to work (except upon some frankly cooperative experiments in farming). There had seemed to be almost an eagerness for dependence on Paul Bickford among the few farmers I had seen that day in Vermont. Not a slavish dependence, perhaps shrewd. It was not that Paul Bickford was Uncle Sam or Uncle Sam was Paul Bickford; it was rather, I thought, a recognition among those who needed it of a training and leadership and confidence they themselves did not possess, and of the necessity of it to them. That is not slavery but an encouraging common sense among common men. I had seen that eagerness elsewhere. I wondered if the farmer's desire for rugged independence even in New England was not a myth. What he wanted in the hard hills of Vermont as well as in the deep topsoil of the Mississippi Delta was a living on the land. And despite the politicians and the poets, or both together, I doubt that he erects any impregnable philosophies between himself and the fulfillment of that desire.

Bickford drove me back to Bradford. The little town looked substantial and secure in the quiet darkness. It had been there a long time. It had had an appreciation of intelligence for a long time, if a library indicates appreciation of intelligence. The first incorporated library in the state had been established there as far back as 1796. It stood in the dark in an ugly brick and granite building; but there were books in it, and men could learn. Despite them, despite the fact that there is less illiteracy in Vermont than in any other New England state, less even than in any state in the East, men had not learned the way on the land to a satisfactory independence.

The boys and girls were going off to the crowded complex commingling towns, and where the independent yeoman pushed the plow the trees came or the professors—or Paul Bickford. Like the Orange County farmers impoverished in independence, I preferred him. We said good night, and he drove back to Lake Morey with his head full, I knew, of the price of Pearly Norris' pullets, the bugs on the back of John Brook's squash leaves, and the tragedy of the tippler who had to pay $17 to Vermont civilization for his crime. Independence for all is a magnificent ideal, but I think the more practical question in New England is whether there are, or could be, enough such young Yankees as Bickford to go around.

XXV

After the Arrowhead, Absentees

THE FOUR-FLUSHERS IS A POKER CLUB in Portland, so Edward
E. Chase reports, which abandoned competitive individualism in 1932, and turned social-minded. Maybe so. Certainly
they still take poker seriously in Maine. So seriously that Mr.
Chase, who is in the securities business and is chairman of
the board of the University of Maine, has found his reports
of the Four-Flushers' deliberations the best vehicle for a solemn satire on subjects of public interest, at home and abroad
in this land, from Passamaquoddy and the Republican party
to the Townsend Plan and a managed currency. As secretary
of the Four-Flushers, Mr. Chase has reported the suggestions
of the club that Passamaquoddy power be used to electrocute
the blueberry maggot, and that the Republican party stop
using stale bait.

I did not find it necessary to agree with the reports of the
secretary in order to be amused, and enlightened in amusement by them. But after I had met the secretary and read his
reports I wished that the Four-Flushers had made a philosophic examination of Maine's recent reception of those who
came in direct or indirect response to its state-supported wel-
coming, children and shoemakers, tourists and organizers for
the C.I.O. If the losers among the Four-Flushers had been
able, as the secretary says, to reform the game on the ground
that their losses were evidence of social mismanagement,

they might be able to work out a system under which, when a player or a state called for cards, only aces would be forthcoming. That would be a help to Maine and some other states as well.

I came into Portland from the children's camps in the woods and the shoemakers in the towns to meet Mr. Chase in the Eastland Hotel. He did not look like the Fool Killer. He did look immediately grim instead of witty, shy, silent, even a little hard-bitten under his close-cropped hair. The humor in him came out accompanied by an almost unwilling smile. When he talked about the people of Maine from the Blue Hill where he was born to the ends of the state, the sharpness of his understanding and his occasional impatience with some of his countrymen were warmed, I suspected, by a sentiment even more secret than his wit.

"Why, the best people in Maine live around there," he said when I asked him about the Carroll murders in South Paris which made a mystery above a mess.

The coast up toward Passamaquoddy seemed to him sad. For a long time the brightest boys had been leaving and the girls had for husbands only the boys who were left behind.

He talked about Maine's ancient separation of mind and spirit from the rest of New England. There had been involved the familiar differences of Episcopalians against the Puritans, Free Trade Jeffersonians against the Federalists, and the old competition of Portland and Boston. Beyond all that, Maine bulks above New England like Texas against the western side of the South. Both are regions alone (the size of Maine must be gauged by its neighbors; it sits off as no other American state does, touching the border of only one other state). Maine's sense of separation grew almost pompously in a political feeling that it was a sort of reservation of righteousness when, with the exception of little Vermont, it alone voted the national Republican ticket in 1936.

In March, 1939, *The Sun* of Lewiston, where the shoe strike had been smashed, declared in reference to Federal concern about it that "it ought to be as impossible to fine and imprison Maine employers under a Federal law as to send in a German army to take Maine over." (But many Down Easters do not feel that way about Federal funds, the Townsend Plan, and Passamaquoddy.) In the New York World's Fair, Maine stood apart from the joint exhibit of the other New England states and put on a show of its own—a very good one, too, with real live Maine fish swimming in such a replica of Maine water as fooled the fish if not the customers. Fortunately the sense of independence does not always go to the extreme of that Maine man who was questioned regarding his patriotism back in the days when the second Ku Klux Klan had spread far from the South to political power in Maine.

"Are you 100 per cent American?" he was asked.

"I'm 200 per cent American," he replied. "I hate everybody."

I can testify that that is not characteristic of most men of Maine. If I saw any such, they kept it from me. Indeed, they were such happy hypocrites as made me think they were among the most hospitable and friendly people of earth. And if Maine does stand apart, it welcomes the incomer (if he does not represent the C.I.O.). The outsiders have come in from all directions. They are not only the children who pour through Portland on the first of July to fill the camps, they have also been the French-Canadians who fill the mills. Even more significant, maybe, Maine has been served or has suffered, been developed or exploited (perhaps all of them), by a capital which in great degree has been absentee.

There is local money in Maine. There never was such an absence of cash as cramped the South. But the most important enterprises are and have been for a long time under the control of men and capital from outside the state. There seems almost to have been a limit to the size of businesses remaining under local ownership. Native families built banks, woolen mills, shoe factories, and, in the old days, ships; but railroads, public utilities, pulp and paper, and cotton textiles have tended to go into the hands of men far away.

"This foreign control has been resented," Edward Chase told me, "but it has been due more to the reluctance of Maine capital to assume the responsibility of ownership than to the zeal of outsiders to exploit."

Maine towns built the parts which were put together to make the Maine Central Railroad, but its control went soon to the Boston & Maine. And when after forty years control was regained by Maine people, the local rejoicing did not create a local resistance to the temptation to sell again when high prices were offered by outsiders. The Bangor & Aroostook Railroad—the potato line which is probably as consistent a money-maker as any road in America—always has depended largely upon outside capital. The story in utilities has been much the same. Even though the cracking of the Insull empire brought some local control over power back, important influences continue to be exerted over it by outside interests.

"Incidentally," Mr. Chase said, "Maine is one state where considerable benefit was derived from Insull's activities, through the investment of several millions in industrial promotions. Five cotton mills, two of which were practically in liquidation, were purchased by the Insull people, and substantial sums spent in reconstruction. While these ventures haven't been profitable, the industries have remained. It is due largely to this fact that Maine has lost few of its cotton spindles in the last twenty years. The same Insull money built a fine newsprint mill at Bucksport."

Maine capital had done its share, he thought, in the development of the paper industry, but the dominant influence in many of the leading enterprises, Great Northern Paper, S. D. Warren Company, St. Croix Paper, was that of men who do not live in the state.

One thing I think especially pleased him. Even on paper it ought to be punctuated by one of his slow, half-secret grins. "Maine people do not usually sell out for nothing," he said. "As a rule the men who have come to Maine to buy business enterprises have paid through the nose and lived to regret it. It might have been better for Maine to have resisted the appeal of a price, and to have placed a higher value on the control of her own economic destiny; but the advantage of the moment has usually been with the Maine trader."

I had come to meet him at the dinner table in the Eastland, by two industries in which outsiders are in considerable measure involved, shoes and children. In Maine sometimes they seem a long way apart. But geography has crowded the swarming summertime camps of the children of the country into clotted clusters around the lakes and ponds and little towns just west of Lewiston-Auburn, where in 1937 in a very real sense the state of Maine confronted the C.I.O., the National Labor Relations Board and seemed to have a good-sized Maine woods chip on its shoulder even for the Government of the United States. I am certainly not capable of assessing all the virtues in that controversy. Still it pleased me as a perhaps perverse parent with a child in a camp to know that our well fed darlings had gone to the Maine woods to get close to nature at a point less than twenty-five miles away from the scene of the strike where guardsmen camped for days to preserve, I gather, the civilization of the state of Maine.

It would be hard to find a road which seems further from the angry complexities of these times than that one on which I came across a green mountainous New Hampshire to the camp country around Lake Sebago in Maine. It was quieter still because I came on Sunday. On the Saturdays in that summer not only in Maines' store in South Casco but in fifty little other towns boys and girls would be buying cheese and crackers and olives and strawberry push-ups to supplement the entirely adequate diet provided by the camp commissaries. On the weekdays the trees would hide them in the woods, around the lakes, where they danced and rode horseback, in the craft rooms where they hammered out pieces of pewter to take home as decorated ash trays to their papas. (They come high, those ash trays.) All together these children in the green make an industry which Maine regards with benign satisfaction even if argument does persist between the camp directors and the Fish and Game Commission over whether each fourteen-year-old must pay a license to catch one fish.

The Maine Development Commission reports that there are over 200 camps in the state (which has a twelfth of such camps in the country), with accommodations for over 15,000 children. Not every cot is filled with a child every year, but estimators normally count 13,000 children in the woods during July and August. They also report that the price of the boys' camps runs from $250 to $400, that of the girls' from $250 to $500. I gather that $300 would be a fair average. As I multiply, that means a total of 13,000 times $300 equals $3,900,000. That is not all. My Elizabeth spent $14 in pocket money on God knows what. Take off $4 for the self-indulgence she inherits from her father. If 13,000 other children spent $10 apiece, that comes to $130,000 worth of crackers and olives and ice cream and candy which went to the stores of Maine. In addition a great many parents made a great many trips to deposit or collect or see the children. I should not dare figure that sum. Best & Company of New York provides the uniforms at the Gulick camp of Sebago Wohelo, where my girl went. It represents other camps, too—a dozen or more, with a total of a thousand children, perhaps. At $50 a child, that's an item of $50,000. Best does not have all the business; some similar money comes to stores in Maine. Then there are the railroads and the doctors.

That is the money that comes in. A good part of it undoubtedly stays in Maine. The taxgatherer and the butcher, the grocer, the carpenters, the caretakers, the cooks and the storekeepers all get a share. But the profits do not in very large measure stay in the state. Less than a quarter of the camps in Maine are run by Maine people. More camp operators come from New York than from any other state, more from Massachusetts than from Maine. Indeed, more than half the camps are operated by people from those two populous states. A majority of them are schoolteachers, with preachers and doctors following in number at a distance behind.

A red-faced young man in a garage in South Casco stopped beating on a tire rim long enough to show me the way to the Gulick Camps. They are among the oldest camps in Maine, started early in the century by Dr. and Mrs. Luther Gulick, who were prominent in the beginnings of the Campfire Girls and the Boy Scouts and other similar movements for boys and girls. Timanous is their boys' camp. They have two camps for girls, Sebago Wohelo and Little Wohelo. (Wohelo is a synthetic Indian name compounded of the first two letters of work, health, and love. Christening camps is often an interesting business: A Mrs. Baldwin runs Baldy, Mr. Gans operates Gansmere, a lady named Wilder has the Wilder-ness Farms.)

More than thirty of the camp directors have both boys' camps and girls' camps. Some have further divisions into junior and senior camps in which the teen-agers are separated from the tots. And even in the woods there is a racial and religious separation. There are about forty camps (some among the best camps in Maine), which are exclusively Jewish. Most of the other camps follow the rule of the prep schools and keep the Jewish quota down. There are camps for Christian Scientists. There are rugged camps and ritzy camps. One girls' camp, it was reported, even had a hairdresser in constant attendance. In some of the best camps, on the other hand, they even wash their teeth in the lake, which is all right for the children as Sebago is Portland's water supply. But around Sebago Lake sanitation is sharply watched at the camps by the public combination of the state which guards the camp industry as precious and Portland which drinks the blue waters which lap the shores before the camps.

At the Gulick camps that Sunday they were resting beyond preparing. The boats were in the lake. The horses were across the road in the long barn. The cabins had been swept. There were even trunks at the foot of some cots. There was still a childless peace over everything. But within a little while the cabins which sit apart and at odd levels following the contour of the big-bouldered slope would be swarming with girl-children in shorts. It did not seem a very pleasing prospect to me. I have four girls of my own who both plague and please me. The idea of a hundred of them day after day in the summertime seemed appalling. Dorothy and Halsey Gulick seemed rather pleased than dismayed. They are a young couple, that is to say in the late thirties. Halsey grew up in the camp his mother and father founded, and Dorothy was a camper and a counselor before she became the wife of the director and so half-director herself.

"We don't have any disciplinary problem," Halsey said.

Laid up with a twisted knee, he was calmly carving a chain of wooden links out of a long block of wood. Other chains hung about the central cabin, which sits with wide windows high above the lake. Below was the swimming and boat pier, the diving tower and boards. Below, too, the children would sail the Cape Cod Nimblets and paddle the big war canoes.

Across the water were islands in the lake which the camp owns. Sometimes the children sleep there. "It's not any problem. Sometimes the children who have the most trouble in schools make the best campers. All of them learn quickly to do what the group of all the campers expects of each camper. It's a sort of rule by public opinion, I suppose. At any rate, it works."

I am sure it does. But I thought of myself in a camp as I know I would be, the dismayed center of the riotous chaos of a couple of hundred children. Halsey Gulick, however, whittled and talked in calm, waiting for his charges. All winter as head master of the Proctor Academy in Andover, New Hampshire (where he has worked out some very interesting ideas in shop education which conceives of hand work in the building of boats and the understanding of motors not as vocational training but as the use of vocational problems in the training of the mind), he had had a little world of boys to manage. Then he was looking forward to more boys, and girls, too, in the three camps he operates. I had the feeling that despite all the responsibility they would mean, they would mean pleasure to him, also. For a moment even I thought how pleasant it would be to sit in this room above the lake and hear the call and clatter of all the congregated children in the open cabins among the trees. Then I thought of mothers and fathers and skinned knees and runny noses. The idea passed.

They fed me well in the long empty dining hall. Some of the counselors had already assembled. They talked about their camps and other camps. Not far off, somebody said, a man was building a new camp with cabins so constructed that if it failed as a place for children the cabins could be used as coops for chickens. There was more free, good-natured talk about this industry for children in the woods. I wanted to stay longer listening. But I had to be going up the road to see other camps and beyond the camps, but not far from them, the people who make shoes in Maine. They are, I think, closely related to the New England children in the camps. It is a pity that such a little distance can separate them so much when at last they must come together in common fortune and then perhaps in unfamiliarity and surprise. Maybe, I thought as I rode to Raymond and then, twisting north by Panther Pond and Rattlesnake Pond (there are no poisonous snakes in Maine) and Long Lake to the camps around Casco and Harrison—maybe the children are sent to touch the wrong earth. Under the most excellent arrangements and with the best care the fed and schooled adolescents of the New England upper middle class go in summer to touch and understand the tended forest and the clear water. But the Indian is with the arrowhead.

Life grows in Lewiston about a United Shoe Machinery Corporation machine. I am not quite sure, so far as these children are concerned, whether the new Indians are the United Shoe Machinery Corporation or the C.I.O. I am sure that the young Yankees live on an earth which both will shape, and where their meeting will be at least as complicated as the meeting of the Pilgrims and the people of Massasoit.

It is not only the children who move to Maine. The Massachusetts children might learn that some of the men in Boston who most lament the departure of Bay State industries preside over a system in shoes which makes easy their departure. It is undoubtedly true, as a committee of the General Court of Massachusetts charged in 1939, that some Maine towns were promising low wages and no unions to such shoe plants in Massachusetts towns as would make the trip across New Hampshire. But it is also true that the leasing system of the United Shoe Machinery Corporation, which has a close relationship with the First National Bank of Boston, makes it easy for plants to move. No large capital is necessary to go into the shoe manufacturing business since the manufacturer does not buy his machinery but leases it on a royalty basis. This has fostered fierce competition. Furthermore, according to such an authority on New England as Malcolm Keir, the leasing system has worked to create the unions from which the leasing system now helps the manufacturers to run.

"Not only has the leasing system retained small-scale operations and resulted in specialization," said Professor Keir in a report which he prepared for the Governors of New England in connection with Southern railroad rate pleas, "but indirectly it has fostered labor organizations. Since the employers in the industry were not fortified by aggregations of capital, and because their intense competition with each other prevented mutual cooperation, whereas the localization of the industry brought workers in close contact, the conditions were propitious for aggressive unions. The unions were most active in the old shoe towns of Massachusetts.

"Of late years, therefore," he went on, "employers have moved their manufacturing operations into New Hampshire and Maine where unionism was unimpressive and wages were lower than in Massachusetts. The shoe towns north of Boston suffered more from this kind of loss than those south of Boston. Manchester, N.H., and its adjacent towns gained from the overflow, and likewise Auburn and Lewiston in Maine."

But the United Shoe Machinery Corporation keeps its big offices on Federal Street in Boston. In general the shoe unions stay in Massachusetts, too, at least so far as Maine is concerned. Powers Hapgood, director of the C.I.O.'s United Shoe Workers of America, who spent fifty-six days in a Maine jail when he was trying to organize Lewiston-Auburn shoe workers, claimed only 50,000 members in America at the same time he made a wish which was the expression of a need for 300,000. Other unions claim 40,000 more.

In Maine the real, important absentee in interest is the United Shoe Machinery Corporation which, with a practical monopoly of shoemaking machinery, makes just as much money when its machines work in Lewiston-Auburn or Bangor (where the city council appropriated $30,000 for a school to teach people to work in the plant that was moving from Massachusetts) or Mechanic Falls as when they work in Haverhill or Boston or Lynn. It does quite as well, indeed, when they are installed in the Middle West. Of course, it would be wrong for the United Shoe Machinery Corporation to rule its patent properties to serve the old shoe towns of Massachusetts alone. Furthermore, it is in business for profit, not patriotism, and it is doing quite nicely in an industry in which manufacturers and workers sometimes seem equally caught in a competition close to chaos. Still and yet, when disturbed business men and patriots in Boston study the disappearance of old industries in the new dispersal of industry, they would make no mistake if they contemplated 140 Federal Street as well as the grasping, promising tactics of states and towns and chambers of commerce in towns far away as both Mississippi and Maine.

I walked along the same Androscoggin River which in New Hampshire cuts the paper town of Berlin in two. It cuts Lewiston and Auburn apart in Maine. Also, in a real sense it separates French-Canadian Democrats on one side from conservative Yankee Republicans on the other. They had been making shoes and cloth along the river there for a long time. The French-Canadians had come down from the poor crowded farms of Quebec, and the factories had come up more recently from Massachusetts for the labor of their children grown into big boys and girls through the parochial schools. They vote the Democratic ticket in Lewiston, and not long ago a Democratic Christian Scientist was elected Governor of the state from the Catholic town. But it was a Republican Baptist druggist from Newport, Maine ("The Rexall Store" on the main street), who sent the National Guard during the strike in 1937 to spend nearly a month of spring in Lewiston-Auburn.

It was peaceful enough when I was there. Everybody was happy, an Irish policeman told me.

"Of course, we've got poor folks here," he said. "We could use some more jobs. But we haven't got as many soreheads as we used to have."

"Do many of the children from the camps come here?"

"Not often. I guess they get off the train at Portland or Augusta. But there are plenty of them out there in the woods. I guess in July the're more kids than grown people between here and New Hampshire. And they've got a lot of other kids over there."

"Where do they come from?"

"Oh, hell, everywhere! A lot of them are rich kids from Boston and New York. It's nice business for Maine."

In Maine that week I did more wandering, riding to the little towns which want the factories and need jobs in them for their people as much as little Mississippi towns do, as much as bigger towns like Lewiston-Auburn, and are as ready to make any promises and to defend them; to more camps, to general stores which recognize the child trade as a blessed addition to the farm trade. I remember that between the children and the shoemakers the Shakers live in a little town called Sabbathday Lake. There were not many new members now, a man who rode with me said. The world surrounded their Christian communism and came to buy their chocolates. Not only Sabbathday Lake was subject to pressure and change. Nobody knew what New England the children were growing to in the woods, or what Maine was developing around the lasts and the stitchers. Not even the Four-Flushers can take the element of chance out of that change.

XXVI

The Road North

It is axiomatic, says Kenneth Roberts, who was born in Kennebunk down in the point of Maine between New Hampshire and the sea, that you are not really in Maine and don't know what it ought to look like, until you've crossed the Kennebec. Beyond that river which splits the state, he suggests, men from below it have the impression that only with the use of ice axes and trained guides can the intrepid enter a region where, with the screaming lynx, the land is shared by hardy lumbermen who subsist on seal blubber diluted with grain alcohol. I can testify as expert about that naïveté. As one from far south of the Kennebec I knew better, but I feared worse. Long, long ago I cut the teeth of my literacy on a stirring volume called *The Motor Boat Boys on the Kennebec* and I can still report that those boys moved dauntlessly on an adventurous stream. Therefore as we left the Statehouse in Augusta and passed the beautiful old Blaine Mansion where the Governors live, I was glad to have as guide on the road north, at the end of which there are more potatoes than panthers, young Keith Field of the Maine Development Commission.

In general I distrust such guides. Development commissions in most states specialize in showing identical bathing beauties sporting upon indistinguishable shores. They throw jewels in your eyes which can be as blinding as sand. But

Keith Field's specialty was potatoes, his virtue was that he knew the north like a neighborhood ("Hi, Harry, how's Ethel"), and that in his own unofficial person he was a pleasant and typical young man of Maine. He had begun his career at twenty as a salesman on a commission for the telephone company ($15 a week drawing account, but you got fired when you were $30 in the red). He did not get fired. To the amazement of himself and the telephone company, he ran his commissions up to $100 a week, whereupon the telephone company fixed salesmen's salaries flat at $23. He quit. He got a job on a newspaper at Gardiner; but a flood washed the press away, and the paper died with the press. From a newspaper supply salesman he heard about a job up in Presque Isle in big Aroostook County, which is as far from Gardiner as Gardiner is from Boston. He talked five dollars' worth on the telephone, went up by airplane and got the job. What was more important to him and to me, he began to get as newspaperman an understanding of the great Maine cash crop of the potato, which made him one to help when the state of Maine began to tell the world in new amplified terms about the virtue of the potatoes in the state of Maine, and of the people who grow the potatoes and the earth out of which potatoes grow.

We crossed the river and headed the Plymouth north. There were stone piers in the Kennebec to which, Field said, the log booms were tied. There were pulp logs coming down. He explained the traffic on the stream, the laws which keep it open for everybody's wood. At Waterville there was not only Colby College but, more interesting to me, a whole railroad siding full of the snowplows of the Maine Central Railroad. We had lunch in the Governor's town of Newport, where we were met with a certain special hospitality which seems to go with native hotel-keeping in Maine. Manager Joe Day had, I remember, two symmetrically placed gold teeth in the front of his mouth. A pretty waitress served us with a pleasant democracy which is something altogether different from city familiarity. The strawberry shortcake was properly made of biscuit dough. I asked why some people dared make it with cake. That has been a question which has puzzled me across America, but the waitress in Maine gave me the only satisfactory answer I have ever received.

"It's just plain laziness," she said. "You can buy cake at the store."

Well fed, we went on to Bangor and stopped there to examine the unromantic remains of the old-time Devil's Half Acre where once the saloons and whorehouses waited the roaring spending of the spring-freed lumberjacks. They are as gone as the girls and the bartenders and the gamblers who waited in them and the big lusty boys who came down to get a hell-raising and a hangover for a year's work in the woods. I guess that was pretty poor pay. Still I should like to have got to Bangor before the greater wisdom and the greater goodness entirely prevailed. But the ancient elms on a street called Broadway are worth remembering, rows of them on the sidewalks and two rows in a green esplanade between. We stopped by the waterworks to see the salmon pool in the Penobscot where every May and June the gamy fish make their way up the falls to spawn, and where the first one to find his way to a hook has the honor of being plattered on the White House table. In Orono most of the people I wanted to see at the university were out of town, but we stopped on the steps of the agricultural building to discuss her pretty efforts in humanity with Bruce Minor's blonde secretary who was nursing an injured English sparrow for which she had made an aseptic gauze hospital bed in a shoe box.

It is a lonesome road beyond Old Town where they make the canoes and where probably the Indians working with modern equipment do a good deal better job than Hiawatha. The houses were farther apart, and gray and grim in their loneliness. Some of the barn roofs were as swaybacked as old dying horses. There was an old man, bearded and ragged, pushing a wheelbarrow in Olamon. He was talking to himself like a distraught Santa Claus. Across the Penobscot at West Enfield was Howland.

"I don't know what they make here," said Field, "but sometimes it stinks like hell."

It is paper. There was no productive smell in the air when we passed. We stopped to get gasoline at a Gulf station which bore on its front all the signs of modern advertising, and at which oil and gas were dispensed with the methods of modern merchandising. Behind it the men's room was a privy. It is by no means an institution either antique or unknown in Maine. But south of Lincoln we came to an industry which is rarer than it used to be not so very long ago. Behind the high board fences and under the watchtowers above them, silver-fox farming had boomed; and afterwards people had suffered as well as the foxes. The gray fences and the wire ones had run up around the little town of Lincoln almost as building lots had been staked off in Florida. Local people took a flyer in foxes, and local people lost their shirts if only the foxes lost their skins.

We pulled the car up in the yard by the watchtower and the keeper's house of one ranch which was still in operation. A man in Bangor, official of a fur firm which also operated in New York, had bought up a group of the bankrupt ranches. Young Ed Southard in blue work shirt and trousers came out of the house. We told him we'd like to see the ranch.

"I'm not supposed to," he said, "but hell!"

He unlocked the door in the fence. We went in to meet a smell customarily encountered only in zoos. In long cor-

ridors in the grass within were wire-bottomed wire cages
filled with the foxes. The original breeding stock, he said,
had been brought from Prince Edward Island, and in the
boom days pelts had sold from $100 to $150. The average had
gone down to something like $26. There were 375 animals in
the ranch we saw. The foxes not to be kept for breeding are
killed in January, when the fur is best, but I am not sure in
such a manner as not to hurt the foxes. He showed us the
wooden tongs with which the fated foxes are caught about
their necks. There were deep claw marks in the hard wood.
When so caught they are stunned with a blow, and while
stunned their necks are broken. Thus the ladies get furs without scars.

"That's something none of us like to do around here,"
Southard said when he described the process.

The breeding must be as carefully watched as the killing
is done. Female foxes are in heat only three days in the year
—in January or February. While they are breeding, men
watch from the towers and record the matings. Careful records are kept on each fox. Their ears are tattooed for identifi-
cation. They get from one to seven puppies in a litter. That
year they had had two litters of eight. They had also had
some trouble with the deliveries: some of the young had
been too big.

He showed us puppies and also the one fox on the ranch
which was tame enough to handle. Southard had raised her
on a cat. The fox has a terrible bite. Sometimes in the past
when they had put two in a cage, all that would be left of
one of them would be tail and bones. But the pet fox seemed
tame enough, though shy even in tameness. While I was
watching Southard handle the pet an old cow eating grass
betweeen the cages gave my shoulder a sharp push with her
muzzle. I jumped. Southard drove her away.

"She's bullin'," he said.

There were more ranches up the road, a bigger place with two towers and a number of places which seemed not only weather-beaten but abandoned. The woods began. We rode, as it seemed to the stranger, through the wilderness. Despite the fact that the forests have been cut back from the coast, and that Maine has shipped its trees for a century to the world to build houses and print newspapers, 15,000,000 acres of forest land still remain. That is an area equal to all the land devoted to farming in New England. All of it seemed to stretch back from the highway, which carried us through it. The lynx and the bear and the white-tailed deer are in there. A mile from the road, Field thought charitably, a man like me would be forever lost from the world. We passed through townships with so few people in them that they have never been organized and are governed by the foresters of the state. There is a band across Maine between the capital and the great fields of Aroostook where even at the most crowded point less than 10 per cent of the land has been put into cultivation by man.

But the world opens beyond the forest. Almost precipitately, it seemed to me, we came out of the forest to the big fields and the rolling farms of Aroostook. Four-fifths of the county is still a wooded wilderness, but the remaining fifth where the potatoes grow makes it one of the richest agricultural counties in America. (Like other agricultural counties, too, it can sometimes be among the most broke.) In the East, certainly, it is one of the biggest. Three states are smaller than this county. As Americans count, it may be at the end of the world. It is a pleasant and productive end, in the lively little towns of which local pride waxes mightily and competition, too, whether it be over which town has the fastest trotting horse or over which ships the most potatoes.

Beside the road the fields spread wide. The half-buried potato storage barns emerged from the earth. Near Houlton there was the stain of potato starch in a stream. In the lobby of the Northland Hotel men were talking about the effect of the weather on the potato crops in New Jersey and North Carolina. We went across the street and found lively, confident Bernard Esters putting to press the last section of the fat edition of *The Houlton Pioneer Times* which commemorated the hundredth anniversary of Aroostook County. It fairly bulged with business. I was interested in the page advertisement of the A. & P. Food Stores, not merely because they promised to buy $12,500,000 worth of Aroostook's farm products in Aroostook's hundredth year, but also because the page recounted that eighty years before a young man from Maine, George Huntington Hartford, had gone down to New York to begin the Great Atlantic & Pacific Tea Company. But in the historical feature stories one item of significant history was not presented: In the hundred years in which the Aroostook farms had been spreading where the forests had been, over the whole of New England farms and acres devoted to farming had decreased.

With Esters and young Norman Leighton, who had prepared the literature about the patriots and the advertisers in the edition, we went back across the street and drank to the hundred years. Afterwards Esters, as editor, had serious business with a down-state politician who looked like Robert Louis Stevenson. Field and Leighton and I ate heartily, then in the cool summer night (a good night for potatoes) Leighton drove us across the Canadian line to Woodstock, where the stores were full of pictures of Their Majesties the King and Queen. Back in the United States we stopped at a roadside dance hall where the boys and girls were stirring mightily to the strains of swing. They perspired in the night which the moon and stars did not warm. We went back to our car and passed a couple kissing. If Aroostook were the end of the world, I thought, America might begin there as well as end.

XXVII

Potatoes and a Priest

IN THE EARLY MORNING we came into the main street of Presque Isle, where the cars of the potato planting town and country are parked in the middle of the wide street and the offices of the potato buying and selling companies look down upon them. On the road north, washed fertilizer bags had been drying on the fences in the sun, fences which reminded me of those in the cotton South. There were more of the half-buried storage houses. There were tractors in the wide fields, a few horses, but not any mules (the mule is as rare in New England as the Negro). If there had been Negroes on the streets, Presque Isle might have seemed in its brief summer a thriving market town for cotton or tobacco. The same girls as in the South sat in the drugstore, the same coatless men walked the streets. There was not only the same Woolworth's where Keith Field bought some bright trout flies for twenty-five cents apiece, but the same farm implements and farm machines were for sale. As the morning warmed, even the sun seemed the same.

It is an interesting arrangement in paradox, I think, that if the American goes far enough south into Florida he will come into the North again occupied by Yankees fled from their snow. If he goes far enough north to that big plug of

Aroostook which lies between New Brunswick and Quebec, he will come into the South, or at least a land where living is shaped in patterns similar to those in the cotton-growing Mississippi Delta. The little sober steady struggle for a living on the small hilly New England farm is left behind. Agricultural ideas spread wide as the valley in a big speculative masculine farming. In Aroostook you come to the one-crop, cash-crop, high-hope, long-chance farming that has made men expansive and kept them poor down below Virginia. There are other similarities.

There may be, as the men of this North say, a lot of politics about the talk of malnutrition on this richest land in Maine, but some of it has been there as well as in the South. There is need for diversification in crops (and a growing practice). And north of Caribou along the green valley of the St. John River there is sometimes a poverty among the Acadian French which is at least equal to the poverty of their relatives who went with Evangeline to Louisiana, sometimes even almost equal to that of the Negroes who plow the land for the planting of the cotton there. But in farming as well as in marketing, the Maine farmer who has so often taken a beating on the richest Maine land is trying to use intelligence to get out of difficulties as real and as discouraging as any encountered anywhere in America.

While we rode north Keith Field had worried out loud because of a report that Dr. Allan Roy Dafoe had said something in the papers about taking the Dionne quintuplets off potatoes because they were getting too fat. Maine is sensitive about the suggestion that potatoes are fattening. Dr. Dafoe and the Dionnes in Ontario were not so far off that they should lack sympathy for the little French who are not fat among the potatoes. Across the years the same impression plus the increasing year-round availability of other foods had cut the consumption of Maines' big cash crop. In 1909 everybody in the United States consumed an annual average of 4.2 bushels of spuds. In 1937, when Maine began its advertising and marketing program, it had fallen to 2.8 bushels. At that time the farmers figured that if the 1909 consumption per eater could be regained there would be a market for 175,000,000 bushels in excess of the 391,000,000 bushels raised throughout the country that year. If the American ate a nine-ounce potato a day instead of the seven-and-a-half-ounce one he was eating, that would mean a market for 75,-000,000 more bushels.

The figures sounded like some long Southern talk about the effect on the cotton crop of adding an inch to the Chinaman's shirt tail. But Maine went to work to do something about the situation. It was the first party in interest as the leading potato growing state. In Aroostook alone, from as much as 170,000 acres planted in potatoes, producers make from 200 to 450 bushels to the acre. Yet in seven of the ten years before the marketing and advertising program was begun (with a self-imposed tax of a penny a barrel on the growers) potato men had lost money. A farm-mortgage debt of $30,000,000 had grown with the potatoes.

With $25,000 appropriated by the legislature and $100,000 to $150,000, depending upon the size of the crop, from the barrel tax, Maine set out to advertise the potatoes of Aroostook as "State of Maine" potatoes, but at the same time undertook to make the advertised potato of the State of Maine mean something in quality in the grocery stores of the land. (That "State of Maine" label means graded quality now on a bag of potatoes, on a box of blueberries, on a lobster's claw. Money spent to advertise low-quality goods would hurt rather than help Maine products, and Maine seeks its money's worth in the realization that the buyer also wants his.) Anybody can sell any potatoes grown in Maine anywhere, but not as "State of Maine" potatoes unless the size and quality meet the standard. There are starch plants for others; they talk about scientific studies to make cellophane out of spuds.

There was some grumbling at first about the tax, about the plan; there has also been a good deal of early success. For the first time the Maine potato went ahead of the Idaho potato in price; in a glut year Maine moved its entire crop of 52,000 car lots of graded potatoes to market. It may be too early to count the long-term benefits. Maine and its farmers are convinced that the program carried on under the direction of the State Department of Agriculture and the Maine Development Commission is on the right track and a clear one. They do not say much about it in the Statehouse in Republican Maine, but the advertising and marketing program is only half of the plan of salvation. In the last voting before I was there, the farmers of Aroostook had voted around 99 per cent for Federal potato crop control under the AAA.

We found Frank Hussey in his office as president of the Maine Potato Growers, Inc., the big co-operative of the county, and he took us out to see the potatoes growing on the Hussey family Maple Crest Farms. He is a young man, lean, alive, who had been twelve years farming since he graduated from the University of Maine in 1925. He wore that day in his little office on Main Street calf-high boots over his long trousers. His shirt collar was open at the throat. I remember his strong fingers when he pulled the brown loam back from a young potato plant's roots. He was the third generation in potatoes. His grandfather had come from central Maine to Aroostook when his father was five years old. He had come because he was broke.

"When I see the rocky farms down there," Hussey said, "I'm glad he was broke and did come."

Now on five farms, Charles E. Hussey & Sons, Inc., grow both table and seed potatoes. The limy soil and cool moist climate of the valley not only produce food worthy of the trade-mark of "State of Maine." Of increasing importance is the further fact that production in Southern areas depends largely upon healthy seed potatoes obtained from Northern-grown plants. (There is an interesting Northern-Southern combination here. Since the prime quality of seed potatoes is their freedom from disease, Maine operates beds for foundation seed in Florida where test plots show early any disease in sample plants before the big fields are planted in Maine.) The seed potato, says Dr. Malcolm Keir, is one of the very few commodities produced in New England that have nothing to fear from Southern competition. Hussey had been in my town in North Carolina to sell seed potatoes to dealers there.

"I found Yankees there, too, when it comes to price," he said.

He took us into big insulated storage barns, across a fifty-acre potato field where a tractor was cultivating the plants. He explained the crop rotation involving oats and clover and timothy between the plantings of potatoes. The most serious land erosion in New England is in Aroostook. Too much the old method of running rows up and down the hills continues to be practiced, and there is sometimes nothing to impede water running down mile-long-looking rows. Maine (and in this case that means Aroostook) spends more money and a larger proportion of its farm income on fertilizer than any other state in the region. Hussey showed us how wiser farmers were co-operating with the Soil Conservation Service. He pointed to the rows which ran with the natural contours of the land.

"In the old days, if a man didn't plow a straight furrow we'd fire him," he said. "We fire him now if he does."

By Southern standards, it is a swift farming. The growing season is only ninety to a hundred days long. Planting starts from the 1st to the 15th of May. Digging begins in the last

week in August and may continue to the first of October. It
is then that the big demand for labor comes. All the spare
labor in the towns takes to the fields. The Acadians come
down from the St. John River valley. People come from
cities as far south as Boston, even cranberry pickers from
Cape Cod. They get from five to eight cents a barrel depending upon whether or not they are fed, and they pick from
fifty to a hundred barrels a day. The Farm Bureau in the
county fixes the price every year. (Once there was, someone
told me, a report that the C.I.O. was coming. There was
preparation for war, but no war came.) The picked potatoes
go into the half-buried storage barns or the lines of storage
houses beside the tracks of the rich Bangor & Aroostook railroad. The big dealers and the little speculators buy and
grade the potatoes. Then Aroostook counts a year which is
rich as race horses (new automobiles now) or poor as the
parishioners of Father Soucy have seemed always to be, good
year or bad.

Sadly enough, a good part of Aroostook even in good years
is only less poor. Evangeline only lost her lover, but some of
her sister Acadians (never to be confused with French-Canadians, Maine men say) have in the generations found lovers
who turned out to be husbands growing gnarled-handed and
stooped-shouldered. Together they produced a plentiful
progeny who were generally poverty-caught at home if they
were not in effect crowded out of the little farms to seek a
living far away. Sometimes, so crowded out, they were lost to
the Church. So young Father Soucy reports, and the Father
not only knows but has, beyond his preaching, extended his
ministry to include the living bodies as well as the immortal
souls. You begin to hear about the young priest before you
reach Aroostook, about his co-operatives, about his productive politics for his parishioners, about the faith Protestant
agriculturalists have in his zeal for the rural welfare of the

children of his Church. Field and I set out north to find him.

The road beyond Caribou ran quickly into what seemed a poorer country. Frank Hussey had moved from the big house beside the barn into Presque Isle to get his children off the high-speed highways. There are apparently no speed laws in Maine but not much crowding on the roads either. Certainly there was not much traffic north of Caribou. There were still some big barns by the highway, some of them with French names painted on them in big letters. There were poor houses, too, some looking little more than lumber-camp shacks.

I remember one new unpainted house; it would be small, I thought, against the big cold of the Aroostook winter. But there were electric wires running into it and a radio aerial above it. There was a row of disreputable-looking log cabins in Cyr Plantation (a plantation is a governing and taxing unit in the empty reaches of Maine), and a schoolhouse not more than twenty by twenty-five feet which bore the name Governor Brann School. A carnival had its tents up in Van Buren, its Ferris wheel turning and music blaring for the French folk in the border town. People are never too poor for carnival. We crossed the bridge into Canada to St. Léonard, and I remember still the pretty French girl sitting on the porch there. All through the French country they sat on porches, like girls waiting, and they seemed to me prettier than any Frenchwomen I had ever seen, far prettier than the women of their race in France. Beyond the pretty girl I laughed at swift border change. There was a big familiar red and white truck loaded with bottles and the sign painted on it shouted: Buvez Coca-Cola Glacé.

We looked at Maine from Canada. The green hills ran up from the banks of the river and looked richer for the distance. You could feel the temptation with which an imperialist might look across a frontier. The St. John, however,

does not border poverty or problem—it runs in the midst of
them. A huge Catholic church looked as if it might be a load
as well as a light for the people. But, looking at it, I remembered the queer conversation of an Aroostook Mason. He
indicated, I thought, a pretty clear cleavage in the country
when he asked if I was a Protestant. He was obviously relieved when I told him that I was a Methodist though not a
very good one. So I was surprised later by what he said about
the big Catholic churches in the poor, crowded little Catholic
towns. He had thought at first, he said, that they proved a
sucking clerical exploitation, but he had been mistaken. If,
he declared, the money spent on the sum of the Baptist and
Methodist and Presbyterian and Congregational churches all
went to make one church, it could be a big one, too. That
seemed logical to me. Competition can be as costly as monopoly even in religion. But in New Brunswick the state as
represented in Edmundston by the sad-looking *palais de justice* made a poor comparison in brick and stone at least with
the church.

We turned beside it back into America across the international bridge upon which drivers are enjoined not to speed
their horses faster than a walk. Beyond it America began at
a beer joint run by Joseph Guerette, a paper factory and a
sign set up by the Rotary Club of Madawaska. America began also in this most northern town in the East with sleazy
tenements. There was a two-story tar-paper one. The land
did not look as pretty as it had seemed from across the river,
nor as simple. We headed south by Frenchville, which strings
out long beside the road, by St. Agatha, to the little village
of Sinclair, which lives off the fishermen who come to try the
waters of Mud Lake and Long Lake. The rectory of Father
Soucy stood behind the little church in the trees on the shore.
He was not there. Nobody answered our knocks. I remember
that the three-inch risers on the steps to his porch made me

wonder if an old priest had been there before him whose knees were tired and stiff.

We stopped at the Dodge Inn and played skee ball on the porch decorated with soft-drink signs while the obliging proprietor in voluble French phoned Fort Kent to see if he could locate the priest. (There had been no phones until Father Soucy came.) Our play on the porch, in which Field vastly excelled, brought the children of Sinclair to watch us. A small boy with very bad teeth tried unsuccessfully in scant fisherman's English to coach me to victory. Field took my quarters, time after time. Then the innkeeper came back. We might find Father Soucy in Fort Kent, he said. Who could tell? He was a very busy man in his Studebaker, Father Soucy. A woman stood behind him as he spoke, and soon, I noticed, Father Soucy would have another citizen of Sinclair to christen. The north country would have another young mouth demanding food.

A slim young Frenchman with the English of a wider world stopped the trade involved in the sale of a mattress to a middle-aged *mère et père* to direct us to the rectory in Frenchville of the Church of St. Luke. Father Peter Hamel came out on his porch behind the undeceiving imitation marble columns. An affable gentleman in a solemn black cassock, he wore also a rather jaunty panama hat and smoked a long black cigar. He phoned again.

"Yes," he reported. "You will find him in Fort Kent. His heart and soul are in his co-operatives."

So we came at last to Fort Kent and learned at a grocery store run by one of the Father's brothers where we should find him. (Two other Soucy brothers run two other grocery stores.) But first, by accident, we found Elmo Dow, fish and game warden of the district. Field, the fisherman, stopped to talk to him. Big plans for fishing on Moosehead Lake were on foot, Dow reported. He had already sent the men in with the boats. The Governor and the National Commander of the American Legion and other notables were going in by plane. Dow was joining them. He spoke to Field about another newspaperman at the capital who was not generous in sharing his Scotch on fishing trips.

"To hell with him!" said Dow. "He's just a little too tight."

From his big, freehanded masculinity we went to the spiritual strength of the young priest in the parlor of a friend's house down a little side street. The room was furnished with new furniture out of the machine age of America, such furniture and hangings as a man or a woman might buy in Montgomery Ward or Sears, Roebuck anywhere in America. But the young priest in his cassock was conscious of the old Church behind him. He was also, I think, conscious of his own dignity and strength. Someone has described him as a "go-getter"; so in the same sense was St. Paul. The phrase smears them both. In English that was good but not always certain, he told us about the credit unions he had established among the Acadians, the creamery, the breeders association, the plans for a co-operative selling organization to handle the needlework of the women. Occasionally he flung his hand out in a gesture which was both definite and abrupt.

Father D. Wilfrid Soucy was thirty-six years old then. He was dark with thick curly hair brushed back from his forehead. His white teeth seemed too large for his mouth and made it ugly—and strong. There was a look of leadership about him despite a certain air half of shyness, half of pride. As he talked, there seemed to be nothing theoretical about him. Obviously there was nothing inconsistent in his use of liberal co-operative ideas as a son of the conservative Church. He was not interested in changing economic patterns but in helping his people as Catholics out of economic distress.

"They are poor," he said. "The girls have to go away from

301

home. Often they marry outside the Church. They are unhappy and lose their health. If we can help them, they will
not have to go away. We can save them for the Church."

He does not come out of the deep poverty with which he
deals. His father was a business man in Fort Kent. His three
brothers all run grocery stores. He went to St. Francis Xavier
College in Antigonish, Nova Scotia. As young priest he served
for six years in Westbrook, town near Portland where Rudy
Vallee grew, and where French people still make textiles of
cotton and rayon and silk. Soucy had become interested in
Catholic Action and went to Boston College to study, special-
izing in co-operatives. He had been back in his native Aroostook three years as priest of the little parishes of Sinclair and
Guerette when I saw him; but his work in co-operatives was
only about a year old, though old enough to have attracted
attention not only in agricultural circles in Maine but among
co-operative workers throughout the country. His practical
application of his studies to his parishioners in Aroostook began by accident. A man who was organizing a co-operative
creamery of a sort asked him to come and speak to the
farmers.

"I will come," young Soucy said; "but I'll have to tell them
what you are organizing is not a true co-operative."

"Come nevertheless," said the man.

So Soucy began his ministry of co-operation. The creamery
formed then was not a co-operative but a stock company in
which the members subscribed $10 stock for each cow they
owned. Then they got a pure-bred Ayrshire bull from New
York State. That beautiful animal is the central figure of the
St. John Valley Ayrshire Breeders Association. Soucy organized five Federal credit unions with the church as the unit
in Sinclair, Guerette, St. Agatha, Daigle, and Stockholm. He
persuaded the power company and the telephone company
to run their lines into Sinclair. Rather casually he spoke

about a Federal rural electrification line to the power company; no such thing was necessary he was assured.

As the economic ministry mounted in addition to his spiritual ministry, he got the State Highway Commission to build a road which cut more than thirty miles from his traveling between Sinclair and Guerette. It was a long riding on old Sundays when he had to fast till Mass was said after forty miles of roundabout road. He told me about that road: He knew a druggist from Augusta who knew that the man in authority in the Highway Commission had a friend who was the priest at Machias. So Father Soucy spoke to the Bishop in Portland, who spoke to the priest in Machias, who told the man in the Highway Commission how bad Father Soucy needed that road. Today the road is the best one in a section where the winter plays havoc with the surfacing—a joy to fishermen in Mud Lake and Long Lake as well as new speed in his service for the priest.

He needed to save all the time he could. One week in addition to his work as priest, he drove a thousand miles and delivered fourteen lectures on co-operatives. There are twenty-five communities to which he must go. He praises and scolds and fixes his people in the purpose until he can come again. It is never long before he comes. But the education is, he thinks, the essence of the co-operative. Both the co-operatives and the education are desperately needed.

"Co-operatives should be started," he told me, "when people are poor."

They were poor enough in the St. John valley. The people had lost their farms, he said, because the Federal land banks lent them more money than they needed. They spent it without wisdom. They borrowed money, and they grew potatoes.

"Potatoes!" Father Soucy said once. "Nothing but potatoes. A one-man farmer will put in twenty acres of potatoes, spray them, tend them all summer. If potatoes sell for two dollars a barrel—and how many times in the last ten years have they?—he'll make a little money. If they sell for seventy-five cents a barrel, he will lose a thousand dollars.

"Little farmers like our people in the northern section of the county can't afford to gamble like that. But for many years false prophets have told them that mixed farming can't pay up here, that we're too far from the markets."

He shook his head. "They would only trust a priest. What I have done is for the honor of the Church. I am not the whole thing. If it is a success, it must develop leaders. It is an educational process as well as an economic plan. They must study. Men must learn to lead."

He was making final plans when I saw him for the biggest, perhaps, of all the things he had done for the so many little people of the valley, so many that they have to be identified by numbers because the Acadian names are often alike. The Federal wages and hours law has hit the sisters of Evangeline. Crocheted baby clothes and outfits for older children have for many years brought some money into the Acadian homes even if the money represented sweatshop wages for fine work paid by dealers in New York. The law put an end to sweat-shopping, but also to income. Father Soucy had organized a co-operative enterprise to produce the garments and made contracts in New York to sell them. More than two thousand women were already signed up. In the past they got about twenty-five cents for a day's work. His plan would make it possible for them to earn at least a dollar. There are, among his people, fifty-eight hundred families with one or more crocheting women in each of them. He was going to have a yarn mill. The state of Maine was going to help them put sheep on the land. He counted on at least $2,000,000 a year from the crocheted clothes. That would be a lot of money in the St. John River valley.

The past was counted in smaller sums. He wrote me after I came away about the credit unions: "In their first months of operation they have saved $1,800 and lent $2,100 to those poor people which goes to say that the people have paid back the money lent and quite fast at that. This money would not have been saved otherwise because nobody goes to the bank to deposit a 25¢ saving and they do it regularly in the credit union. They can borrow when in need for the smallest interest possible, on small loans 1% per month for the money left to pay and they don't have to have security. Yet strange to say we have not had any bad loans yet and the reason is this: Give the poor people a chance to be honest and easy will be everything."

It is a poor land still there on the St. John. You can see the poverty there as you can see it in the South. You can see it, when a boy grins, in his rotten teeth. There is not enough yet on all the children-crowded farms for all the girls to stay at home—or all the boys either. The Federal Land Bank sells farms and sometimes the Escovitzes buy them. There are still too many potatoes. Sometimes there is even too little to eat. Soucy has struck at the poverty, but it is a big dragon which will not die from the first wound. It is much that he has faced it and is not appalled or afraid.

I looked at him sitting there in the little parlor in Fort Kent. He has a priest's hands, apparently a priest's quietness of spirit. But I suspect this young priest is a driver, a driver for the Lord and the Church and their people, their little people, their poor. I wondered if sometimes a little laziness did not whimper in Jean or Alex behind the young Father's back. He has had them out in winter cutting poles for the telephone wires that came in. He had them plant as a free community enterprise a National Youth Administration farm which was officially begun too late for cultivation.

The work runs before them in his plans. The women will

be crocheting. The men will be laboring. And Father Soucy will be behind them, in the field with them, speaking to them, scolding, praising, to break the poverty that has sent the girls out to be lost to the Church. He has more time now. The Bishop has given him an assistant. Somehow through one of the Federal government agencies he got some secretarial assistance. When he went down to Orono, in the spring before I was there, to the University to tell Maine what he was doing, he enlisted the enthusiasm of important people— Protestants, most of them—in the work he was doing.

Perhaps his will runs ahead of him. He was planning to organize a co-operative to help the lumber workers, who only get about forty cents a day after furnishing horse and wagon, he said. Finally he planned a co-operative for potatoes which would eliminate the middleman, "the A. & P. and those trusts." He said it like David, and I thought of Goliath who is not always to be laid low with one stone. Certainly he undertakes formidable enterprise in Aroostook.

A young priest will need the Lord's strength to accomplish it. He is strong and young; but I remembered the low risers on the steps at the rectory in Sinclair, and I wondered if even a young priest about the business of his people and their Lord ever tired. As a Protestant and a stranger, I hoped not. And I hoped, as Field and I drove southward, that the earth might become as rich as it looks from across the river, and that the girls and boys might all stay home fed and safe and happy on their old lands and in their old Church. They have been a long time poor on the margins of the wilderness.

XXVIII

High Tide and Low

1

IT WAS STRANGE IN SUCH COLD to be mosquito-bitten, but even in summer the breezes from the Bay of Fundy were chilling in the street by the mess hall in Quoddy Village; and the mosquitoes seemed to be the more voracious for warm blood in the cold air. Young Richard P. Dawson of Providence did not seem to mind the cold. He was Mayor of Quoddy Village, where the National Youth Administration was giving vocational training and work experience to the young of New England in the abandoned village built to house the workers on the Passamaquoddy tidal power project. Patrick Joyce of Boston, director of public relations in the boys' government, shivered. I shivered with him and slapped where a mosquito had attached itself to the back of my hand.

Up the street there was a tentative, preliminary note of music. The Fourth Work Experience Group at the Quoddy Regional Project was at the end of its time and training. Its 285 graduating members had been at Quoddy in interesting time. During their stay the unionized staff had risen in organized protest which approximated revolt, the boys themselves had struck in sympathy. Afterwards the director had been removed, and the union in effect upheld. Now under the new director, young Maine schoolteacher Harry Gilson, who had been vice president of the union, the group was having its commencement and farewell. The boys were going back with some training and more hope to look again for jobs. The girls of Washington County by busloads were coming in to tell them, while Waddy Akins' orchestra roared its rhythms, some tenderness maybe of good-bye. But on the dance floor there were more signs of hotfoot than farewell.

Mayor Dawson smiled. He seemed more like a collegiate young man of the world than a youth ("the youth" is a dreadful uplifter's phrase for the young) rescued for training from a New England family in difficulty. He spoke with slightly amused but also entirely serious sympathy, from which his own fortunes seemed detached, about the sadness of the evening. Some of the big boys from slums of the cities had wept. It was not unmanly; many of them, he said, were leaving the only decent living they had ever had. Despite the government's training they were not going to find it easy back at home. With less sentiment he spoke about the girls.

"These girls are different from any I ever saw," he said. (I think he was going to marry one.) "If a man goes with a girl once, he is expected to keep on going with her and her alone. It's funny, but that's the way it is."

Keith Field and I had come down the long empty stretches of U.S. Route 1 from the potato country by Houlton and Amity and wide Grand Lake to the most eastern American emptiness and poverty in Washington County. Fewer people live in it now than there were when the Maine boys came back to it from the Civil War. Lumbering has lagged. Farmers have not gotten rich, and fishermen have suffered like farmers. The blueberries have the acid soil they need. The long road up from the populous East is long enough for the tourists by the time they reach Ellsworth and the turn-off to Mount Desert Island. Beyond are poor people on a poor land unless they be the sardine-packing Peacocks or the Roosevelts who began to come for the summers a long time ago to Canadian Campobello Island. Long ago there was a boy among them who used to come across the bay to sit on a nail keg in Eastport while the fishermen talked about the tides. That was before Dexter Cooper, the engineer, made the plans to harness the power in the twenty-six foot rise and drop of the big tides. Later, of course, the boy became President of the United States. Passamaquoddy became big argument. The powerful power companies in a New England free of all such public power projects fought it. The New England Council opposed it. Even the President himself at last seemed to lose interest in it. Now the tides are gnawing at dams that were to restrain them, and back of bankrupt Eastport they still hope desperately, sometimes angrily, in the President's name. He knows, they say, as the boy on the nail keg both the need and the power. Somehow, they believe, he will find a way, despite the power companies and the politicians, who are sometimes the same—a way to run the blood of power across the blueberry plains to stir new living in a stagnant land, to make living cheaper and better in the whole New England around it. (And most Maine politicians, while steadily voting the Republican policies on everything else, publicly agree with Washington County about Passamaquoddy.)

We came into Quoddy Village at both an excellent and an unfortunate time. It was commencement day (if that term applies to the completion of the term of an experience group). As graduates, the boys (eighteen to twenty-five years old) were at dramatic point in their lives. The staff was busy discharging them with encouragement. Nevertheless we got as guide about the village gay, tough-talking Tom Foley, chief of both the village police and the fire department. Foley, who was a retired battalion chief of the New York City Fire Department, had been brought up by the Army to guard against fire the deliberately cheap construction village which the engineers built to house workers for five years. He remained when the NYA in 1937 inherited the quarters after the construction army had disappeared.

In his car he showed us about the temporary town which looked in 1939 as if it would last a good many more years than the engineers planned it to last. The boys on the project keep it in condition. But the $2,172,000 village—the engineers thought they were going to spend $40,000,000 on the project—does not compare in appearance with Norris, Tennessee, which TVA built as a permanent town when it began the construction of Norris Dam on the Clinch (Norris cost $3,800,000).

Foley drove us about its streets. He pointed across the bay, where the engineers had so briefly worked on the project which it was promised would generate more electricity than the combined capacity of all existing power stations in the state, and so would provide cheap power to farms throughout Maine and to industries, which so might be encouraged to come into the region. The power from the tides, it was promised, too, would make possible the development of the bauxite clays about the bay to produce aluminum. Foley drove us on, by mess hall and dormitory and the cottages of the staff. There was a big model of the complete tidal power project, and the boys at Quoddy were building an even better one. As we passed the dormitory a huge Negro shouted, "Hey, Chief!" and we stopped for Foley to write his autograph in the big boy's book. Foley told us about the boys. He likes to think of himself as their philosopher, guide, friend, and protector.

"Why, hell," he said, "they tried to blame everything around here on our boys! Every time anything wrong happened they blame it on 'em. I went down and told 'em to cut it out. Why, we never had a bit of scandal left behind. That's more than you can say for a lot of college towns."

In passing, he pointed out one of the triangular fire alarms with the hammer beside it for banging it. He stopped in front of the administration building, talking more about the boys. He liked them, and they were a good-looking lot. All their work in the shops was over. They were ready to go out and demonstrate to themselves the value of the vocational training and guidance the government had given them in this project which began as an experiment, but from which similar youth training centers in other regions have been copied. He did not mention the fact, however, that about a month before the whole project had almost blown up when the irritation between Leon R. Crowell, the director of the project who had been brought there from the direction of the Pickwick Dam Training Section of the TVA and the local union of United Federal Workers of America (C.I.O.), headed by Anthony Zill, had come to a head which Washington had to lance. Foley had been a member of the union's grievance committee.

As early as April the union had put a piece in *The Eastport Sentinel* saying that the conditions at Quoddy Village from the standpoint of the employees' welfare and the project's future "were becoming progressively worse." But the final storm did not break until May, when Director Crowell fired Zill on the charge of insubordination because he "flung" union demands on Crowell's desk. There was considerable argument over nice distinctions between "flung" and "put." The union members poured into the administration building in demonstration of protest. The boys on the project struck briefly in sympathy. (There had been another boys' strike in the first group at Quoddy due in part to the fact that one of "the youth" sent up for work experience had already had experience as a labor organizer.) Wires were rushed by both sides to Washington. In the confusion desperate Eastport, which had lost the millions of Quoddy, got the report that the Work Experience Project was going to be closed, also.

So the protesting politicians joined the clamor. Compromises failed. Telephone messages were misunderstood. In the end—whatever Washington may call it—the Washington decision was an almost complete decision for the union. Crowell was pulled into Washington but was associated with the NYA in 1940. One of his associates and supporters left the service. Another was sent to duty on a similar project in far-off South Charleston. Harry Gilson, vice president of the union, was made director of the project in Crowell's place. (Since he got elevated out of it, there are grapevine reports that he has had some troubles with the union himself.) Later the union got from Washington a substantial part of all its demands about cheaper medical care for the staff, promotions, and the like.

Going over the story I remembered a phrase a Federal forester had used in New Hampshire, "We're a long way from the wigwam up here." They were a long way, also, at Quoddy. Crowell, who must have been an able organizer and who had an excellent record at Pickwick, seems not to have been a very tactful man. But Zill, the statistician, and some of his colleagues in the union must not have been very easy to bear. Zill was already a member of the union when he was sent up from Washington, where he had been connected, as a statistician, with WPA. Crowell got the idea, perhaps from the union's public statements in *The Eastport Sentinel* about the situation at Quoddy getting progressively worse, that the union was formed to "get" him. Such a purpose was passionately denied. Whether the union meant to badger him or not, he was badgered. He and the young big Zill became fire and powder to each other. The whole situation to a stranger seems angry and sad.

After all Crowell was a hired man, too. Some of the things

the union did not like were done by Congress and, under
Congress and the Comptroller General of the United States,
by the Administration in Washington. Whatever may have
been the merits or the demerits of the May-time crack-up at
Quoddy, Crowell seems to have had a genius at the last for
separating himself from sympathy. Once he threatened to
throw off the place the local newspaper correspondent who
furnished all the news about Quoddy to the conservative Republican newspapers of Maine. He made some comments
which were not relished locally about the efficiency of Eastport WPA workers and the action of Eastport in requiring
Quoddy children to pay tuition in the Eastport schools. He
was strict in his discipline with the boys—too strict, they
thought. And near the end, by a miracle of mischance, he
grew a mustache which, almost hair for hair, was a replica
of Hitler's. Placards appeared about the dormitories which
caricatured him as *der Führer*. When Zill "flung" or "put"
the union demands on his desk that day in May, Quoddy
Regional Project had as much morale under discipline as in
general attends the prelude to a mutiny.

But peace reigned when we rode about it not many weeks
later. The group had completed its training without hitch
if with some excitement. Our guide, Chief Foley, had to go
and get ready for the farewell exercises. So we got into our
car and followed him toward Eastport until he turned off to
go to his house upon a beautiful eminence which long ago
the local people learned to call Snob Hill. There is nothing
temporary about the houses on that hill; the Army engineers
built the colonial houses, which sit upon it high and proud,
for the Army engineers. Altogether, I was told, the nine
houses on that hill with land and drives and water and sewerage cost around $250,000. They do not look worth it, even
if they do look the residences of a rich city suburb set off
from a little sad town in Maine.

2

Eastport is sad. Sardine canning is not what it used to be there. Before Passamaquoddy was begun with an original allotment of $10,000,000, the population of Eastport had been falling steadily at every census since 1900. In the most eastern city of the United States (Lubec is farther east, but it's a town), boys found it harder to get a job at home long before the Passamaquoddy project of the WPA. Then suddenly the old dying town jerked to life with that allotment of $10,000,000, and the prospect of more, to harness the tides and electrify the land. The boom was formally inaugurated with a parade, a banquet, and a dance on July 4, 1935. By July 19, Lieutenant Colonel Philip B. Fleming of the U.S.A. said that local landowners were charging $4,000 an acre for land. By August 18, the Passamaquoddy project was employing 1,000 men. By November 23, employment reached its maximum of 5,042. But by January 7, 1936, a general lay-off of labor started, due to lack of funds; $5,000,000 of the original $10,000,000 was taken away, though later two of this second five million was restored. By July 1, just three days less than a year after the parade, the banquet, and the dance, Colonel Fleming issued the gradual but complete shut-down order. Eastport had had a year, and what a year! Old houses got new bathrooms in the hope of new boarders. Old residents got new ideas about values. There was little delay from boom to bust. Eastport quickly had wasted what substance it had had left in 1935 in riotous hoping. In 1939 it still looked like an old woman who had danced all night under the erroneous impression that once more she was young—and was going to be rich and young forever.

They still hear the music of hope. But there is bitterness as well as hope now. I remember talking to R. C. Emery, mayor of the town and editor of *The Eastport Sentinel*. He believed that Passamaquoddy would be completed. But he knew that power company money and power company influence were at work every day in the politics of Maine to prevent the completion of Passamaquoddy, which he also knew promised cheap power and new prosperity for the people of Maine. The day I was in Eastport, his paper carried an editorial comparing those who oppose the Quoddy tidal power development to those who once opposed cast-iron plows, automobiles, and the other items of advancing civilization. Men in Eastport spoke of power lobbyists with a bitterness which would make most public power advocates sound like emissaries of the Edison Electric Institute. Republicans said the Republican party in the state was loaded with power's representatives. They talked about a gentleman so much at home in his lobbying at the capital that he wore his bathrobe in the lobby of the politicians' hotel in Augusta.

The faith of Eastport, if angry, was firm. I was lucky enough to get a copy of a special edition of *The Eastport Sentinel* which had been published when Dexter Cooper, the engineer whose plan and dream was Quoddy power, died on Campobello Island in February, 1938. A Minnesota boy, he saw the tides of Quoddy first when he came to Campobello on his honeymoon. The urn of his ashes was buried on the island. (His house there, which cost more than $30,000 in 1925, was advertised for sale for $12,500. "Reason for sale, death of owner.")

We could see Campobello clearly from Eastport, even the roof of the house of the boy who used to come over in the summer to sit on a keg of nails in the store and listen to the talk of the fishermen. Eastport had not grown richer since. There was a financial agent in charge of the town's finances, put in by the state of Maine. A lot of the people were as poor as the town they lived in. Maybe, as some said, WPA was the biggest industry there. Nevertheless men still hoped that the boy from the red house on Campobello would yet make power surge from the tides in the terms of Cooper's plan. Claims that steam plants could make power cheaper than the tides left them angry and cold.

3

Certainly there is power in those tides. They lift and drop boats like elevators. I remember the tie lines on Carroll Peacock's Chris Craft cruiser at the wharf of the Peacock sardine packing plant in Lubec which permitted it to rise and fall with the more than twenty-foot tides. Wharfs that are flush with the water at one hour may be green, scummy walls above it at another. On the same powerful tides Lubec has not suffered as Eastport has. Its population in 1930 had fallen from the past. But more owners of sardine packing plants now live there than in Eastport. Furthermore though it is only two and a half to three miles by water from Eastport, Lubec is forty-two miles off by land. That cushioned it from the swift destructive Quoddy boom. There are rich men in it. A man who ought to know told me about a citizen enriched by sardines who went down to Boston to buy his clothes from Edward L. Dunn, the most expensive tailor in New England, and then wore the suits in Washington County without either collar or tie. There are poor people there, too. Indeed, there is a lane of diminutive scabrous-looking houses running up from the water to the highroad which is as poor as anything I saw in New England. The rough lane itself looked as if it would be a watercourse when it rained. In a window was a tiny but proudly placed American flag.

Carroll Peacock, slim, dark-jowled, took us in his cruiser from the wharf plant of R. J. Peacock Canning Company (the biggest packers of the little herring) out on the waters of the bay. Big as the output of his company is, his plant in

Lubec (Peacock also packs in Portland) is an unimpressive pair of buildings running out on piers to which the sardine boats come; but his fleet of boats is equipped with the best modern ship-to-ship and ship-to-shore radio telephones (you can phone any one of them from where you are now for the phone tolls to Boston and something like $3 more). For our benefit he talked to one of his captains. From somewhere out there the boat captain called him "Carroll." They spoke about another boat which did not answer its call. The captain had heard him, but he was "dreadful faint." They thought he was close to the docks in a town. We signed off and headed across the narrow sound between Lubec and Campobello Island.

There were flocks of gulls on the badly washed earth-filled dam which the engineers had built between Treat's and Rice's islands. Originally this dam had been wide enough for three trucks to pass upon its top. Not one could cross it now. The fill gapes from the landing pier beside it. There was only a succession of big teeth between the gaps which the tremendous tides had made. Other dams, over which railroads run, are faced with granite and so remain intact. Peacock swung out into the sound again and then closer in to the shore. We could see clearly the two Roosevelt houses beside their green water tower and windmill. Mrs. James Roosevelt's house was red with a gray roof. The house of her son, the President, had a flattish roof with flat-topped gable windows in it. Farther up the shore in a white house near Welchpool, Dexter Cooper had lived and planned.

Nearer at hand Peacock, the sardine man, explained the weir on the shore before the Roosevelt houses. Weirs are made of fences running from the shore out into the bay with the entrance to the trap the only place where the moving herring seem to be able to pass. So they go into the trap. "Putting the drop down" is closing the weir. Then men go in with seines and get the herring, which are soon on the way into the cans. A big reel of a seine was on a float near the weir.

From the water Lubec is a hill town which rises from its shore in a round slope to the spire of the Congregational Church which has been a landmark for mariners for a hundred years, Peacock said. "The Saxby gale blew a higher spire down."

We went through the canning plant with its big pots and long tables. There was a smell of oil and fish, but the idle plant was waiting in cleanliness. Indeed, the whole town of Lubec waits for the whistle to blow when the sardine boats come alongside the dock. When it does blow, at any hour of the day, women put down their brooms and their dishes and their babies, and run for the sardine plant to clip or oil or pack sardines, never knowing how long their labors may continue, nor when they will return home. All that depends upon the quantity of the fish which the boats have brought to the pier. The fingers of the women fly, and no higher wage would displace them with men. "Packed like sardines" is a packing by women; bigger-handed men would take vastly more time to get the herring into the cans. But the women and the men in Lubec are affected by the movement of plants to Portland. A sardine packer told me freight rates pulled the plants down the coast. All Maine sardines were sold at a price plus the Portland rate of freight, which means that the Eastport and Lubec packers must absorb the difference between the freight rate from Portland to destination and the rate from Eastport to the same destination. The railroads decline to take the blame.

"The industry from Portland to Eastport along the Maine coast," a railroad executive told me, "is controlled by not over a dozen individuals, and it is unfortunate that they cannot seem to be able to compromise their commercial difficulties and compete on a level that would enable all of them to make money. There are only four packers in Portland, and three of them have plants in the Eastport-Lubec district, so that the terms of sale are practically in their own hands. It seems, therefore, that they might change the base price and eliminate the differential between Portland and Eastport without the railroad entering into the picture, if they so desired and could agree among themselves."

Certainly as they go south they come nearer the point at Lewiston-Auburn where the C.I.O. made its fight in Maine. As fish packers look up wistfully from Massachusetts the labor situation from the employers' point of view seems almost idyllic in Washington County. As they move south the packers may move to new labor problems, but the market is south, too, in the South. This does not mean that Southern states may take the sardine industry away from Maine. It is easier to lure manufacturers and bankers than the schools of herring from the North. It does mean that Maine sardines are a food product for poor people which must be sold cheaply. In the sardine industry the Southern Negro and Southern cotton are as important as the little fish and nimble-fingered women of the state of Maine.

Maine canneries use cottonseed oil in packing the fish, which not only is cheaper but, because it has a lower free fatty acid content, keeps longer than olive oil. But Scandinavia and Italy together got a big head start in shaping the taste of the world. So American sardines have found their biggest market among the Negroes of the South. It is a cheap market, poorer than it ought to be, as the South knows and as Maine should begin to understand. There may be a close connection between a slum street in Lubec and a cabin in the cotton. And even this American market has its disturbing lapses. They tell a story in Maine that the sardine packers were alarmed to action by the fact that there was a big drop in sardine consumption coincident with the beginning of national prohibition in the United States. The packers got one of Maine's first citizens to study that decline in order to recommend procedures to offset it. He did. He collected masses of material on the drop and the cause. Then he made his report: "Pack a sardine that a sober man will eat."

That is slander. But it is the mildest of the tall tales which they tell in Washington County about the industry in the old piratical days before pure-food laws made the industry the cleaner, more careful one it is today.

4

From Eastport we drove back toward Quoddy Village and the Indian reservation on Pleasant Point beyond. On the way we picked up two local boys, Lester Musslo and Morris Taylor. They were on their way with groceries to the camp of Musslo's grandfather, Grant Wilson, on East Bay near Pembroke. The grandfather was a fisherman. Last year, the boy said, there had been few fish in the weirs, and this year the fish were being rejected by the buyers.

"It's awful poor business," he said.

I asked them about the Quoddy boys.

"They're pretty tough guys," young Taylor said. "Some of them have been in reform schools and places like that."

"Only the girls like them," said Musslo, "and girls like any strangers."

Certainly the girls seemed to like the Quoddy boys as much as the local boys disliked them. We saw that clearly later at the crowded dance. But before we went back to Quoddy Village we circled the Indian reservation. The Indians looked very white. There were no copper warriors to be seen, but some slight, pale young men were pitching horseshoes. There were two Indian basket stores and a

Catholic church. Women were sitting at the doors of the little gray wooden houses on the bay shore. There was an old Indian woman with a handkerchief around her head. But there were young women, some of them pretty and none of them brown squaws. One was nursing a child.

Back on the highroad again we saw a little man we had seen first at Quoddy Village. He had been there asking questions as we had been. He looked like a Jap, but he said he was from Honolulu, the most western American city, and he had been in Eastport, the most eastern American city. It was a circumstance which pleased him. The very blonde woman with him said she was from Canada. When we passed them again on the road he was taking a photograph of the blonde woman and two middle-aged women who somehow looked like the tradition of missionary Christianity in Massachusetts. As a group they looked a little odd by the side of the road in Maine.

At Quoddy in the mess hall the boys at banquet were being told good-bye. Director Harry Gilson was telling them that the interest of the project would continue in "each and every one of you." While he talked the juveniles of the village crowded like merry young scavengers about the kitchen door and received the spare drumsticks and surplus wings. There was a long applause after Gilson finished, and then out they poured. They were, I thought, a good-looking company from the huge Negro, whose blow in a recent boxing match had sent a young Italian by airplane to a brain surgeon, to the grinning young Irishman still on crutches after an operation in the village hospital for ingrowing toenails. They were dressed in their best. Some in flannels which would have been in good taste down the long coast in Bar Harbor, more in carefully pressed suits which had been pressed many times before. I thought, looking at them, that they were like—though a little older—the boys of a high-school graduating class in any not too fortunate American community.

It was difficult to believe, looking at them, that in overwhelming proportion they came from families on relief, and that they had been brought to Quoddy because they needed the help of Quoddy to find even a minimum of security in the New England in which they lived. Fortunately for me, Anthony Zill, the president of the union, had made a study of these boys in his official capacity as supervisor of testing and statistics. Zill may have been a troublemaker for Crowell, but as a statistical sociologist he assembled with care and skill the facts about the boys who struck when he was fired, though that last item did not get into his statistics.

The boys were, as might be expected, from the poor of New England—about half of them of foreign parentage, more than half of them Catholic, most of them from homes which were equipped with such conveniences as light and water and sewerage, but in which the father did not have a job or worked for the WPA. Most of them had had some jobs before they came to Quoddy, but few of them had found anything approximating steady employment. Most of them had been suffering from undernourishment, Zill said, before they came, but their chief physical defects were in teeth and tonsils and a need for circumcision (less than one per cent of them were Jews). The average was a young man of twenty, weighing 143 pounds and standing five feet seven by the doctor's measuring rod.

One thing in particular worried Zill:

"Quoddy workers were asked what is wrong with the world. The question was intentionally made broad enough to allow for all possible interpretations, and so that replies would not be directed. Despite the fact that something was wrong and evidence testifying to that fact abounded about them 25.7 per cent replied nothing, 13.1 said they didn't know, while

22.3 per cent omitted answering this important question. There is reason to believe that a great majority of this last group felt that nothing was wrong with the world. Thus 51.1 per cent of the workers failed to show any social and economic awareness at all. Those that did have an answer showed a significant absence of radical opinions and were more or less stereotyped in their responses with a tendency to emphasis on human weakness. . . . The fact that approximately 50 per cent of the workers who have reached maturity in most respects fail to recognize that anything is wrong is definitely disturbing."

That even the poor young felt that all was right with the world did not surprise me. Even when bad, the world is pleasant to the young. What disturbed me most was the revelation that, by Southern standards at least (probably by national standards in what has been called "a nation of fourth graders"), the boys who were deemed to need special assistance from the government in finding a place in Mr. Zill's bad world had had considerable educational opportunity. Nearly half of the boys had completed high school. The average for the whole group was completion of the junior year in high school. Furthermore 94.4 per cent of the communities from which they came had public libraries, and two-thirds of the boys claimed the possession and use of library cards. The average Quoddy boy had read 2.6 books in the month before he came to the project, and among these Yankees by far the most read book was *Gone with the Wind*.

Such schooling and reading among these boys drawn largely from the population on relief may not compare with the progress by Exeter and Andover and Groton through Harvard and Yale. Still it seemed to me a considerable amount of formal education and educational opportunity. The conjunction of education and difficulty disturbed me. We have put so much faith and hope in formal education in the South where we too much lack it that evidence of its failure in practical terms in New England where it has been provided longest was confusing to a Southerner. I expect it should also be basis for consideration in the North.

These were the boys who met the girls who began coming in the early dark by the busload from the surrounding towns of Washington County for the dance. I do not know so much about the girls. Washington County has provided no Anthony Zill to count their characteristics. It is a pity, maybe. As they stepped from the busses and skipped across the space to the recreation hall they were pink and white, fluffy and dark-haired and lively and golden-haired, and all very young. Nothing seemed wrong with their world. But there was an untabulated world behind them. A good many of their fathers, also, were on WPA, the boys told me. One young male cynic from the city declared that the people around Eastport were never too poor to go to carnivals.

Some of their mothers came with the girls in the busses. They were sensible-seeming women. Certainly they did not seem to come out of poverty, nor riches. They wore the vague look of concern which mothers wear everywhere at dances. It seemed to me, despite some whispering that I heard about a pint in the men's room, that the party was at least as decorous as a senior prom at a New England college that early summer. I am afraid that simile is not precise enough unless college proms have advanced in decorum since I was attending them some time ago. But there was nothing solemn about the occasion. The music wailed and patted its feet. The girls moved slim shoulders. They were very pretty in the clothes, cut from the same models, machine-stitched in the same factories, that the girls like them were wearing then in Keokuk and Goldsboro and New Bedford. They moved to the same music with the same eagerness.

I thought as I watched that maybe the Roosevelt boy who

used to come over from Campobello and sit on the nail keg in Eastport had brought power into Washington County, though it might not be tidal but biological. I am not sure now. The statistics do not show that the local boys have gone out into the world and left the local girls behind to a choice between New England spinsterhood and catching a boy at Quoddy. Of course, almost all statistics are out of date before they are in hand. But the last counting in Washington County before I was there showed more single males over fifteen years of age than single females of the same age. In Eastport there had been more unattached girls than unattached boys, but not in a proportion to make any multitude of old maids.

Whether the best boys departed and the best girls were left behind is something that does not get into the statistics. It is instead only the basis for an argument as old as the movement from Europe to this country and from the old East to the opening West. There is a logic to support the view that the strong and independent have always dared and filled the new lands and left the difficult old ones. Since American pride is based upon that thesis, it has generally been accepted in America. But the wastrel and the irresponsible move also. The man who pioneers the new land may be running away from the problem of the old one. In so big an argument certainly a stranger would not dare (a native might hesitate) to say whether the fall of population in Washington County had come from the loss of its best or the welcome departure of the worst of its young. Probably there has been some of both. In some degree at any rate the President through the NYA played Cupid when he sent the boys in to train their human powers in the vacant village from which the tidal power-makers had departed. Love not only laughs at locksmiths; it laughs even at a world in which there are not enough jobs for the young.

Waddy Akins' music blared above the feet of the boys and girls. The paper streamers stirred above their heads. The mothers watched. The attendants were busy at the soft-drink stand. I noticed that the big Negro watched but did not dance. Tomorrow the boys would be on their way back to Boston, back to Providence and Fall River and Vermont. Not all of them by any means had jobs waiting for them. Nobody knew what would happen to them with their little more experience and skill. Nobody knew then with any certainty what had happened to the boys of the three earlier groups which had come to Quoddy, stayed for six months of intensive vocational training in a variety of trades and occupations, and then gone back into the human maze of New England. But if there had been some masculine weeping over the return to difficulty before the banquet, it was quieted now.

We went out from the music into the darkness and rode away. The music was gone. Once on the road, I thought I smelled the fires with which fish are smoked. A few days before, I knew, Ed Ramsdell's smokehouse and stringing shed over in North Lubec had burned when the smoke fires ignited the walls. We stopped in Pembroke for gas, and then went on.

"Where's West Pembroke?"

"We're in it."

The village was only darkness. I had read about it in Editor Emery's paper. Harry Ashby of Meddybemps had been found guilty of coming down there and poisoning six of Theodore Jones' cows. *The Eastport Sentinel* had reported: "The trial, one of the most sensational in its implications in the recent history of this county, was based on the familiar 'triangle' situation, and in its course, a long series of depredations, ranging from the beating of a dog to death and the burning of a whole stand of farm buildings, was

326

shown to have occurred during the four years leading up to the crime for which the respondent was being tried."

Such things, I knew, happened in the darkness in dark villages and the darker insides of skulls everywhere. But fortunately, also, everywhere they are rare. On the January night when Harry Ashby slipped down to poison the cows other men were sleeping in good conscience after hard work in the deep snow. Now in the summer behind us the young poor of New England danced upon the most decorous occasion with the girls of Washington County. The girls knew they were pretty, and only 50 per cent of the boys (fewer than that, that night, I think) thought anything was wrong with the world. We drew up beside a big elm before the door of Herb Allan's fishing camp in Dennysville. In the dark, men were gathered about a car where they had been listening to the report of a prize fight on a radio. On the ground beside them a long salmon lay white in the black grass.

XXIX

Portrait of a Fisherman

HERB ALLAN GOT OUT OF THE CAR to welcome us. He is a big man, masculine and good-humored. Until his successor had been elected the night before at the meeting in the Red Men's Hall, he had been president of the Dennys River Salmon Club. His father before him had kept an inn there close to the famous salmon pool which swarms with the hard-fighting fish. Keith Field asked who had caught the beauty lying luminous in the grass, and a young man from New York with black fishing whiskers growing out of a white city skin claimed it. He was modest about its size, but when Field offered to photograph it he said that he had brought color photography equipment along and was going to take its picture himself in the morning. Herb Allan stowed the fish away in the sawdust around the ice in the basement of the barn across the road. Then he took us up to our big room with a pair of double beds in it. We asked him if he would join us in a drink.

"I never refused but once," he said, "and that time I didn't hear the invitation."

The drink he poured himself was diminutive, but he drank it slowly, talking frankly and heartily about the fishing, the luck the fishermen had been having. The fish on the lawn had not been an especially big one, he declared. A man from Massachusetts, I think he said, had caught a salmon the day before which was close to twenty pounds. One of his other guests stopped by the door, and we asked him in. He was a small nervous man. He poured himself a drink, and I noticed that on the hand that held his glass the nails had been bitten close to the quick. We sat on the edge of the big beds, and he talked softly and with almost pleading sensitiveness about fishing and dogs and game and tackle.

"A man never has but one real dog in a lifetime," he said. "Does he now? Does he?" He shook his head. "Only one. Mine was a Llewellyn setter and she died two years ago. I'll never have another like her."

He told us about her. She must have been a wonderful dog. Her remembering owner was a business man down in Massachusetts and a successful one, I gathered; but on the edge of the big bed he seemed a sad man, too. He had come a long way from home for fishing, and he was lonely. What he liked to do, he said, was to get away on a swift stream or watch the dogs in the brush. He talked in sad condemnation about what the New Deal was doing to business. He felt that things were being done that a sportsman could not approve. The politicians did not please him. Some other aspects of man in his world had hurt him: He had been a young lieutenant in the Navy in 1917–18 and he remembered standing by while an oil tanker, that had been torpedoed, burned. The water all around her was flaming oil. Men in it died before they could swim. Even the men in the lifeboats were consumed. Standing by, he said, they could not get to any of them; and he could not get away from the memory of them. (His memory reminded me of a story I had heard in Eastport about hard-up and lawbreaking fishermen who poured kerosene on the water, lit it, and scooped up by the netful the little herring lured to the flame.)

"I love nature," said the sad small man. "I know where there's a nest of plover near where I live. There aren't so

329

many of them left. And I wouldnt' tell anybody in the world where it is."

"How much do you fish?"

"Not much," he said, "—two or three times a year; but I work on my tackle all the time."

"I'd like to see some of it," Field said.

Our guest went out and brought some of it back. He had about $2,000 worth, Field estimated. There were calfskin books of hand-tied flies which he got from A. Carter & Company of London (they were the best, he thought, in the world). He showed us a Leonard rod which William Mills of New York had made for him—a light lithe thing which presented suppleness to the salmon's strength. They might use a ton of bamboo in assembling the one rod. I gathered that the rod had been made for his hand as a suit of clothes might be made for a man. I also learned that to the sensitive hand no two rods are ever exactly alike. He flexed the rod which he loved with his thin fingers.

"William Mills," he said, "doesn't load a rod up with a lot of hardware."

I examined his flies. Ignorant as I am of such things, they looked like jewels against the leather. They represented not only art but understanding. Men had tied them in knowledge of the salmon's hunger and the salmon's eye. They made sport in the pool but they made beauty merely sitting in the box. The fisherman spoke of them lovingly. He laughed.

"When my boy was born," he said, "the doctor came out and told me that he had arrived with a rod in one hand and a gun in the other."

We laughed with him.

"When are you going fishing?" Field asked.

"Four o'clock."

"What about going with you?"

"Fine! I've got plenty of equipment. I've got another rod

almost as good as this one for you. I've got plenty of stuff. That will be fine. My guide's coming at four."

"How about you?" he asked me.

"Not at four," I said. "I'm an old man. I'll sleep."

After we had gone to bed he came in to report to Field that he had his line in soak or something like that. It seemed to me that he came in later to make another report about it. But when I woke at eight in the morning Field was still asleep in his bed. We went down to a bountiful Down East breakfast. Outside, the fisherman's guide was sitting whittling under the elm tree where he had been waiting since four. Upstairs our fisherman was sleeping soundly among his tackle. The salmon that day were safe from his beautiful flies.

XXX

Up to Boston

BEYOND A BRUSH-GROWN CEMETERY and the blueberry barrens, I remember, we came suddenly into a street where a dowager was descending with the aid of a liveried chauffeur from a limousine. There was a station wagon parked beyond it. All the shops suddenly looked like suburbia. The land had changed. We had crossed more than a county line. We had, indeed, in Ellsworth come to that coast upon which the rich summer squatters cool themselves, and out of those outposts where only Maine people live. At Ellsworth, the woman's clubs of Washington County were saying that summer, the highway commission had seemed to contrive to make it appear that road development in Maine comes to an end. At that point, they said, the main road seemed to run southward to Mount Desert Island and not eastward to Lubec and Eastport, Machias and Quoddy. Something does happen there. West of Bar Harbor, certainly west of the Penobscot, the coast thickens with the houses of capitalists and ambassadors, writers and scientists, and other lesser folk with the same personal problem of heat and happiness. Before them all Maine runs out in fingers into the sea blue enough for anybody and cold enough for anybody who wants to turn blue.

But boys and girls were swimming in those waters; they would have to be, I thought, a hardy race for that. On those shores in the summertime most of them were the far extreme

332

from the boys and girls in Eastport and Quoddy. The boys
had not come up to Maine for any formal productive experience. Those who came and swam and fished and sailed were
vacationing from the elaborate training which the well-to-do
in New England have long provided for their young. And the
young New Englander out of Exeter and Andover, Yale and
Harvard is often beautiful to behold. I never saw the boys
who went to China in the clipper ships. I have no knowledge
of the appearance of the young Yankees who began to build
the mills. But as a matter of simple masculine aesthetics I
doubt that they were any better to behold than the young
Yankee breed which still holds the old Yankee money. I do
not know about the rest. Nobody can count how tough and
shrewd their minds are. They may be better gentlemen than
men. The highway I followed ran out of their summertime
by their schooling, through the industrial towns to Boston.

"Up to Boston," they say, and "down to Maine." A president of the Rotary Club of Boston (there are Rotarians in
the Athens of America) told me confidently that the reversal
of the prepositions came from the old seagoing days. Perhaps
it does. But New England's Merriam-Webster Dictionary referred to the fact that in England a gentleman from London goes down to Scotland. On the American shore there
seemed to be some confusion as to where "Down East" begins. Bostonians go down to Gloucester. But Down Easters
are Maine men, and Maine men begin at Kittery. The true
Down Easter may live farther up ("down") the Maine shore.
There is at least a legend that long ago big Barney Beal of
Columbia Falls had to beat up fifteen men in a Portland
saloon who undertook to deride a Down Easter. His fists may
have spread the allegiance down ("up") the shore.

Certainly something less pleasant has spread north toward
Down East. I drove alone out of Maine through the farther
thickening beyond Portland where the roadside stands, which

had been grim in the spring, were garish in the summer. I remember that I thought that in comparatively richer York County the grasping for the traveler's nickels was a sadder spectacle than the difficulties of the Catholic Acadians in Aroostook or the old stagnation in Washington County. There was some sense of faith and dignity along the poorest roads in the north and Down East but in the south in York the roadsides grimaced seeking trade. Behind them are the clean shores and the green woods—they can be scarcely seen. Maine at its beginning puts its worst foot foremost in brazen smearing of a magnificent road.

(I knew that the road hid a good land and a lovely shore. I had spent a week end at York Harbor after the summer meeting of the New England Council there. I remember standing on a high rocky promontory with Dudley Harmon and watching two sailboats come slowly and uncertainly out of a cove into the wind. Harmon, long, lean nervous Yankee who carries his cigarettes in tin boxes of fifty, would as the active executive of the New England Council have no difficulty in making anybody think all New England is perfect on that shore. Fortunately for New England, however, he is such a regionalist as knows that his region contains not only fair shore but ugly road, too. He knows its problems as well as its pleasantness. And I think the hope of New England—as also the hope of long-term usefulness of the Council, which is a great deal more than a chamber of commerce of New England—lies in such concerned knowing by such men.)

It is like escape to turn inland from the great gut of U.S. Route 1 into New Hampshire beyond Portsmouth by the market gardens and the old towns. It took time and a tradition and not merely a rich man's money to make the old school in the old town of Exeter. The boys were gone that day, but I had seen them when I came before from Boston with Herbert Elliston, financial editor of *The Christian Sci-*

ence Monitor, to see his student son, Steve. From Steve, who was thirteen that year, and from Dr. Lewis Perry, the principal who was wearing a red vest with his Tuxedo as a member of the Tavern Club in Boston when I met him, and from Myron Richards Williams, A.B., director of studies in the school, I learned a little about it. To me as an American with no pretensions to pedagogy (indeed, with a tendency to prejudice against professional pedagogues), the old school, now so richly furnished, made sound sense. They speak much of democracy at Exeter. It is there, but it ought to be understood. In the first place it is a democracy of young intellectual aristocrats. Though professors are human and names are potent everywhere, Exeter is not concerned as some other New England schools are with the place and position of parents. It has fourteen to seventeen hundred applications for three hundred places. It can choose, and it does, from the best. Furthermore, though every student gets from endowed Exeter an education which costs more than he pays, even the self-help students ("holders of foundation grants") must have a minimum of $500 with which to pay for their schooling. The "flat rate" is $1,050 per year. Obviously that eliminates the actually poor, though even those who pay all pay less than they would in no better but more pretentious schools.

In general, Exeter, under the direction of five well-to-do gentlemen trustees, who include a member of the House of Morgan and the chairman of the First National Bank of Boston, maintains a disciplined intellectual democracy of the upper middle class. (As I count, that is as high as our classes go in America.) Under the gift of Edward S. Harkness, the boys in classes limited to about twelve to a teacher (well educated, well paid teacher) get close and intimate instruction. Under those teachers and outside those classrooms the boys have to work, and hard. No pets are pampered intellectually. And discipline: "There are no rules at Exeter until they are broken." ... "Liberty tempered by expulsion." But the boys get the idea.

"They don't tell you not to do anything, they advise you not to."

The boys understood, however. Maybe they understood too well for their own comfort. Perhaps, as the school suggests, "the rigors of the law of elimination are frequently exaggerated by schoolboy fancy; for it is one of the most natural things in the world to enhance the glory of mere survival by painting it as difficult or rare. As a matter of fact, dismissal is a remedy that is applied pretty sparingly." Nevertheless, the system is designed—wisely—to give meaning to survival. Not the boys who might enter but the product which leaves is its concern. Its teaching plan is personal, but its purpose is a part of the creation of an American leadership based upon brains. I hope it works. If it does not, I do not know anything else that will. And I am not sure that it does.

I asked about that. Elliston and I had gone from young Steve's room in Dunbar to the office of the director of studies in Jeremiah Smith Hall. I remember it was a gracious room with Chinese vases on the mantel, a portrait of a lady on the wall. From the top of a bookcase a bust of young Augustus looked down upon us. Mr. Williams was a gray gentleman in gray clothes. He talked at first to Elliston as parent about the fact that young Steve had been proposed as one of the boys to take a special new science course of two years which would necessitate his dropping Latin. The two men sitting there, the New England gentleman teacher and the intellectual British journalist, made an interesting picture. Elliston was listening, pulling at his pipe. Williams explained. Elliston punctuated his listening with, "Yes, quite." He would talk to Steve about it, he said.

Then Williams took me about the school. For the seven hundred carefully selected boys there is a magnificent plant.

Andover's plant may be, as Mr. Williams thought, more impressive to behold, but it would be hard to think of anything lacking to make Exeter better equipped to turn out such boys as it wants to turn out. We went into classrooms and libraries, dining rooms and recreation halls, and by Mr. Williams' own pleasant quarters in one of the dormitories. Outside under the trees I asked him the question that bothered me: "Does Exeter, which does as good a job in America as any other school—do Exeter and Harvard, Exeter and Yale, bring out men of the vigor of those who returned after going from boyhood to China on the clipper ships?"

It was not a new question to him. It is certainly not a question to which there is any certain answer. But the feeling kept plaguing me in New England that the great things in New England had been done by generations with little formal education—by men who had learned in the forecastle and the mill. And that the great troubles had grown in times in which their sons had been formally much better educated than they ever had been. The lawyers and the preachers had always gone through formal schools. Daniel Webster was an Exeter boy. There were others. Senator George H. Moses of New Hampshire himself reported: "I was once asked by a Principal at Phillips Exeter Academy, 'How did you happen to become Minister to Greece?' And I answered, 'Because I came to Phillips Exeter Academy.' And that is true." But it was also true that he had gone as a delegate to the Republican National Convention which nominated Taft, who appointed him.

Vigor was not all, Williams thought. From education a man might get more joy out of his own life, and others might take more pleasure from his company. It was undoubtedly true, I agreed; but it was sad still if tougher other men were able to deprive cultured gentlemen of wealth of their world. (Unfortunately, some of the best educated men of New England have kept their money while their region has lost its mills: there is a new skill in conserving investments which seems to have succeeded the skill in developing new enterprises at home.) We walked back to Jeremiah Smith Hall and to the chairs beneath the bust of Augustus.

Director Williams thumbed through a list of students who had graduated twenty years before in quest of something like the vigor of the young Salem ship captains, the toughness of the Yankees who built the towns of Lawrence and Lowell just below us on the road. I remember that he mentioned John Cowles of Des Moines who was not only a successful newspaper publisher but also producer of the picture magazine *Look*. He had become Exeter trustee. He was from Iowa, and since two-thirds of Exeter's students now come from outside New England perhaps its meaning in terms of New England leadership is restricted. For a long time boys have come from far away. It may be significant that while old Exeter never produced a President, three Presidents (Lincoln, Grant, Cleveland) sent their boys there to school. In general Exeter and all such schools get the second and third generations from greatness. It can train them well by high, stern standards, but a school cannot maintain strength where biology does not.

I drove down the road the little way under the green trees from school to factories. Exeter is not responsible for Haverhill, where town and shoe workers together have had their troubles. It seems, indeed, to be almost in another world. And that may be one of the troubles. Haverhill was already a prospering shoe town when its most famous son, John Greenleaf Whittier, wrote his famous poem in celebration of the barefoot boy. He called shoes, which he had helped to make before he began to make verses, "the prison cells of pride." There was no chamber of commerce to protest then. Furthermore the poem seemed to do no damage; the damage came later when towns in Maine, New Hampshire, and Vermont as well as far away pulled twenty-three shoe plants out of the anciently unionized town in three and a half years.

Nor is Andover which sits farther down the road beside them responsible for the state of Lawrence and Lowell. But in them a stranger has a feeling that cruder forces are operating to fill and empty their mills than are even contemplated in the schools. The graceful buildings at Exeter designed by Ralph Adams Cram, who married a Confederate captain's daughter and gave his heart's loyalty to the Jacobin pretenders to the British throne, belong to a cloistered world beside the grim brick cliffs of the old mills on the Merrimack. But education goes forward in the old mills, too.

I remember that in Lawrence I drove down Essex Street straight toward a huge sign under the clock in the old Everett Mill: "To Let." I went in to find Russell W. Knight, young Irish real estate man who was in charge in the almost cavernous countingrooms of the old mills. He had done a good job filling them up with the new diversity which is as welcome in Lowell and Lawrence as it is in Fall River and New Bedford and Manchester. In his mill I met the Marums, Jews from Germany where the family had been rich from almost as many generations of knitting manufacture as the generations which had followed the building of Lawrence by the New England capitalists in 1848. But the Marums had been dramatically and completely destroyed in Germany. Aryans ran their factories in Germany in that summer before the Aryans went to war. The Marums began again in a space in the big old Everett Mills in Lawrence. They seemed like children. Julius Stern, the brother-in-law and the oldest, who had once been a banker, was the leader, but Claire, thin and brown-haired, who spoke a soft English in a soft voice, and young blond Hans and solid dark Arnold were in the factory when we were there. They had had trouble getting just the machinery they wanted, but they had done well. Knight had rented them more and more space. It was not easy; but they were young, and they worked around their own machines and the people who worked the machines for them. They had been hurt, but they were not afraid. New England remained for them the new world with promise in it. They made a light in Lawrence for me.

I did not hurry. I knew Boston would be there when I got there. So I took the indirect road and went by Salem where the young men had taken their education in the forecastles between the Derby Wharf and Canton. Some of them had come back rich men and captains in their twenties. Some died in the Philippines, and some lived and never got rich at all. They were poor in the midst of a quick riches like that which had built the big houses in Natchez. But there was a McIntire in Salem to guide the competitive display of the Derbys and Crowninshields. Unfortunately he could not guide the wealth-making which followed the wealth from the ships. It spread from the mills in the tawdriness which so often in New England has engulfed the old towns. Beauty almost is a sign of failure. Success is shown where wealth has only spread its slums. Sometimes the crowding lasts beyond the wages. (In Salem the witch-mind may last beyond the witches: It pleased me to learn that when the Puritans and the Catholics together undertook not long ago to raid the birth-control clinics in Massachusetts, with seven clinics to choose from, they picked the one in Salem where the witches were hanged.)

Maybe it is a miracle in ugly Salem, where they have altered the Witch House to house a drugstore, that lovely Chestnut Street remains. In its brief length beneath its old elms, it is perhaps the noblest street in America. I left it to look at the houses on Essex and Federal streets and around green Washington Square. But I came back to its old mellow brick and picket fences and white porticos. It gives you a feeling that America should have proceeded very nobly, very confidently in nobility from those houses under the trees. Perhaps it has. Even if it has not, as some shacks of tar-paper and tin on the road to Boston may indicate, the street is good nevertheless. There was a moment for a few in which there were both the money and the art for great dignity in serenity in this land. Men made it who learned the world from the wharves, the warehouses and the docks. They marched in it, not puzzled. In Chestnut Street the image remains, even if for the young, and the old, the dignity and serenity are not easy to attain.

XXXI

Saltonstall and Salem Street

THE YEAR THAT LEVERETT SALTONSTALL was born in Chestnut Hills with a silver spoon in his mouth, in the mouths of Henry Adams and John L. Sullivan life tasted like ashes. Young Leverett was delivered into the rich and aristocratic household of Richard Middlecott Saltonstall on September 1, 1892. Exactly six days later in New Orleans, James J. Corbett in twenty-one historic rounds took the world's championship away from the big boy from Roxbury. And in the months before and after, Henry Adams, the introspective grandson of President John Quincy Adams, returning from abroad, found that "everywhere was slack water." The American people "were wandering in a wilderness much more sandy than the Hebrews had ever trodden in Sinai." Mr. Adams, who was beyond fifty, learned to ride a bicycle that year and awaited the second election of Mr. Cleveland. The last was an advent "which led to no deeper thought than that of taking up some small notes that happened to be outstanding. He had seen enough of the world to be a coward, and above all he had an uneasy distrust of bankers. Even dead men allow themselves a few narrow prejudices."

The year was important to more people than the baby. Mary Baker Eddy established the First Church of Christ, Scientist, in Boston. Calvin Coolidge was at Amherst. Louis Brandeis was member of the conservative law firm of Warren

& Brandeis. John Greenleaf Whittier died, the last of the flowers of the flowering. A Democrat was Governor of Massachusetts. John Francis Fitzgerald ("Honey Fitz") was a member of the Boston Common Council. Martin M. Lomasney bossed the Irish, and his Irish bossed the city. David I. Walsh was a student at Holy Cross. Charles William Eliot had been for twenty-three years president of Harvard and James Michael Curley had been for just eighteen years on this earth. William Dean Howells, who had moved from Martins Ferry, Ohio, to Louisburg Square, published two novels that year. A year before and for the third time, Mr. T. Jefferson Coolidge, who had his office in Boston as treasurer of the big Amoskeag Mills in Manchester, New Hampshire, called the attention of his stockholders to the trend of the cotton industry southward.

Forty-seven years later I went up from Tremont Street by the corner of the Common to see the baby of those times who had come to the Governorship in ours. There were pigeons eating crumbs about the subway station. People were coming from luncheon in the restaurant on the street level of the Park Street Congregational Church. Up Park Street I passed the door of Houghton Mifflin, which in survival beyond the flowering of New England now publishes a number of good books by Southern writers. There was the show window of the Anti-Vivisection Society with a horrendous display of the cruelties of scientists. I went by the Union Club and across Beacon Street to the Statehouse. With the aid of more than one Irish policeman I found my way to the office of Russell Gerould, who had come from *The Boston Herald* to handle the press relations of the Governor. He was not in his office when I first came, but some of the others of the staff were there.

There was a small dark Irishman who said of his Governor, "This guy makes Abraham Lincoln look like a second rater."

But pretty young Mrs. Marsh recalled the sun on the Common to me when she said, "I think the Governor's a man of mighty poor judgment myself when he could be out riding horses in Dover to be spending his life with all these problems and people."

It is a choice certainly. Without lifting his hand, Leverett Saltonstall would have such an economic security as most men only hope for. Without stirring his brain, he would still be a Saltonstall; and the Saltonstalls are not only aristocrats stemming from the first Massachusetts past—also, according to Charles Francis Adams, of all the ancient New Englanders only the Winthrops and the Saltonstalls were entitled to armorial bearings before they came across. Since Sir Richard Saltonstall came to America with Governor Winthrop on the *Arbella* in 1630, there have been ten of them in a straight line to this Leverett to graduate from Harvard. (One of the Leveretts was Governor of the Massachusetts Bay Colony; the Leveretts were determined Tories in 1776.) But the Saltonstalls had not been, Governor Saltonstall insisted solemnly in the 1938 campaign when he needed poor men's votes, always rich. His grandfather had had to sell his wine cellar to put his son through Harvard. It would seem wonderful if such a metaphor for poverty did not get a laugh from modern Massachusetts. The Governor's wealth came largely from his mother's side of the family. She was a descendant of Peter C. Brooks, who made money as a merchant which was afterwards multiplied in real estate investments in the West, part in Fort Dearborn which became Chicago. Such a background led naturally to the legal-financial career as that unique but not rare institution of the Boston trustee, as it also led to the Porcellian Club at Harvard and the Somerset Club in Boston. It was not enough: Leverett Saltonstall went into politics and joined the Elks.

I saw some of the other aspects of that choice he made after

344

I saw the man himself, tall, slim, long-jawed, in the chaste and pleasant office in the Statehouse which Bulfinch designed. They speak of him as "homely" in Boston. In his campaign for Governor, one of his supporters said that he has "a South Boston face." (South Boston is old Irish ground.) He is not pretty, but he did not seem homely to me. There is a mechanical quality about his expression, but his eyes and his graciousness warm the mask of his face which unwarmed might serve in a pageant about witch-burners. I had the sense that I must remember that not only was the first Puritan Saltonstall a gentleman but also the first American gentleman Saltonstall was a Puritan. I expect the Governor has a conscience as long as his ancestry. But the Puritans were by no means always grim. They made money and rejoiced to have Gilbert Stuart paint their pictures. The Governor did not bend perceptibly as aristocrat, but he seemed a man designed to be painted in oils as the Portrait of a Gentleman. There is high color at his cheeks, new gray across his dark hair. I suppose his shyness is more apparent than real. He is democrat enough to make Irish and Jewish politicians and me like him.

Nevertheless there is a wall behind which he does not hide but stand. He is a Saltonstall, and he does not deny it to be also a politician. He is an Elk, but I can no more imagine him slapping a back than having his back slapped. He is conservative. How should he be anything else? But he is not slick, expansive, sharp-shrewd promoter conservative: he seems the conservative (maybe it is the Boston trustee pattern) who conserves. Such conservatism is generally more careful than imaginative; it may sometimes be more concerned about dividends than about people. His own supporters say Saltonstall is not brilliant. If not sparkling, the brain in his long head seemed studious and sound. Everybody says he is honest (they don't say as much about every man who has held office in

Massachusetts). It is an honesty, I think, which exceeds that of some of his supporters who would call in the lawyers to see how far, legally, honesty has to go. Democrat that I am, I liked this Republican: he seemed to me in a difficult Massachusetts a simple aristocrat with the deepest honesty which is humility. That is much, not only in a gentleman but in a Puritan. I am not sure that it will be enough in Massachusetts now, but the God of the Puritans knows that it will not do any harm.

Names apparently mean much in Massachusetts politics. Blood and money may antagonize, they also appeal. If a candidate's name is not Saltonstall or Lodge, it had better be Walsh or Tobin accompanied by first names derived from the saints. It took Irishmen and Italians as well as Yankees to elect Saltonstall; but in a real sense, when he was elected, not himself alone but also his class regained both possession of power and responsibility for the problem. In the Governor's office the Irish Democrats, James Michael Curley and Charles Francis Hurley, might have been guilty of waste and worse; but beyond the Governor's office the Yankees who have always controlled finance and industry had not been entirely successful in the same years. Now again the Yankee ruled the Statehouse as well as the banks and the mills. But he was under no illusion about the pleasantness of power:

More than 800,000 persons in Massachusetts then, or 19 per cent of the population, were receiving public aid.

At least 10 per cent of the population, Governor Saltonstall found, would in all likelihood have to continue receiving aid indefinitely (67 per cent of all cases receiving aid from local welfare boards were unemployable). The cost in 1938 to the state and the localities was $57,000,000 for relief outside of institutions. Of this, even the economical Republican aristocrat believed, $40,000,000 appeared to be an inescapable continuing minimum.

That was only half the problem.

"For many years," Governor Saltonstall said, "our industries have been declining. Even during the period from 1920 to 1930, when industrial employment throughout the United States increased nearly 20 per cent, that of Massachusetts declined. During the last nine years, industrial occupation has fallen off in Massachusetts even more sharply than it has in the rest of the country. Since 1930, industrial jobs for some 85,000 of our people have ceased to exist. Today it is estimated that we have in Massachusetts some 250,000 employable persons for whom, because of this shrinkage of work, there simply are not at the present time any jobs. This means that about 820,000 people, or nearly 20 per cent of our population, have for this reason to be looked after in some way other than by private employment."

I had come along the road by some of this problem before I went into the office of the tall man in the Capitol. In his office I remember that I asked him a question which was too brutally simple for the complex difficulties of Massachusetts: "What are you going to do?"

"Mr. Gerould will get you some material on what we've done."

He lit a cigarette, and the smoke went up by his long face. The ways of escape were fairly familiar, but not easy: thrift on the one hand—he quoted Coolidge about that in some of his speeches; advertising, promotion, encouragement on the other. But organized labor did not like the conservative Governor. Some manufacturers were still reading the advertisements and the persuasive letters from the South and from New Hampshire and Maine. And while everybody in New England is for thrift, in Massachusetts as elsewhere that thrift is always preferred which cuts closer to somebody else.

He told me a story, smiling about it, but I don't think he really thought it very funny. It was about one of his own conservative supporters who wrote him, "Frankly, I do not think you have struck out strongly enough for economy." There were other such letters from impatient taxpayers in the state in which the cost of state and local government had run from $175,000,000 in 1919 to $425,000,000 in 1938, while the state's pay rolls were falling more than $150,000,000. The Governor who was not finding slashing simple accepted the frank opinion. But a telegram came not long after the letter from the same man: "Withdraw all support if you permit closing of Worcester Teachers College." The two together made a parable for his preaching to the state. It may help him cut a few million dollars from the cost of government in a state in which even Yankees demand more and more of government all the time.

But Governor Saltonstall knows that thrift is not all. Not long before I saw him he had used another word to describe Massachusetts' need: "Jobs."

"If we can bring back business—and with it jobs—most of our worries about taxes and economics will be over."

"How are you going to get them?"

"Of course," he said, "a lot depends upon the national situation."

He had been worried, I knew, about a case in which the RFC had apparently been prepared to lend money to a Massachusetts mill with which to move out of Massachusetts to the South. I rather shared his opposition to that, Southerner though I am, and though also I knew that a good deal of Massachusetts money may have been loaned by Massachusetts men to do approximately the same thing.

I knew, too, that a committee of his own General Court had just completed a report which showed that not only the South but the poorer states of New England had been pulling at the manufacturing plants of Massachusetts. The whole thing seemed to go together like a design.

In Massachusetts, Governor Saltonstall inescapably represented a wealth which was being pulled at from below. The Irish politicians had not run up the cost of government in Massachusetts. They had been merely the instruments of demand. The poor Irish and the Italians and the Yankees who had been left behind had taken more and more in taxes to shorten the human distance between the Saltonstalls and the slums.

And in America, New Hampshire and Mississippi, Maine and Tennessee were using every device available to them to take from Massachusetts its old and big accumulation in the production of wealth. Even within Massachusetts, Fall River tugged at New York, even at Boston. There was a process in progress. It did not seem very pretty. It did seem very natural. It is no new radicalism. Sometimes, indeed, the radicals cry most loudly against it. The C.I.O. (which some New Englanders as well as some Southerners consider radical) cries as loudly as chambers of commerce when mills run away. It is not a new thing. I expect the English mills did not regard it as very respectable procedure for Samuel Slater to slip the plans for English machines through the English laws to begin the industry in Pawtucket. There is the tariff to remember, and it created not only wealth in New England but poverty to envy it in the South.

I looked at Saltonstall. I liked him. But in the Statehouse of Massachusetts, with all the best and richest Yankees behind him, he seemed to be like a man standing before a tide— a tide in comparison with which those tides which roar out of the Bay of Fundy at Passamaquoddy seem less than a ripple. Saltonstall walked to the door with me and said good-bye. I went out into the anterooms where many people were waiting, but not so many as had been waiting. When he first took office there had been four hundred people a day out there in those rooms seeking jobs. I suppose they were all loyal Republicans who expected the Governor to realize that they had helped elect him and therefore to make places for them. There had been, somebody told me, thirty thousand applications for fifteen hundred jobs. It sounded fantastic, but no more fantastic than the fact that one out of five people in the old Bay State of independence and thrift was receiving some form of public aid. And that there was not industry to which they could apply any skill if they had it to apply.

"But the thing that puzzles me," I said, back in Gerould's office where the newspapermen come for facts about the Governor, "is that, with need growing and industrial income falling, I don't see anywhere any such poverty as we have everywhere in the South."

"I don't think anybody's suffering," somebody said.

"Are they feeding on the fat of the past?"

"Maybe."

"Don't think there are not slums in Boston," said a slim, dark-haired young man.

I regarded him. "I'd like to see them."

"I'll show you."

So I set out with Roland Sawyer, who had come from Maine by newspapering in Concord, New Hampshire, to the staff of *The Christian Science Monitor*. In Maine his family had been making moccasins for three generations. They began long ago when there were Indians to cut and bead and paint them. Now not only were the Indians gone, the competition among the palefaces was not getting any prettier. So shoemaking lost and newspapering got one of the best young minds I met anywhere in New England.

We walked down beyond School Street to Washington and across Union and Blackstone streets to Salem Street. I had been in the neighborhood before when the streets about Faneuil Hall were crowded with pushcarts and magnificent vegetables and bargaining peddlers and customers. I had been impressed then by the fact that in Boston the food market and the money markets are so close together. That does not mean that meat and mouth are always so close. Even on this middle-of-the-week day there were peddlers and carts and Italian sidewalk salesmen. In bakery windows there were round dirty-rinded but promising-looking cheeses. Some of them were big and round as layer cakes. Sawyer and I exposed a joint ignorance when we asked about bulbs in a box and were informed by a fat and obliging but mildly scornful shopkeeper that it was garlic. There was a cart of crabs.

"This," said Sawyer, "is the North End which is supposed to have the worst relief."

It did not seem oppressively poor. I glanced upstairs and met the solemn eyes of a beautiful old white-headed man who was leaning on his hand and looking gravely out of an upstairs window. Children were playing in a blind alley. On Prince Street there was a whole succession of bakeries with windows full of beautiful bread. Then a Chinese laundry. On a brick wall of a tenement the anouncement was written in chalk: "I love Frankie." There were more carts of vegetables. Around another corner were the frayed remnants of a political advertisement: "Retain Keliher the Humane Sheriff."

"He died the day he was defeated," Sawyer recalled.

There were plenty of children in the streets. Their balls bounced from brick walls. They shouted back and forth to one another. There was music.

"It may be a WPA band," Sawyer thought.

An unshaven blind fat man overheard him. "Naw," he told us, following his ears, "it's the kids."

He moved past us and felt his way through the crowd of children and adults to the fence around the school grounds. There was the band. A Catholic Father in a brown habit with the sun beating down on his bare head directed the band of

351

little children. Their music roared high above them in the yard between St. Anthony's School and the public bathhouse on North Bennett Street. The crowd against the fence listened appreciatively. The children marched back and forth to the time they made with their own horns. The priest seemed, pleased with his players.

(It is hard for a Protestant Bible Belt Southerner to realize the power of the Catholic Church in New England. It would be hard to overestimate it in those cities where the French and the Irish and the Italians are congregated. The Italians have a reputation for being more independent and less consistently devout than the French or Irish. The French and the Irish, devout as both are, do not always like each other's company. In some places there are two sets of parochial schools. There have been some lively controversies about them. There have been some other differences within the Church. Some Catholic labor men have been sharply critical of the attitude of the Church toward labor. Even devout Irishmen sometimes talk in a lively irreverence about William Cardinal O'Connell, the head of the hierarchy in New England. I heard one call him "Dollar Bill" and "Gangplank Bill"—this because of His Eminence's supposed predilection for travel. But the same man said of the convening of the College of Cardinals to elect a successor to Pope Pius XI, "The Cardinal didn't want to go. He knew those guineas would hit him up for some more dough." Like the rest of us, undoubtedly, the Catholics have difficulties among themselves; but on questions of religion and morals, both of which are wide enough sometimes to spread a long way, the power of the Church is tremendous. Politicians know it. Some Protestants hate it and fear it. Some schoolmen charge that it is insidiously destructive of public education. But its charities are tremendous. Essentially it is a vast conservative force which sometimes seems strangely more closely allied in economic thinking with the employing Protestant Yankees than with the multitudes of Catholic employees. It is the rich church of poor parishioners. It is big enough to hold much fault, but it is incredible that it should be so big and powerful unless it met the deep hungers of the multitudes who pour into its doors.)

We stood listening while the music-making Father led his melodious children up and down the yard of the parochial school.

"I'd like you to meet Clem Norton," said Sawyer. "Let's get my car."

In it we set out to meet Clement A. Norton, superintendent of Commonwealth Pier and member of the Boston City Council. I am glad I met him. We found him in his office, which is lined with the sources of a vast information about practically everything in the world. There was a set of *The New York Times Index*. There were bound volumes of *Time*. These familiar sources were supplemented by an extensive and ingenious filing system of his own in which he kept clippings and articles, pamphlets and speeches. He had big scrapbooks, too.

"I've got it all here," he said. "Ask me anything, it's here."

"Cotton picker," I said.

It was not a very good suggestion. He was disappointed, I think, though he pulled out some material bearing on the subject. He not only collected as he read. Each year also as unattached bachelor, he made a trip to Europe. In Ireland he had, I was told, made speeches in support of De Valera telling the Irish in Ireland how much the Irish in Boston love De Valera. He sent back letters on his travels to the Boston newspapers. I had read one of them describing a bum on a bench in Vienna seen from the window of an apartment which once had been set aside for royalty, but in which an Irish city councilman slept. From such a store of information he talks rapidly and steadily, with his voice rising oratorically from a whisper to a roar and dropping back again. He snaps his fingers often for emphasis. Altogether he was the liveliest pessimist I met anywhere in New England. You had to catch his ideas and his words as they flew.

". . . anemic neutrality . . . corkscrewy . . . nit professors will say anything . . . New England is in for a worse slapping than it can imagine . . . the tip-off will be when all the banks close again . . . New England won't give up the cushion . . . I live better than Hitler. I have orange juice and California salad and smooth roads to ride on . . . you couldn't buy a glass of orange juice for $15 in Russia . . . the crack-up is going to be worse in the cities and New England than in the South . . . the South is already down and can move only one way . . . Baltimore and New Orleans will store cocoa beans which are the basis of candy on their piers for nothing. I want to meet competition here but there's a banker who says, 'No' . . . two thousand stevedores in Boston, and there never will be work for more than a thousand of them again. Those that work can make $25 a week. Rest won't try to find other work. And one chowderhead among them can stir them all up . . . what we need is brains . . . the next President will be the last one . . . Roosevelt is plowing a dark sea . . . I'm for him for a third term. I don't know whether Massachusetts would vote for him, but disaster if he is not elected . . . New England won't give up its cushion . . . the taxes are higher in Boston than any major city in the United States . . . New England Power has gone Irish Catholic Democrat . . . New England is going to get slapped . . ."

The night came down on his talk. We left his office and stood in the dusk on the pier while his automobile waited. New England, he was certain, was moving complacently toward disaster. The whole country would be in it, he thought, but New England would suffer most because it had most to

lose. The liberals, he believed, must be ready to take over
when the crash came. There seemed little light in the darkness for liberalism or anything else. He stood like an Irish
Jeremiah shouting the need for quick repentance under the
threat of woe. I doubt that Boston hears him any more than
other places have listened to other similar prophets. I hope
there is no need to hear.

Sawyer drove under the railroad tracks above Atlantic Avenue and then turned out in the darkness onto T Wharf. All
along it the little fishing boats of Italian fishermen were
moored. The old wharf is not only the center for the little
fishermen as the big Fish Pier at South Boston is the center
for the bigger boats. (Boston is the big port in the fishing industry of New England, which means $25,000,000 a year for
fishermen for sea foods which retail for $100,000,000.) Also
old T Wharf or part of it, in an age which delights in the
quaint, has been pleasantly remodeled to conceal some small
modern apartments between the masts of the little trawlers.
We went up a flight of stairs and found Frances Sawyer, grave
and pretty, in the wide-windowed living room like a ship's
cabin.

Of course, I was to stay for dinner. But we compromised
about that and went out to dinner together to the Capri Restaurant, up one flight of stairs at 145 Richmond Street. I was
lucky again. Not only was the food good. Also Avy Orlandi,
the manager, was having a party that night for his intended
bride. There was special music. The bride and her friends
sang songs and danced. It was very merry, with a touch of
such undisturbing melancholy as good merriment needs: I
remember that the Italian girls sang with great feeling "Way
Down upon the Swanee River." We were all a long way from
home. The Sawyers and I felt almost a part of the bridal
party. I drank my Chianti alone though I drank it in good
company. Also I drank it to Avy Orlandi and his bride. May

they have long life and many diners. But their best customer will never come again. He used to come regularly.

Long ago when Avy Orlandi was much younger—perhaps his father ran the restaurant then—in those days it was on Parmenter Street, near Hanover. Then sometimes they would get a call from the Copley Plaza. They began to expect such a call whenever they saw in the papers that Enrico Caruso was singing in Boston. The Copley Plaza would phone, and they would get very busy in the kitchen at the Capri. The chef would make something special and fine. The word would go out from the kitchen, and when Caruso came in his car the street would be full of Italians waiting to shout at him. He would come in. He did not want anything special and fine. He would have just the most simple thing.

"Oh, something very simple," said Avy Orlandi. "Something like we eat at home."

That was a long time ago, too, as a bridegroom counts time. Caruso died in 1921. In that year young Leverett Saltonstall was a member of the board of aldermen in the town of Newton. Many rich people live there and not, by Salem Street standards, many poor. He was born there, and he lives there still. But nobody knows better than he does now how close the poor are to the quiet "bedchamber" towns where rich men sleep, how close the hungry states are to Massachusetts.

XXXII

Capital of Dilemma

ON SCHOOL STREET IN THE SHALLOW LAWN before the nondescript City Hall the statues of Benjamin Franklin and Josiah
Quincy seemed colored by a dust that did not devour them.
Franklin, with his head down, seemed sadly thoughtful, but
Quincy was erect above lower extremities draped in a remarkable cloak. Behind them debris chutes brought to the
lawn the rubbish of a WPA modernizing process within. Past
them went the politicians and the taxpayers. I went in with
them to find Joe Kelly, who was to take me to the Mayor. In
the old building, which seemed like nothing so much as a
down-at-the-heel Southern courthouse in a poor Southern
county, a good many Bostonians seemed to have the same
idea. We went up the steep stair to the iron fence across the
crowded room and to the Irish policeman who stood on guard
there. Somewhere beyond him was the young Irishman, beautiful as an angel, who after other, florid Irishmen and pale
Puritans had come to Boston's power in the days of Boston's
difficulty.

Not only had taxpayers been declaiming in Faneuil Hall
about costs at home with a zeal which equaled the ancient
crying there about crime far away. Also, not long before I
went to see Mayor Maurice Joseph Tobin, a statistician from
the suburbs had snarled at Boston. From his own practically
private post office of Babson Park (near Wellesley), Roger

Babson had referred to Boston as "our good neighbor"; but he moved on from that sweet salutation without any fiscal compassion.

"The estimated annual tax burden on the average family," reported Babson, who had graduated from M.I.T. before Tobin was born, "already tops $250. With a population of only 781,000 and annual assessments soaring above a billion and a half dollars, Boston is obviously inviting a fiscal hurricane."

Almost the statistician seemed to rejoice in despairing for his good neighbor. He spoke of the "strangled city," "the responsible citizens maddened to desperation," "fantastic assessments," "taxpayers' strike," "political gang." He shouted a sentence which ran through melodrama to anticlimax, "But whether Boston turns to such graceful default (by reorganization of debt), or welches like a common bankrupt, the city plainly needs careful study."

Such study as he proposed sounded rather like a postmortem examination. But if the old City Hall was not marked with opulence in the midst of so many surrounding banks and trusts and other agencies of private invested wealth, certainly the company in it did not look disturbed.

Even the poorest of them outside the iron fence waited complacently, with the endless patience of the poor everywhere in the offices of politicians. Beyond the fence was the even more familiar politicians' club. In it a very much at home young Jewish lawyer was making calls on the phone. An immaculate elderly Irishman sat with his middle-aged daughter. They seemed to know the whole stream of men who passed back and forth through the room. An Irish lawyer came in to sit down and talk city finances with the Jew at the phone. He said of the money being spent on the City Hall to try to make it do instead of a new one, "They might as well throw it right out in the street."

"Some day," said the Jew, "this will be a museum."
Two sportily dressed men met each other in passage.
"Playing any golf, Tom?"
"Not much these days."
They kept coming, a lame Italian with a cast in one eye, a man with a remarkable mustache composed of two waxed inch-long tufts of blond hair one below each nostril. Then Joe Kelly, the Mayor's secretary, came and took me in. In the center of a big room the Mayor was talking to the newspapermen. It was a private office without any privacy. Around its walls, by its windows and its doors, sitting, standing, talking, silent, there were more people than there had been in the anteroom. The Mayor sat on one side of a gleaming table. I sat down at the end of the row of four reporters on the other. He was talking to them in a very low, pleasant voice. He is undoubtedly good-looking—even, after the pattern of young movie actors, beautiful. He has dreamy appealing eyes, a long straight nose, slick dark brown hair. His lips are full. That day he wore a double-breasted gray suit, a green tie with thin black stripes in it. He smoked, and as he talked, so quietly in the crowded room, he gave the impression of nervousness and an almost pleading persuasiveness.

Afterwards he took me to his desk in the corner of the room. He is no playboy. He understood the seriousness of his job in the seriousness of Boston. It was because of that situation that a fusion movement, headed by Henry Parkman, Jr., of old Republican and Codfish background, put him forward. He was an Irishman to mark the Irish protest against the Irish James Michael Curley (whose reputation for personal brilliance exceeds his reputation for the best public service). There was a crack among the Codfish Yankees, too: When Parkman, as Corporation Counsel after the election of Tobin, strongly opposed an increase in rates by the Boston Consolidated Gas Company, Charles Francis Adams, who is not only "g.g.g.s. of John Adams" but also director of forty-seven corporations, testified that Parkman had "broken the faith." It was not quite clear whether he meant the faith in high gas rates or the straight Republican ticket.

The year Tobin took office, he was thirty-seven. In that year, also, according to the Boston Municipal Research Bureau, the adjusted tax rate of Boston exceeded the average of the twelve other largest cities in America by 49.5 per cent. In all but one depression year Boston's adjusted rate (worked out for comparison purposes by the Detroit Bureau of Governmental Research) had been the highest among large American cities. More and more the rich moved to the country or the independent "bedchamber" towns. (Babson lived in one.) In 1938 relief from all sources in Boston among the poor who remained was costing $100,000 a day, *The Christian Science Monitor* reported. There had been tax defaults and "take-downs" of buildings to save taxes. There were no buyers for the big old houses on Beacon Street and Commonwealth Avenue. Bad and extravagant government may have helped push the situation to a head, but Boston is a city of 800,000 people by night and 2,000,000 by day. Its richest suburbs are beyond the taxgatherer's reach. Maybe a man from a distance can never become a Bostonian, but a gentleman born in Milton, educated in Cambridge and living in Newton may be the perfect Bostonian though his name nowhere appears on Tobin's tax books.

But the beautiful, soft-speaking young man who was born in Roxbury and lives in Jamaica Plain was not—for publication at any rate—discouraged. He told me how great a city Boston was, with its factories, its ports, its fish, its banks. He had himself risen slowly in the New England Telephone & Telegraph Company in the Boston where the Scotchman, Alexander Graham Bell, made his first phone call. Then he moved up more swiftly as member of the House in the Gen-

eral Court and of Boston's school board. He knew his town.
He remembered in approval what the old damned NRA
had done for Boston. There was need for redistribution of
wealth. It was proceeding. He recognized the difficulties of
Boston and the New England of which it is the capital. He
was not depressed by them.

"Don't ever think New England is licked," he said. "It's
not."

He repeated it while we walked across his office, by the
working and talking men who shared it with him, to the
door.

"Boston is not licked. It never will be."

It is difficult to understand on Milk and State and Devon-
shire streets how it could ever be poor. I went out of the old
City Hall into streets which seemed as full of trustees for invested fortunes as the streets around old Faneuil Hall were
full of pushcarts. The big First National Bank alone had
$600,000,000 on deposit. There was ten times as much in all
the New England banks, and that was a gain of 220 per cent
in thirty years. Nobody knew how much money was represented by the trustees in less glorified offices. And nobody
knew where the money was invested. The First National
Bank reported that millions of dollars from Boston and surrounding territory had gone to the South for the establishment of new cotton mills.

Suddenly it seemed to me in those narrow little streets,
which Bostonians say were laid out long ago by wandering
colonial cows, that Boston is the capital of a dilemma. It did
not seem to me that the financiers were any clearer in their
heads about the way they were going than the cows had been.
Of course, the cow at last heads for the barn. The financier at
first heads for the profit. I am not critical of either the banker
or the cow. There is no milk from the cow that does not
come home. There are no dividends from the investment

361

which does not go where the profit is. New England accumulated great capital in the beginning by struggle and thrift among the snow and the stones, and on the not less difficult sea. It grew in a spreading industry and ingenuity ashore. It is in those banks now, but it does not stay in those banks.

Capital goes where the profit is greatest or surest. That is sound sense in finance on State Street or anywhere else. But bankers and trustees are also citizens. They are citizens of New England, and no people in America, I think, not even the Southerners, have a greater love for the earth beneath their feet than the Yankees do. Nevertheless while the economic leaders of New England are giving their time, their interest and their money as citizens to such agencies for New England development as the vital and intelligent New England Council, they are also sometimes acting as capitalists to create the competition elsewhere which may destroy industry at home.

I put that question tentatively and timidly and got from a New Englander, anonymous but informed, a forthright answer.

"New Englanders have learned," he said, "as I have that in the investment of their money, and the money that is entrusted to their care, they must do it facing sound facts. Millions of dollars have been lost by sentimental investment. These same people have a love for their communities and contribute rather liberally toward making conditions in these same communities such as would warrant investments therein.

"Take my own case. Very few have contributed any more to New England than I have, trying to make it a place where people felt justified in living, where my children could make a living, and where one could bid for capital in the open market. At the same time, I have felt compelled to liquidate many of my family holdings in old New England industries and invest in other industries, often in other sections of the country. As it is, the family fortunes have been held fairly well, and are worth a little more today than when I first had charge. Had I remained in the same investments that existed, I should very much doubt if we would have a quarter of the property we now have.

"I think the people of the South and West, more particularly the South, have never learned the principles of work and save. This is natural, for they could sustain themselves year-round in reasonable climate, but the New Englanders learned that they had only a few months in which to prepare necessities to carry them through the winter. The old New Englander probably had sentiment for his home, but he was forced by the necessity of food and heat to invest his time in his economic needs."

The strange thing is that often this thrifty Yankee has saved to make jobs for us wastrels in the South and elsewhere, while men and women who come under the tent of thrift which is supposed to cover New England go without jobs, and tax rates must go up to feed them in cities like Boston even if the cities do not go bankrupt under the burden like Fall River. In the South I had heard so much about absentee ownership that I had not contemplated the home aspects of the money that goes away. If absentee investment, welcome as it always is, makes problems as well as jobs, it seemed to me that there were two aspects, also, to the investments that go away. If I know a dilemma from a cow, there is one in men and money in New England. To add the ancient metaphor to the old cow, I don't think anybody can blame a banker or a trustee for grabbing the safer horn. But it is not necessary to deny the existence of the other horn of the dilemma at home. There were a million men and women in New England who would work if they could get work. It was safer, surer, however, to put people to work far away.

But the thrift goes on. There is not only a thrift which continues in New England beyond the sharper pressures of the stones and the snow. There is also, I think, a continuing tradition of hardheaded honesty in finance in New England, which may be described as "unimaginative" by some New York financiers who imagined almost every possible way to sell suckers trash before 1929, but which seems to me to be a very valid and valuable residue of the Puritan tradition.

There have been too smart boys in Boston finance, there have been some dumb ones, too. Ivar Kreuger is a ghost who still walks State Street arm in arm with the ghosts of some Yankees who sold his stocks. But in Boston keeping, the $11,350 of the Fund for Assisting Students at Harvard College grew without a penny added to $485,882.28 between 1838 and 1939. Benjamin Fanklin's £1,000 of 1790 grew in Boston in the hands of the Massachusetts Hospital Life Insurance Company (which has no hospital and is not a life insurance company) to $329,360, which was used in 1894 to establish the Franklin Institute, a technical school for boys, plus a $98,604 residue which grew from 1894 to 1931 to $523,661. Some early New England fortunes have grown at almost similar rate and in similar safety. Such long-term evidence did not impress me as much as the evidence of present thrift.

Between 1920 and 1930, when the New England textile industry was suffering its swiftest decline, the deposits in the mutual savings banks of New England rose from $2,000,-000,000 to nearly $3,500,000,000. And from 1930 to 1938, when New England and America seemed to be scraping bottom, the volume of those savings not only stood—it grew. In general these were the savings of little people which made the savings deposits in New England $504 per capita as compared with $160 for the remainder of the country.

I learned about thrift pleasantly as I like to learn about other things at good luncheon in good company. It had be-

gun to rain outside but it was pleasant in the little dining
room in the Union Club. I had gone to meet David H. Howie
in his office in the Fiduciary Trust Company which is high
up in the big building full of investors and financiers at 10
Post Office Square. He is, I think, one of the wisest of the
younger financiers of Boston as well as one of the most can-
did and friendly. He has a bright eye, a round face. He wears
a trim mustache. He has, I felt immediately, an almost emotional reverence for the old integrity of the best Boston
finance, a love for its institutions, but a supple intelligence
ready with amusement for human aspects of the modern city.
We went from his office to the sedate and unchanged quarters
of the Massachusetts Hospital Life Insurance Company, the
oldest corporate fiduciary in the United States, to meet Edward H. Osgood, its president. A slight gray man, Mr. Osgood
was waiting for us in the old paneled rooms (which make the
new offices in Post Office Square look dangerously pert) under
a portrait of an early predecessor, Nathaniel Bowditch of
Salem, whose famous *Practical Navigator* was probably more
important to New England than any other New England
book. It was guide for the ships without which there might
never have been much money to save or invest.

Paul C. Cabot was waiting for us at the club. A man named
Cabot in New England may be an eminent physician, a professor, or a banker, but to a stranger he must be also a symbol
almost like the big Codfish in the Statehouse. This Cabot, I
think, was with some thought presented by Howie beside
Osgood as symbol of the fact that the old order does not
merely preserve. Here, with old blood in him, was a young
man of Boston who in fifteen years with a young Saltonstall
and a young Paine had built up the State Street Investment
Corporation from a net worth of $100,000 owned by three
shareholders (themselves) in 1924 to $38,341,347 owned by
5,675 shareholders at the end of 1938. Also this Cabot, who

was growing bald under his dark hair, was man of the same generation as young Irish Tobin in the City Hall. He was three years old in Brookline when Tobin was born in Roxbury. There was another detail: Paul Cabot had married Virginia, daughter of Frederick Shepherd Converse, professor of theory and composition in the New England Conservatory of Music. Virginia's sister, Louise, had married Junius Spencer Morgan, Jr., partner in the House of Morgan of New York.

Though New York financiers may be nice people and make nice relations, Boston financiers are not prepared to admit that the money men in New York are either so wise or so sure as the money men in the Boston tradition. Names like those on the directories of the Massachusetts Hospital Life Insurance Company, the State Street Investment Corporation, and the Fiduciary Trust Company not only read like a first lesson in genealogy, they also mean faith far away from Boston in little banks in little towns.

I suppose it is characteristic of me as one of those thriftless Southerners from a South in which we have sometimes been more occupied with food than with finances that I remember in greater detail than the conversation the little clams on the shells, the codfish cakes with strips of white pork fried crisp, the sound white wine, and the blueberry pie. But there was good talk besides about finances and New England, Saltonstall's efforts at economy and the cost of the insane in Massachusetts. (Has New England more insanity or merely more care? It has high suicide rates, while the South has high homicide rates.) I remember after coffee looking out across the Common in the rain.

The rain slackened, and David Howie and I walked to Bosworth Street to see John Kiley. An Irishman in Boston, his knowledge of Boston goes back beyond his present importance in real estate and his directorship in such an old Yankee institution as the Massachusetts Hospital Life Insurance Company. He was young in the time when Martin M. Lomasney was the boss of more of Boston than the Eighth Ward. In Bosworth Street he has a gay, wise Irishman's contact with reality. He knows his own Irish, and I think he can see the Yankees with a clarity they themselves do not often attain. Most important, he knows the Boston of both. Yankee bankers depend on his judgment. Politicians appreciate his shrewd sense. I asked him about the rich and troubled Boston of them both.

"It does not seem real," he said, "to think that vacant land in the Back Bay in 1870 to 1880, when it was being improved with new houses, should have sold for more or as much as land and houses combined today."

But it is real, real as young Tobin knows, and the landowners, too.

"Old-fashioned houses that have to be remodeled sell for from $8,000 to $10,000 on the sunny side of Commonwealth Avenue and at about the same price on the water side of Beacon Street. Houses on the south side of Beacon Street and the south side of Commonwealth Avenue sell for from $5,000 to $7,500. This is about one-fourth their former value." (And vastly less than their continuing city tax assessments.)

A good part of what used to be meant by Back Bay and Beacon Street had fled to country spaciousness in a tribal migration from a high tax rate on high real estate assessments. The trustee and the banker can come in to make their money and go out to pay their taxes. But the rich in moving to the country on the always open highways have passed the poor on the road. Nobody has counted those who have left the old precincts of propriety along Beacon Street and Commonwealth Avenue. In the city when I was there, however, more than 50,000 people depended on the direct relief from the public treasury for food and shelter. I wondered if around the old town but safe from its taxes in towns without slums there were an equal number of old ladies and children and gentlemen, too, living on trust funds left by the dead.

"Our suburbs have grown at the expense of the city," Kiley said. "I think that if we had an on-the-level census and we did not have the relief problem—which brought a lot of people into the city that formerly lived here and found it easier to get on relief here—if we had that, I think our population in the city alone would be 725,000 instead of about 800,000. In other words, Boston has about the same population as thirty years ago."

But not the same people. The rich who pay taxes have moved to Newton and Dedham and Milton. (They don't come into town for the winter any more.) They are the poor seeking relief who have moved in; they are also generally the poor who don't get out. Both are impelled by the same motives, I suspect, which moved New England across a continent after it came across a sea. The rich want to get out of as much taxes as possible, and the poor want to get as much relief as possible. The money for investment goes as far off as it needs to go to get the best and safest return. These new migrations were understandable even if the flight of the rich and their money disturbed the poor and the politicians, and the arrival of the poor worried the rich and the politicians. Somewhere in the business was the comedy which with pain almost always accompanies change.

Later I walked up Commonwealth Avenue toward the Harvard Club beside the evidence of the change. There were signs in the windows of flats for rent. There seemed to be almost more doctors' offices than private residences. The esplanade was still green and wide between them. Behind brief lawns in the sun which had followed the rain, the whitestone houses with iron grills at the doorways, the red brick and the

368

brownstone houses remained erect in ancient pride; but the marks of the new migration were on the old avenue of affluence and conservatism.

"Of course, there has been change," Leonard Ware, of *The Boston Herald,* said. Still there were many things that did not change. In Boston if you had been, you remained. Not everything was money and taxes and changing real estate. One recent debutante in Boston was the daughter of an old family; it was only a detail that her father was working on a WPA historical project in the Athenaeum.

But Ware lived in change himself. We went after dinner to his apartment. It was in one of the old houses on the water side of Beacon Street which had been cut up into apartments. His big room looked out across the Charles River lit in the darkness by the lights on the Massachusetts Avenue Bridge. The water was dappled by the lights of cars. The river had always been there, darkness and water. I wondered what Bostonians had looked from these windows on it before carpenters cut the house up into apartments for editorial writers and doctors and couples without children who would stay a little while and pay the rent and then be gone.

"Here's a phonograph record I want you to hear," Ware said.

He turned it on. The voice which came was almost a comic Yankee voice, such a nasal twang as I had not heard in New England. But it was familiar still. Then a band played. Calvin Coolidge welcomed Lindbergh back from France and Graham McNamee announced that for the first time in the history of science, radio would broadcast band music across a continent. We laughed at science and history. I went back to his big windows. The whole of New England seemed moving bright-eyed across the bridge, back and forth. I had the feeling that there was not any past under their wheels, only the present and a future close as the other shore. A window on the water on Beacon Street looks in an old land on a new world, rich and troubled and strange. But good Bostonians have no more to fear now than the first Bostonians did. Tobin and Cabot can make it what they will.

XXXIII

From Pilgrims and Patriots

WE WERE VERY IDLE. We were very merry. We lay in the grass between the croquet wickets and drank Shorle Morle, mild mixture of Rhine wine and seltzer clear and bright as the sunlight in Chatham. Straight off there from the clipped yard was Portugal. Up the long forearm of the Cape were Portuguese. In the green grass behind the white house one seemed as far off as the other. There were nice cries of admiration for the picture of the big fish a summertime fisherman from New York had painted to hang on the side of the station wagon in the parade. And laughter for the legend, "Save Monomoy for Birds Like Us," which, hanging opposite the fish, was to help make the parade demonstration of the alliance of the summer colonists and the "natives" against the proposal to make a bird sanctuary of the long sandy spit which ran in beach and dune down from Chatham toward Nantucket. Visitors hunted and fished there and picnicked among the dunes. Chatham citizens made money helping the visitors make sport. Besides, they said, already there were so many birds that they beat the diggers to the clams.

But as neither native nor summer colonist and so not threatened by either intruding ornithologists or the United States Bureau of Biological Survey, I took the sun in laziness and thought about latitude. I was still a pale shade of blue, I felt, from the one-second swim in the waters off the Chatham

371

Beach Club. But Portugal was off there, so the Pilgrims when they first landed on Cape Cod had come south, if not as far south as they expected. My North Carolina was off Africa. That might explain much in the difference between Americans, Northern and Southern. Walter Raleigh's men had died in the warm, and the Pilgrims had survived in the snow. But I felt no climatic energy in Chatham. The Pilgrims and their descendants were farther north than they expected to be; they got some other things they did not expect either—or want. Old Pilgrim Governor Edward Winslow, who warned those immigrants—now glorified as ancestors—that the fountains of Massachusetts did not "stream forth wine or beer," said also that there were some things New England did not want, and among them were "a proud heart, a dainty poise, a beggar's purse, and an idle hand." Well, the South had had its share of all of those as well as more than its share of the sun. Even Cape Cod ran along its last strip parallel with the mainland from these white houses and green yards by bayberry bush and beach plum and locust tree to artists and Portuguese and excursionists and tourist cabins—a way that contained them all.

Up the road at Provincetown, where the Pilgrims had landed first, there were not only artists painting in classes on the shore and living in trailers in the town; the boats also came in from Boston. And they brought everything! Before I saw Provincetown (it does grow honky-tonky—Greenwich Village—but pleasantly so, good-natured, with a strong nativeness still), I had the feeling from Chatham report that the land there stank as it did in the old days when they spread dead fish over the thin soils to fertilize them. I wished Thoreau could get the Cape's sand in his shoes again and the Cape's new natural history into a book.

There was a legend at large in Chatham that members of

the family of Mr. Justice Louis D. Brandeis, old Chathamites, were responsible for the plan to save birds and shut out station wagons on Monomoy. It was untrue but unchecked. I think even those who did urge the sanctuary were dismayed at the anger and misunderstanding its suggestion stirred. There was a sense of rights invaded, of liberties disturbed, which brought the Constitution close to the cottages. The Bill of Rights seemed directly threatened on that neat and pleasant shore. The long arm of Washington seemed reaching into a refuge where brokers and publishers had been secure before and showing a deference for birds.

We went up-street to see the parade. The Fourth of July means more in New England, I think, than it does elsewhere in America. That War of Rebellion was far away and does not intervene. First there was a girl riding at the head of horsemen. The American Legion, whose members had grown a little paunchy even on the Cape, came in uniform led by a color guard in tin hats. In the red and blue Chatham band a bellows-chested Negro was blowing a bass horn. The Coast Guard men wore blue, the Navy's sailors were in white. And the ladies of the Eastern Star were in white, too, and carried some sort of symbolic hoops bound with flowers. The fire department had not only trucks but a red boat on wheels as well. There was a fine green float manned by members of the Chatham Grange. The Yankee put in his commercial touch: the Lime Hill Turkey Farm ("broilers"), Brown's Bike Shop, the Acme Laundry (Vernon Eldredge had made so much money washing for the summer folk that he had a house as big and white as any of them on Shore Drive). Then came the station wagons, some driven by dignified chauffeurs but more by city summer-men in sport clothes who grinned as participants in a protest against power which did not seem

373

to them to stem from the patriots. On Independence Day
their banners screamed for liberty from the ornithologists
with the ancient vigor of the founders:

CHATHAM WANTS MONOMOY FOR FISHING.

*KEEP MONOMOY FOR CLAMS, LOBSTERS AND CHAT-
HAMITES.*

WE NEED SANCTUARY AS WELL AS THE BIRDS.

And finally, best of all:

> *Birds have the air,*
> *Fish have the sea,*
> *Let's keep Monomoy*
> *For you and me.*

Somebody let off a firecracker back of me, and I jumped.
The parade went on, and behind it the traffic clotted. Joseph
C. Lincoln, who has written more about Cape Codders than
anybody living, moved before his own hedges with a lively
seagoing step. But Ludlow Griscom, the ornithologist from
Harvard, somebody in our car said, looked subdued. Before
the big house they had rented, the rich Fleischmanns of Cincinnati, or some of their guests, watched the jam of the spec-
tators which had succeeded the march of the parade. We got
to the Chatham Bars Inn and the bar in it, and drank to
American liberty and independence while we waited for the
traffic of free Americans to thin on the streets. Afterwards we
ate at a long table in the windowed dining room which looks
out across the green salt meadows to the sea over which the
Pilgrims came. And the patriots followed the Pilgrims. And
Irish girls brought in lobster thermidor to us.

I had to leave that afternoon. I had come a long road; but
I had to go back over much of it and "rake over," as they say
in Vermont, and there was a man waiting to tell me something I ought to know, down the road off the Cape where the

New Englanders still believe America began. It was hard moving, full of lobster. In the afternoons there is a quality on the Cape designed for sleep. I said good-bye. Or rather I would have said good-bye if my host had not himself been sleeping off his own lobster in his own house high over the sea. At Hyannis, Russell Brothers Circus was helping to celebrate the independence of America. There was another carnival farther down the road. But the elms in Sandwich spread in ancient dignity over the street. I stopped there to speak to some friends. I remember that across the road from their house was an old cemetery on the shore of Shawme Lake. As I got out of my car I read its sign:

> This cemetery closed to all but lot owners and casual visitors. Persons using grounds for recreational purposes will be vigorously prosecuted.
> Per order selectmen.

That seemed proper. Massachusetts that afternoon was being merry enough where Massachusetts—and America—began. There ought to be a little room left for the past to sleep in. The dead had a right to be undisturbed in their dream.

XXXIV

Invitation to the Yankees

MEN DO NOT MAKE THEIR TRAVELS as straight as crows. Roads twist to go by farms, around barns, over hills, and to the narrowest crossings of the brooks. Even some city streets in New England, they say, twist among the offices and the banks as the cows wandered in the lost green grass. The Pilgrims when they landed in Massachusetts were headed for Delaware. It was a long time before Nathaniel Bowditch, the Navigator, sent the ships of Salem straight on their enriching courses in a system which swung about the certainty of the sun. And still sometimes neither the Yankees nor the stranger among them can be quite sure where they are going. They may not even be in entire agreement about the way they have come. I remember that, when I first went North as Southerner, I was lost in Boston, and I wondered whether I was any more lost than Boston was. A little Italian boy set me straight for a dime.

Maybe then what I have to report is not the travel but the traveler, a traveler from the antithetical South which New Englanders understood was gallant maybe but thriftless certainly, gracious in legend but violent in fact. From such a land I came with the secret respect which all Southerners have learned for the Yankees. It was the recruit before the fighting and the politician after it who said that one Reb could beat ten Yankees. The veterans in Alabama passed on to their sons a reticent respect for the boys from Vermont. Undoubtedly some Yankees came down whose departure from points North must have occasioned as much rejoicing as fury was occasioned by their activities in points South. Some such still come, and they are not always labor organizers. They may be, indeed, men who talked in loudest indignation about underpaid Southern labor before they themselves began to underpay Southern laborers. And some of the gentlemen who stayed in Boston—courteous, honorable, cultured gentlemen—have sometimes been difficult to bear. They talked of Southern thriftlessness in a South which their tariff system had impoverished, and whose poverty a Northern credit system milked. Some ladies even in the Back Bay contributed funds to help the poor Negro tenants under the wicked white landlords, out of incomes which came from interest rates which kept the landlords hot after the Negroes and the Negroes hot over the cotton.

They were details which did not destroy respect. The Yankee schoolmarms long ago gave us what little learning we had. And some of them stayed to become the mothers of Confederate soldiers. Even today Harvard is not so much the name of a university as a word which chills us even in the warm South with a sense of inferiority. We honored Eli Whitney even if we stole his cotton gin and got paid for our plunder by a slavery to cotton which included us all, white and black. We sat in the shade and talked with admiration of the energy of the Yankee in the snow. We appreciated the Connecticut Yankee's skill (it was a Southerner who wrote the best book about it), but we learned to holler for a Negro when there was work to be done with hands. That is, some of us did—a very few of us really. Most of us white Southerners were working hard through that whole legend and not getting much further than those Yankees who let the forest run back across the cow lot and departed for the West.

Out of such a South I came North secretly respectful. I rode more highways than are followed in these pages. I saw more men than those I have described. And I went out of New England over the same Merritt Parkway upon which I had entered it (I rode in for nothing; they charged me a dime to get out), openly and frankly full of admiration. On the most difficult land, the men of New England made a great civilization. They maintained it. But the very greatness of their accomplishment is the measure of their problem. They never had any reason to hope to be so rich. I expect it is gallantry now and not skill or thrift or industry which is the basis of their determination to continue to be.

The fish and the forests, which were what they had to begin with, were depleted long ago. The water power, which now runs by so many less productive mills, is a resource no longer unique. The region has to spend a billion dollars or more every year to feed itself. A million of the eight million eaters within the land were, when I rode it, people who wanted work and could not get it. There were more old people and fewer young ones in the old land than in most other American regions. Twice as many freight cars—and probably twice as many trucks—brought food and fuel and materials in as took products out. And the more valuable products which went out had, in an America which New Englanders had helped spread to the Pacific, a longer way to go.

But the land remained rich. Not only did it have more dollars than its share in the banks, it had more education than its share in the heads of its people. There was, as a Southerner counts, little heartbreaking poverty apparent in the land. Not only were Yankees rich in Milton and Newton, also the poor were fed (well by Southern standards), even in bankrupt Fall River. Most of the people live in the towns where their poverty can be articulate, where their distress must be met or seen. Furthermore, in the great industrial states the rich did not seem ruthless nor the poor driven (there were exceptions, as wage and hour prosecutions showed; also there were factories which employers said labor regulations had shut up). On holiday the beaches are crowded, the circuses filled. Recreation in New England is not industry for outsiders alone. Neither bread nor circus is lacking. And a good deal more is provided.

"We are living on fat," said a lean, rich young New Englander.

I expect the poor would say, "What is fat but food?" Between them, I think, is an old problem which exists not only within the region but outside it. At home Puritan morals remain strong in defense of possession: The rich have because the rich did; thrift must be protected from the thriftless. But there is also a new—and always new as the other is always old—morality of indignation: The rich got because the rich grabbed; pity is more important than profit. It is not necessary to choose between them to know that taxes have gone up at home (as also in Washington), and that much New England capital goes far away (much of it always did), to make profits and jobs elsewhere than in New England.

That old conflict, under a multitude of philosophies ("ideologies" is the word now), between the rich, who want desperately to keep, and the poor, who need desperately to get, is not restricted to men in New England or anywhere else. It applies to nations and regions also. New England was on the poor side once. Some of that conflict went into the revolutionary patriotism of the American Revolution. It entered the fight between the planters and the infant Yankee industrialists about tariffs. And generally the poor men and the poor lands are more active about the business. The rich scream vociferously at every threat, but it is the poor who act in the streets, in the Congresses, and now around the factories. (These poor, of course, are by no means always hun-

379

gry. They may be rich men, strong men, but somewhere there is generally a sharp stick of hunger behind the lands or men they lead.) And the new rich are always the old poor.

New England lacks that sharp stick. It did not always lack it. I suspect that the greatness of New England grew less directly from the high morals of the Puritans than from the inhospitality of the land to which they came. Time and winter dramatically pointed the need for energy. My back still aches from the stones they pulled out of the fields. The long shut-in winters turned the man to the tool and the book. (In the South, in the winter sunshine between cotton picking and cotton planting there were open fields, gun and dog.) There was the sea: we remember shining sail and forget stinking forecastle. The history of men on the sea has been the history of men who could not make a living on the land. Not everybody got rich in New England. The Southerners had some sharp things to say about the girls who came in from the farms to the mills in the towns while the abolitionists were talking about slaves in the South. (New England spokesmen were proud of the small number of illegitimate children they had.) The West was not opened and the New England farms abandoned by men who went off in frolic. They departed from backbreak and poverty. After them men came into New England from the poverty of the world. Most of them are still poor.

We are better informed about the succession of the successful. They move in the books. They sit in the portraits of Gilbert Stuart, the snuff-grinder's son. They lived in the houses of McIntire and Bulfinch. They went to Harvard. They began to write books. They were concerned with good causes. They made—and make—I think the truest aristocracy America ever possessed. They would have distrusted such romanticization of themselves as surrounded, and surrounds still, the planter aristocrats of the South. But they were more durable. They had a better sense of values. Even at their richest, they themselves were closer to the stones and the snow and the sea. Generally, though not always (there were the waistcoats and houses and yachts of Salem), they distrusted display. They believed in God and education, blood and money. Even now they retain standards which are admirable in a puzzled world. I am not sure they will be standards which will suffice.

These aristocrats are not New England. Only a little more than a third of the New Englanders now are native Americans of native parents. A good many of these have an Irish grandfather or a French-Canadian grandmother. A great part of the Yankees who do survive in New England from the ancient days are poor men, still scratching little Vermont farms or leaving them when grandfather dies. But the New England money aristocrat and the Connecticut Yankee who is the aristocrat of skill do still make the patterns of the land. Thrift and skill, industry, ingenuity and independence are virtues which a polyglot people profess even when some of them lack the powers to participate in them.

Sometimes, indeed, they seem words. Thrift is real, billions are in the savings banks, but the rich aristocratic Yankee Governor of Massachusetts found very little of it in the people's government of Massachusetts. Skill and ingenuity are in New England, but no monopoly of them is there. The Connecticut Yankee is often a Pole. The skills of modern industry are learned elsewhere also. Many more would like to be industrious for wages than are. And independence: A fifth of the people of Massachusetts were receiving relief. Sometimes the words sounded like a Southern shouting about bravery and honor and gallantry to a Southern people who needed clothes and shelter and bread.

And that was very strange. For New England had the only two things the South has seemed to lack: wealth and educa-

tion. Not only do the rich maintain well dressed armies of
bankers and trustees and investment counselors to guard fortunes. Also the workers of New England get wages well above
the wages of men and women working at the same jobs in
the South. (Above them even when cheaper living in the
warmer region is considered.) That continues true even
under the wages and hours law which lifted the wages of
many in the South. For a long time even WPA workers received wages far above Southern levels. Families on relief
in New England towns are much more secure than similar
poor folk in the South.

New England is rich and educated. Not only do the Saltonstalls go to Harvard; also even the boys from relief families
in the NYA work experience project at Quoddy in Maine
had as an average almost completed high school. New England had the first public school in America, and the first college. Its colleges are richer. A full fourth more is spent by
New England on its public-school pupils than the rest of the
country spends. The public libraries are open in almost
every little town.

But the land seemed to me to be as plagued with problem
as the poor, less educated South. It did not only seem so to
me. There have been moments when both labor unions and
bankers were frightened together. Mill treasurers and investment counselors, governors and college professors have
spoken about the threat to New England from other new
competing industrial regions, particularly the South. Sometimes they have spoken about Southern competition in such
high hot moral indignation as their fathers used about
slavery, but I doubt that their chief concern was with the welfare of the new, eager, white, prolific Southern slaves.

The sharp stick was behind the South. And the anger in
New England seemed comfortable even when it was choleric.
In its wealth and education New England was also confused.

He was a New Englander employed by the governors of New England to speak for New England who recorded the fact that when the Southerners started in textile manufacturing to beat the damnyankees on a new kind of battlefield, Yankee machinery manufacturers came to their assistance by selling them machines in exchange for stock. The biggest bank in New England devoted to developing New England has also lent money in the South for plants which would compete with New England. The United Shoe Machinery Corporation by its leasing system has made the migration of industries from the shoe towns a much simpler matter. Business is business, undoubtedly. Such business, however, sound as it may be, is not vastly different from the action of labor in pushing up labor safeguards and wages in New England which, say business men of some of the same institutions that sell machines and lend money beyond New England, has forced some industry out of New England (or pushed it from crowded Massachusetts to rural Maine). Both the labor leaders and the business men are about legitimate business for the money or men they represent. All are right, or none of them are.

None of them, nor all of them together, can build a wall around New England—not short of another war. Indeed, if they could build a wall it would only fence in starvation. But, without benefit of wall, money and men in New England must save it or suffer in it together. Money has learned how to go far off to make its profits while it makes jobs for men far from Manchester and Fall River and Lawrence. But the people of New England have found their way by taxes to wealth. Maybe they have only begun. Certainly where there is much wealth they do not mean that there shall be much distress. If wealth—and the education it can command —in New England does not find a way to work in wage-paying jobs in New England, that money had better make enough in Michigan and Carolina to feed an increasing dependence in Massachusetts. (Of course, Federal relief and Federal spending will modify the process, but Massachusetts spending, for instance, has towered, too.)

Wealth and education have, I think, a bigger job than that. An aggressive, militant, raiding regionalism may serve the South which has little to lose and much to gain. But New England has much to lose and much to save. Its hand would grow weary slapping down the hungry states beyond it. The only possible chance it has lies in helping the hungry up. I think that last is not only the hope of its security but the test of its civilization. We have great faith in education in America. We count on its promises with confidence in its results. We have the reputation of thinking much of money, too. Indeed, the American faith can almost be summed up in free enterprise and free education. No part of this land has had so much or so much faith in both as New England.

Through all his troubles, I believe the rich man like the poor man in New England has wished to use the wealth of the land to keep the living standards of New England intact, to keep the promise of its schools high, though mills might fail and incomes fall. In great measure that has been done. Even with a million men and women unemployed, the living standards of New England seemed to me along all the ways I went, with few exceptions, to be held higher than the standards in the whole land around them, hill-high above the standards of the South. This will be a better America if they stay there. But I think they can only stay there if Harvard and Yale and the schools behind them and the money around the schools can produce a leadership out of an old civilization capable of national creativeness in this time. They must be such men as can help the South come up to New England. Otherwise New England must come down toward the South. Beyond the South maybe; there might not

INVITATION TO THE YANKEES

be a bottom for a crowded land of old people, with a falling birth rate, that cannot feed itself. Unless the process which has already begun in the stress upon recreation proceeded to a widening park, and the trees came back across the little hills. It will be lovely forever, whatever happens.

". . . the Yankees were here and left their monuments in old brick mills beside the streams a long time ago . . ."

The road does not run that way. Certainly it does not go straight as the crow flies. There will be frost heaves in it and turns and twists. But it must come at last to a destination in decency which will include North and South together. North is not merely Saltonstall but Salem Street, also; South is rich man, white man, black man, together. The Yankees once fought a war upon the sensible proposition that this could not be one nation, half slave and half free. They were right, and they proved it. But neither can this nation be half rich and half poor. With a sharp stick behind us, uncertain and undirected in the South, we are fighting about that now. And I count it that the sensible Yankees will be on our side. This time we shall all win or lose together.

Index

387

INDEX

Roberts, Kenneth, 120, 285
Roberts House, 149
Robinson, Edwin Arlington, 99, 100
Robinson, H. O., 230
Rochester Courier, The, 80
Rockefeller, John D., 91, 143
Rogers, James Gamble, 189, 192, 193, 215
Rogers, Willard, 18
Roosevelt, Franklin D., 25, 42, 112, 308, 309, 316, 317, 324, 325
Roosevelt, Mrs. James, 317
Roraback, J. Henry, 188
Rosenau, Milton J., Jr., 27
Roxbury, Mass., 342, 360, 366
Royall, Anne, 212, 222
Russians, 59, 61

Sabbathday Lake, Me., 283
Sacco, Nicola, 31
Saco River, 35, 46
St. Agatha, Me., 299, 302
St. Botolph Club, 22, 23, 27, 30, 31
St. Croix Paper Company, 275
St. John River valley, 8, 293, 297–305
St. Johnsbury, Vt., 261, 265
St. Leonard, N.B., 298
Salem, Mass., 8, 36, 167, 340, 341, 365, 376, 381
Salem Village, 39
Saltonstall, Governor Leverett, 18, 32, 39, 137, 182, 342–350, 356, 385
Saltonstall, Sir Richard, 344
Saltonstall, Richard Middlecott, 342
Sandwich, Mass., 375
Saugus, Me., 7
Sawyer, Roland, 350–355
Saybrook, Conn., 195
Scroll and Key, 190
Sears, Roebuck & Co., 301
Sebago Lake, 42, 275, 278
Seymour, Dr. Charles, 8
Shakers, 283
Sharpe, Henry D., 168, 174
Sharpe, Lucian, 168
Shawme Lake, 375
Sherman, Maurice S., 216, 218
Sherwin, Richard, 242
Silcox, F. A., 38

Sinclair, Me., 299–303
Skull and Bones, 190
Slater, Samuel, 168, 170, 349
Sleepy Hollow, 115, 116, 118
Smith, Alvia Murray, 180
Smith, Ellison DuR., 256
Smith, Captain John, 3
Smith, Mary, 20
Smith College, 236
Snob Hill, 313
Social Justice, 151
Soil Conservation Service, 296
Somerset Club, 10, 344
Somerville, Mass., 229, 230
Soucy, Father D. Wilfrid, 297–306
South Boston, 345, 355
South Casco, Me., 276, 277
South County, R.I., 187
South Paris, Me., 272
Southard, Ed, 288, 289
Southern Literary Messenger, The, 4
Spouter Inn, 129, 139
Springfield, Mass., 7, 221–234
Springfield Republican, The, 231
Springfield, Vt., 240
Springs, Elliott, 177
Stackpole, Edouard, 150
Starbuck, Edward, 141
"State of Maine" trademark, 294–296
State Street Investment Corporation, 365, 366
Stephen Daye Press, 230, 241–243
Stern, Julius, 339
Stockholm, Me., 302
Stonington, Conn., 230
Stratford, Conn., 188
Stuart, Gilbert, 345, 380
Suffield, Mass., 224
Sullivan, Charles, 54
Sullivan, John L., 3, 342
Sumner, Charles, 232
Sunderland, Mass., 8, 237
Swedes, 59, 251
Syrians, 111

TVA, 310, 311
Taft Hotel, 199
Tamworth, N.H., 261
Tavern Club, 9, 335

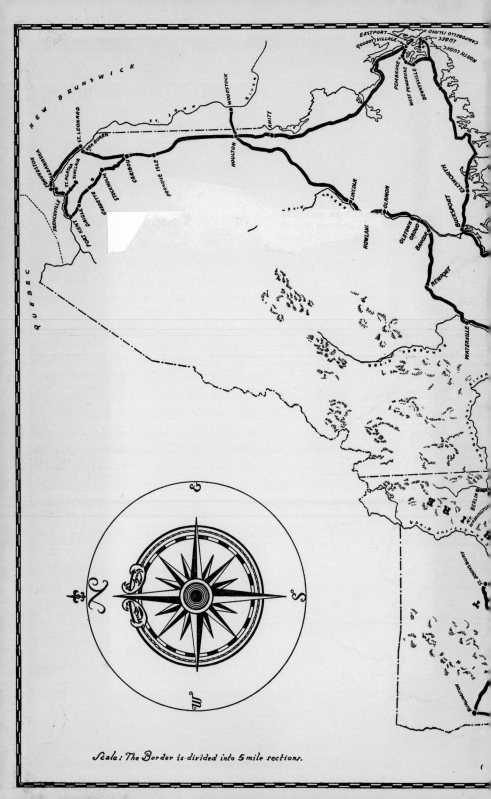

Scale: The Border is divided into 5 mile sections.

INDEX

Taylor, Marjorie, 263, 268, 269
Taylor, Morris, 320
Textile Mills Committee, 131
Thompson, Dorothy, 249, 257
Thoreau, Henry David, 33, 113, 115, 119, 372
Time, 353
Tiverton, N.H., 163
Tobin, Mayor Maurice Joseph, 182, 346, 357–363, 370
Tonieri, Emil, 98
Toombs, Robert, 10
Townsend clubs, 71, 271, 273
Travelers Insurance Company, 18, 210, 213
Treat's Island, 317
Tuckerman Ravine, 54
Tudor, Frederic, 7
Tullock, A. R., 231
Turk's Head Club, 186
Twain, Mark, 167, 212, 233
Twin Mountain, 62

Union, Conn., 21
Union Club, 9, 343, 365
Unitarians, 168
United Aircraft Corporation, 202, 204, 208, 209
United Aircraft Exports, Inc., 207
United Electrical, Radio & Machine Workers, 231
United Federal Workers of America, 311
United Shoe Machinery Corporation, 280–282, 383
United Shoe Workers of America, 281
U.S. Armory, 232
U.S. Bureau of Biological Survey, 371
U.S. Route I, 334

Vallee, Rudy, 302
Van Buren, Me., 10, 298
Vanderbilt, Governor William H., 180–183
Vanderbilt, William K., 180
van Loon, Hendrik Willem, 219
Van Wyck, Benjamin S., 228
Vanzetti, Bartolomeo, 3, 31
Vermont, 2, 7, 9, 12, 14, 37, 42, 45, 135,

176, 235, 238–270, 272, 326, 339, 374, 377, 381
Vermont Agricultural Experiment Station, 249
Vershire, Vt., 9, 260
Victor Emmanuel III, 179
Vogue, 110
Vought-Sikorsky plant, 206

WPA, 73, 84, 90, 129, 130, 143, 148, 163, 187, 197, 245, 255, 256, 312, 313, 314, 315, 322, 324, 351, 357, 369, 382
Wadsworth, Peleg, 35, 43, 46
Walden Pond, 113, 119
Wallace, Henry A., 257
Wallingford, Conn., 17
Walsh, David I., 343, 346
Waltham Watch Company, 85, 109, 110
Wamsutta Club, 131
Wamsutta Mills, 131
Ware, Leonard, 369
Warren, S. D., & Company, 228, 275
Washington, George, 34, 77, 232
Washington County, Me., 307–332, 334
Watch Hill, R.I., 169
Waterbury, Conn., 188
Waterville, Me., 286
Watson, Tom, 217
Webster, Daniel, 34, 44, 51, 72, 77, 337
Webster, Noah, 222–226, 231–233
Webster's Dictionary, 222–226, 229–233, 333
Weeks, Edward, Jr., 28
Wellesley, Mass., 38, 357
Wells, Mrs. W. Storr, 165
West Enfield, Me., 288
West Fairlee, Vt., 262, 267
West Pembroke, Me., 326
West Quoddy Light, 8
West River, 245
Westbrook, Me., 302
Westchester County, N.Y., 8
Westinghouse Industrial Union, 231
Westport, Conn., 15
Westport Factory, Mass., 152
Whalen, Grover, 80
Wheeler, Gerald, 48, 49, 54, 57, 63
White, Peregrine, 122, 126

397

Scale: The Border is divided into 5 mile sections.